"Uncharted is an honest and enc[..] sects our circumstances and brings [..] authenticity, truth-telling, and commitment to help us gain biblical insight on life's most difficult situations is a breath of fresh air in a culture of cynicism."

Gabe and Rebekah Lyons
Bestselling Authors and Founders of *Q Ideas* and *Rhythms For Life*

"If you are looking for insight to help you live out the Bible's declaration that each person, including you, is "fearfully and wonderfully made," *Uncharted* is a wonderful resource and guide. With her characteristic grace and humility, Inés opens up the Scriptures and also her own life to acquaint readers with the kindness of God, coupled with the impact his kindness is meant to have on our daily lives. As a personal friend to Inés, I can also attest that her own life is very much in accord with her message."

Scott Sauls
Senior pastor, Christ Presbyterian Church
Author, *Jesus Outside the Lines, Beautiful People Don't Just Happen,*
and other books

"The beauty of this book and Inés Franklin's words are that they aren't simply written; they are lived. No one can speak with authority on thriving after obstacles unless they have survived them. Inés honestly and gently speaks truth and love while calling us to rise to the calling God has placed on our lives. This book isn't only a resource; it's needed for such a time as this"

Bianca Juarez Olthoff
Pastor
Podcaster, *We're Going There*
Best-selling author, *Play with Fire* and *How To Have Your Life Not Suck*

"I trust Inés Franklin. Her faithful shepherding of God's people, her compassionate pursuit of those struggling, and her diligence to study the Scripture flow from a heart transformed by the grace of Jesus. Her book, *Uncharted*, is so encouraging and representative of the care people receive from Inés—truthful and filled with grace and wisdom from one who has walked the path with Jesus. Through God's Story, her story, and practices that put us in God's presence, I was reminded that my Savior continually invites me to release control to him and to enjoy him. I believe your faith will be strengthened and your joy will increase as you engage with this book."

Eric Geiger
Senior pastor, Mariners Church

"Comparison is a thief—it robs us of the flourishing Christian life. In the place of comparison, Inés Franklin calls us to a deeper, more unique journey: one of simplicity, slowing, and practices that lead to growth and joy. Inés vulnerably and pastorally journeys with her readers, calling them to walk in the transforming presence of Jesus. Walk with Inés as she shares her story; and discover more about your own story along the way."

Tara Beth Leach
Author, *Emboldened* and *Radiant Church*

"In both her ministry and personal life, I have seen Inés Franklin walk in the three dimensions of faithful discipleship at the heart of this important book: discernment, humility, and obedience. Uncharted is not a road map for sudden success. As the title implies, it is a vision for transformational change through spiritual practices and the faith to believe that the outcomes, though not yet visible over the horizon of God's mercy, are as sure as the One who promises them."

Michael J. Beals, Ph.D.
President, Vanguard University

"Becoming a disciple of Jesus Christ is easy... until Day #2. Rather than being a smooth path under clear and sunny skies, following Jesus quickly evolves into a daily challenge that demonstrates the reality of the spiritual battle that Jesus came to fight and win while calling his followers into the contested frontlines of his Kingdom. Inés Franklin demonstrates the power found in blending the disciplines of a student with the spiritual gifting of a teacher, while living the daily demands of discipleship as her test lab for Truth. What Inés shares is worth far more than the cost of the time to read her reflections: the value of her insights stretches into the Hereafter. Read and be encouraged by her lack of platitudes and untested proposals: she's sharing wisdom that has been gained through great commitment."

Bob Shank

Founder, The Master's Program

"It took Inés Franklin eighteen years to produce this book, but it's not what you think. It didn't take her that long to put words together in such a beautiful and compelling way. Eighteen years was the time Inés needed to live the vulnerable life and learn the invaluable lessons you will encounter in Uncharted. Rarely have I encountered a book that is both eye-popping and deeply theological. Don't get me wrong. Uncharted is not a Bible study as much as it is a life study. Inés Franklin's story of redemption flows through the book like a scarlet thread as she unpacks Scripture and dramatically describes her own journey to wholeness. As you read and experience this book, you will take your own uncharted journey, one that will shake and shape you to your core."

Stan Jantz

CEO, Come and See Foundation

"Abraham. Joseph. Moses. David. Paul. Throughout the Bible, every person's story is circuitous. Each is characterized by confusion, fear, and seeming contradiction. For the people of God, this is all very normal. And yet, when our own faith journey fails to follow a straight line, it is incredibly disorienting and scary. We may even wonder if we are following God at all. The truth is, saying yes to God is not simple. It requires courage, trust, and wise counsel—the very kind contained in these pages. If you are currently discerning God's plan for your life and yearning for guidance along the way, Uncharted is exactly the book you need!"

Sharon Hodde Miller

Author, *The Cost of Control: Why We Crave It, The Anxiety It Gives Us, And The Real Power God Promises*

UNCHARTED

Navigating Your Unique Journey of Faith

INÉS FRANKLIN

Fedd Books
P.O. Box 341973
Austin, TX 78734
www.thefeddagency.com

Published in association with The Fedd Agency, Inc., a literary agency.

Cover Design by Andy Lara, Makenzie Odebunmi, and Mackenna Cotten
Edited by Kyle Duncan

ISBN: 978-1-957616-19-3
EISBN: 978-1-957616-20-9

Library of Congress Number: 2022923244

Printed in the United States of America

First Edition 23 24 25 26 27 – 1 12 11 10 9 8 7 6 5 4

To my Abuelita Angela,
you were right.
Thank you for your prayers!
Besitos.

And to my husband, Jim,
life with Jesus and you is a great adventure.
I love you.

"God is for you".

Iris Franklin

CONTENTS

Foreword by John Townsend, PhD xi
Introduction xxi

I. Knowing God's Desires 1
    1. Seeing the Invisible 3
    2. Incomplete Maps 23
    3. Faith Is Not a Formula 41

II. Overcoming Challenges 63
    4. Obstacles Are a Given 65
    5. Questions Are Essential 87
    6. Recovering from Wrong Turns 107
    7. Shame Will Enslave You 127

III. Blessing through Obedience 147
    8. What Not to Pack 149
    9. A Heavenly Mindset 169
    10. Traveling in Community 187

IV. Thriving by Thirsting for God 207
    11. Ambiguity Is Inevitable 209
    12. The Journey Is Mysterious 229
    13. Certainty Hinders Growth 251
    14. The Outward Journey 273

A Prayer for You 286
Acknowledgments 289
Endnotes 291

The faith journey can be confusing.

This book provides a path.

But not in a way we would expect.

FOREWORD

All of us who are Christians have a deep desire within to live the life of faith and follow Jesus. That is the call. It makes sense, because only he knows what the best life is for us. On the surface and at the beginning, this can often seem positive, exciting, and adventurous.

Then life runs directly into us, and the journey of faith seems confusing. It is not as clear or simple as we anticipated. And it often doesn't seem to make sense with our struggles and our questions.

None of us are exempt from the confusion and difficulties of life. We all experience hardship and unanswerable questions, including relationship and family problems, emotional and behavioral issues, health complications, and financial crises. More importantly, we often wrestle with deep spiritual doubts about where God is in all of this. And these concerns can last for years, even decades.

We look to God for help, and that is a good thing, a central part of the journey of faith. We hope that he will resolve our confusing lives and give us a clear path forward. The problem is, we often get answers that sound like God but aren't thoroughly from his Word. For example, have you heard these solutions about how to best live the journey of faith?

"Just surrender to God."

"Here is a simple formula for victory."

"You need to try harder."

"Just pray and read your Bible."

"You're off his path and he's punishing you. Get your act together and it will work out."

Ultimately, these solutions fail us—not because they are totally wrong, but *because they are not comprehensively biblical answers.* They may have some remnant or aspect of the truth, but they don't provide the full perspective of the entire Bible. So these solutions just can't apply to the full human condition. As the saying goes, "Beware the person whose only tool is a hammer, for they see every problem as a nail." And beware the one who only has the simplistic formulas for faith.

Inés Franklin's book *Uncharted* is a refreshing and welcome contribution for those of us who have had difficulty experiencing our journey of faith. Her material is solid and so helpful. She provides a thorough look at what the Bible says about the right path. And her vulnerable personal narratives will engage you.

For a book in this arena to be most helpful, I believe it needs to have four fundamental aspects. Here are the aspects and the ways that Inés's thoughts express them and provide clarity and hope for the reader. I think you will be informed, encouraged, and perhaps a bit surprised and challenged by her content.

Relevance That Connects Us

When we look at the title of a book, the first thing most of us think is, "So how does this matter to my life?"

We're all busy. There are a great number of books, videos, and podcasts to learn from. We must be selective about how we spend our time learning about the faith journey. In other words, the material must be connected to what truly matters to us. It must have relevance. Relevance connects us to the material and to the author. It gives us hope that these words will make something in our lives better.

Uncharted is structured to be highly relevant to anyone who seeks to walk with Jesus in the best way possible. Here are some examples:

The struggles of life. As mentioned previously, no one is exempt from difficulties. Hardship is highly relevant because it gets our attention. We spend enormous amounts of time thinking about, worrying about, having conversations about, and trying to find solutions for our problems. It can be exhausting. But Inés is there with us in the struggles. She makes sure that she covers the matters that are hard for us all and are significant to us.

Confusion. Most of us have found that the journey of faith is not a linear progression. There are ups and downs and reverses, and it is very hard to make sense of it all. Good people suffer and bad people get away with it. People die who shouldn't have. We do all we can, and we still have negative outcomes. The book's content ties directly into this internal conflict, engages us, and gives us a better perspective—one that we can live with.

Our desire for ultimate control over our lives and circumstances. As the book says, we all come from a long line of control freaks. It simply is our nature. We want to feel some sense of security in the journey, and in our lives. So we try to control the actions of God and others to provide that security. You most likely can think of some event in which you could not change someone's behavior, the circumstances themselves, or even your own reaction. It is a daily struggle. *Uncharted* delves deeply into our control issues and provides solutions.

Our need for God to show up. The Christian life is hollow if we cannot see God's handiwork evident in some way. It would be too similar to a life without God, which would be empty. Yet we often ask God to give an answer or talk to us in some clarifying way, and we don't get a response. The book addresses this deep need.

The orientation to live in faith. Nothing is more relevant than this. We were designed by God to come after him in faith. Simply put, Jesus tells us, "Follow me" (Matthew 4:19). Our very existence is based on an orientation, a direction, a stance to be with him and follow wherever he leads. It is as relevant as anything can be. At the same time, following him in faith is not actually simple. We often have no clue as to what the next step should be. The book brings light to that path.

Scriptures That Guide Us

The Bible is God's gift to us, providing us with his grace, wisdom, and guidance. For thousands of years, people have found life and enormous help from the Scriptures.

I confess that I have a bit of a trigger about writers who support their ideas with random passages that they arm-twist out of context. This doesn't help readers understand what the Bible is truly saying; rather, it communicates what the writer wants the Bible to say, and that's a problem.

Inés does not have this mindset; hers is actually the converse. She is a serious student of the Bible, with an earned Master of Divinity degree from Fuller Seminary, one of the top institutions in the world.

When you read through the book, you will see well-thought-out scholarship that you can trust. Your faith journey will be guided safely because of how carefully she has studied the passages you'll read, as she is one who pays attention to the command to "be diligent to present yourself approved to God as a worker who does not need to be ashamed, accurately handling the word of truth" (2 Timothy 2:15 NASB).

Stories That Engage Us

Personal narratives that touch our hearts and minds are integral to a book's attraction and value to a reader. They inspire us, give us examples, and make things real for us. If the truths of a book are its skeleton, the stories are its flesh, as in "fleshing out the meaning" for us.

Uncharted is rich with stories, most of them from Inés's own faith journey throughout seasons of her life. You'll be able to identify with them and think, *me too,* when she describes her experiences. Also, she is one of the most personally vulnerable writers I have read. She chose to be authentic and honest in the service of helping the content matter to people, and you'll be moved by her rawness. Here are some examples:

- What growing up in severe poverty was like for her
- Being shamed by an authority figure in public, which was a scarring event
- As a little girl, being so desperate for hope and love that she came very close to taking her own life
- Falling into destructive relationships out of her brokenness
- Having serious moral failures

What's more, Inés does not follow the simplistic formula of "Then I found God and it immediately straightened out." She knows how hard change and transformation are on the faith journey. And that awareness will encourage anyone who has fallen, recovered, fallen, recovered, and fallen again.

That's not to say that all of the stories are about hard times. You'll be cheered to see how, using the skills she writes about, growth takes root deeply in her heart and life, and things do change for the better.

A Path That Transforms Us

A book that is worth your time investment requires an answer to the question, *How do I move forward with these truths? What are the steps?* We need a path to guide us in transforming our everyday lives. Inés provides us with a framework of best practices for the faith journey: *Following God based on genuine relationship, not obligation.*

Research on successful relationships is clear that going through the motions does not work. A spouse who automatically says, "I love you," every day but doesn't feel it in their heart will not endear their partner to them in any meaningful way. The same is true of our connection with God. He is not drawn to rituals designed to check off the box of spirituality: "For I desire loyalty rather than sacrifice, and the knowledge of God rather than burnt offerings" (Hosea 6:6 NASB).

Giving up our demand to know all the steps. Most of us would like our faith journey to be as predictable as our car navigation systems: "Take next exit, then left in 200 yards, then right in 500 yards—you have now reached your destination . . ." It helps us feel secure in the unknown and gives us a sense of control. The problem, however, is that at some levels, *faith is the opposite of control.* If we knew each step, there would be no need for faith. God requires faith in his Word and his character rather than what we can see: "Now faith is the assurance of *things* hoped for, the conviction of things not seen" (Hebrews 11:1 ESV, emphasis added). *Uncharted* teaches us ways to handle the anxiety of not knowing each step so that we can follow his leading.

Actively seeking instead of passively wishing. The faith journey requires us to take initiative, to make the first move sometimes, even if we aren't completely sure. Sometimes we are so overwhelmed with the complexities of life that we become passive instead of active, relying on God to rescue us. However, psychological research has shown that, with only a few exceptions, a passive approach to life's challenges will not get us where we want to go and will often lead to more problems. God designed life as a co-laborship with him. He does his part, and we do ours: "For we are God's fellow workers; you are God's field, God's building" (1 Corinthians 3:9 NASB). Inés is so helpful in her recommendations about taking action.

Moving toward the messy and finding him there. When I am speaking at a conference, I'll often ask the audience, "Okay, how many of you have ever struggled and been confused in a really messy problem in your faith walk: relationships, family, work, spiritual life?" Everyone raises their hands, of course. Then I'll say, "So how many of you have never had significant struggles or confusion?" No one will raise their hand. Then I'll say, "It's too bad no one raised their hands on this second question. We really needed someone to do that so the rest of us could see what denial looks like."

Because life, for Christians and non-Christians alike, is messy. Not everyone has the same type of messy, or the same levels of severity, but we all live in a world with brokenness. So often we want our faith journey to be clear sailing, but we instead encounter hardship, failure, loss, rejection, and more confusion. Inés goes to great lengths to show that faith as a means of success and clarity is not real, and it is not biblical. But she also shows how we can find Jesus in the storm and connect with his grace and resources to continue the journey.

Living in the right community. We were not designed to navigate faith alone. Our very minds and souls were created to transfer the nutrients of life to one another. Life takes a great deal of energy out of us. We sustain each other with being present, conveying the good, providing reality, and calling one another to action.

Some people make the mistake of thinking they should have all of their needs met by God alone, and that depending on the love, grace, and truth of people is a plan B. Yet, the Bible, and a great volume of research, all point to the fact that we need people. In fact, when we allow someone to bear our burdens of weakness, confusion, and struggle, we are fulfilling the very law of Christ: "Bear one another's burdens, and thereby fulfill the law of Christ" (Galatians 6:2 NASB). Inés provides skilled suggestions for how to let the right people walk the faith journey with you, and how to accompany them on their journeys.

Finally, on a personal note, having been a close friend with Inés and her husband, Jim, for many years, I can validate that not only is this book an excellent guide to your faith journey but that she also truly walks her talk. These words are trustworthy.

I hope you benefit greatly from *Uncharted*. God bless you.

John Townsend, PhD
New York Times Bestselling author of the Boundaries series
Founder, Townsend Institute and Townsend Leadership Group

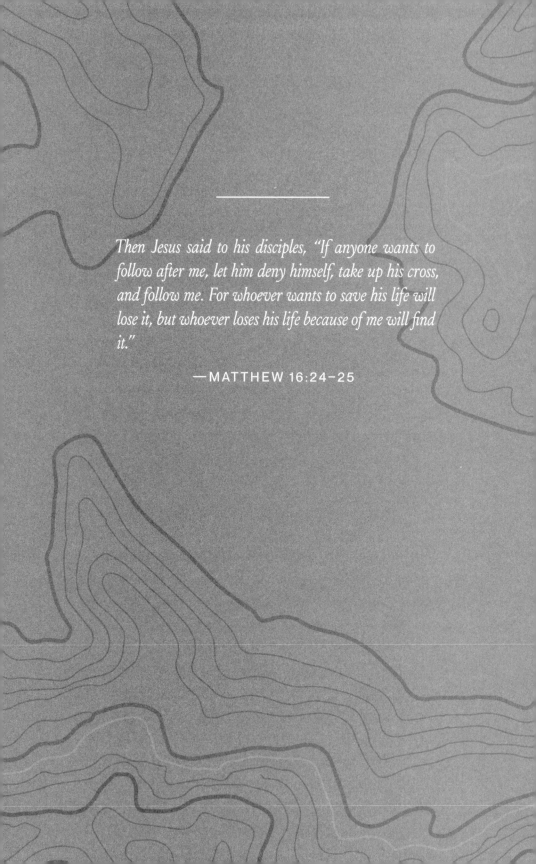

Then Jesus said to his disciples, "If anyone wants to follow after me, let him deny himself, take up his cross, and follow me. For whoever wants to save his life will lose it, but whoever loses his life because of me will find it."

—MATTHEW 16:24–25

INTRODUCTION

It's time we tell the truth: the journey of faith in Jesus is a mystery.

A mystery is something that is not fully understood. It's something we can't completely explain. Some mysteries are frightening. They are events or unexplained phenomena that defy logic and reasoning, and often leave us feeling unsettled or even scared. They can appear menacing and affect us personally, like a dark figure knocking on your door at midnight. It could be a teenage neighbor who was returning from a late-night study session and noticed your water hose running in the front yard. Or it could be a stranger with more nefarious intentions. Some mysteries we can well do without.

On the other hand, some mysteries are beautiful. Even though we may not fully understand them, they fill us with wonder and awe, like a beautiful sunset, the aurora borealis, or the birth of a child. Some are natural phenomena, like the unexplained giant circles that rotate and glow on the water in the Indian Ocean. Others are man-made, like the pyramids of Giza or the Great Wall of China. And then there are the mysteries of the human heart. Love is perhaps the most mysterious and beautiful thing of all. We can't explain why we love someone, but we know that it's real and wonderful.

When we encounter a mystery, we are forced to rely on our faith. We must trust that there is a greater purpose at work, even though we may not be able to see it. This can be a scary proposition, but it can also be an incredibly rewarding one. The beauty of a mystery is that it can lead us to a deeper understanding of ourselves and the world around us. It can challenge us to grow in wisdom and to see things in new and exciting ways.

The beauty of a mystery is found in its ability to take us on a journey of discovery. It makes life interesting and worth living.

When it comes to one's faith in Jesus, the journey can be both frightening and beautiful. Only Jesus knows it fully. For starters, his invitation to "follow me" is a call to deliberate self-denial. He invites his followers to pattern their lives after his own example of self-denial and suffering. To follow Jesus is to put our lives on the line, or die to ourselves, daily, which is what he means by "take up [your] cross" in Matthew 16:24. When we embark on this journey of faith, we are setting out into the unknown, leaving what is familiar behind. We don't know where the journey with Jesus will take us or what we will find along the way. Sure, the Bible clarifies that eternal life with God is our reward,[1] but do we know exactly what that will look like? We know it will be good and that we will be with and know[2] God in a way we now do not, but that's about it. This does not mean we shouldn't stay on the journey. In fact, part of the beauty of the walk of faith with Jesus is the mystery itself. It's what keeps us searching, learning, and growing in him. But the greater wonder is that God, the Creator of the universe, the Alpha and Omega, walks with us, and we walk with him! The surprising wonder is his deep love for us. The apostle John said it best:

> *God's love was revealed among us in this way: God sent his one and only Son into the world so that we might live through him. Love consists in this: not that we loved God, but that he loved us and sent his Son to be the atoning sacrifice for our sins.*
>
> —1 John 4:9–10

The journey of faith in Jesus is a beautiful mystery because, as we walk with him, he leads us into unknown territory. The Greek word we translate into mystery[3] is "*mystērion*" and it refers to something that must be revealed. More specifically, "some sacred thing hidden or secret which is naturally unknown to human reason and is only known by the revelation of God."[4] Jesus opens our eyes to new things and helps us understand God, ourselves, and the world differently. It is a journey that is full of surprises and delights. To us, the unknown is scary, but it is also exciting. It is an adventure that can take us places we never dreamed of going. It requires us to trust beyond ourselves, to trust in him who is greater.

When faced with a mystery, we want answers. We want to know why things happen and how they will end up. But with the journey of faith, there often aren't any easy answers. Each person's walk with the Lord is unique and filled with twists and turns and ups and downs. Often, we set expectations for our faith journey, but then we are bound to be disappointed. This can be frustrating, but it's also part of what makes the journey so beautiful. Instead of having all the answers, we get to trust in the Lord. We get to rely on the guidance of the Holy Spirit, even when we don't fully understand what he is doing.

This leads me to wonder why we would ever buy into the idea that the faith journey is predictable, linear, and easy. Even this famous and often-quoted verse in the Bible, found in Jeremiah's prophetic book, leads to more questions than answers:

> "For I know the plans I have for you"—this is the Lord's declaration—"plans for your well-being, not for disaster, to give you a future and a hope."
>
> —Jeremiah 29:11

This was directed to the nation of Israel as a whole, not to one person, and read to them when they were living in captivity in Babylon. They were slaves living in enemy territory and were told by Jeremiah that they would have to remain there for seventy years.[5] Amid captivity, they were to seek peace and "pursue the well-being of the city."[6]

This passage was likely received as bad news. The Israelites wanted rescue immediately, not in seventy years. To the Israelites, the words of Jeremiah might have sounded utterly ridiculous. The passage isn't a personal promise that if you follow Jesus, your faith journey will go smoothly. James makes it clear in his book that we will all experience trials,[7] and Peter tells us not to be surprised by our suffering.[8] And Jesus said, "A servant is not greater than his master."[9] The journey for Jesus was a hard one, full of tension, surprises, and the worst kind of suffering. Most of the psalms are poems of lament, and for good reason. Yet, none of God's good promises to his people ever failed.[10] The great mystery is that, even in the face of uncertainty and human suffering (at times horrendous), God has good desires and purposes for his people and is faithfully at work to carry out his redemptive purposes. This is the tension of the journey. And it is worth committing to it.

To navigate our unique faith journey with Jesus without denigrating its mystery, we must actively surrender and accept being sustained by the gift of his presence and the faithfulness of his promises. In later chapters, I will unpack what I mean by *active surrender*, but may it suffice here to say that leaning into the mysterious journey with Jesus is not a passive endeavor. Even faith, as defined by the writer of Hebrews, requires action: hope. "Now faith is the reality of what is hoped for, the proof of what is not seen."[11]

The call to follow Jesus is an imperative command. Thus, the goal of this book is to lead us from our obsession with control to an ever-renewing commitment to our faith journey with Jesus. I am convinced that only in that constant state of active surrender will we experience less anxiety, disillusionment, and frustration, and more of God's peace.

And don't we all want that?

I Am Just a Witness

But you will receive power when the Holy Spirit has come on you, and you will be my witnesses in Jerusalem, in all Judea and Samaria, and to the ends of the earth.

—Acts 1:8

Part of the reason this book took me so long to write is that I could not decide how to present my point of view on this important topic. My seminary education equipped me to conduct exegetical studies and present well-organized and substantiated commentary. My role as a pastor prepared me to walk with people in the reality of their stories, to provide a ministry of presence rather than just being the person with all the answers. My experience as a chaplain calls me to say very little and listen with my heart as I comfort God's people. My perspective as a Puerto Rican woman raised in financial poverty by a Roman Catholic family certainly colors my views. And my story, wildly messy as it is (you'll see), has been used by God to illustrate the mystery. This book is not a Bible study. It is not a pastoral sermon. It does not have all the answers. It is not silent (yes, you will hear my Puerto Rican passion). And it is not a memoir. It is a witness that includes a little bit of everything that makes up this daughter of Christ. You get all of me here, but I pray you hear God's voice well above my own.

At first, I thought it would be cool to organize a book called *Uncharted* rather untidily, but none of us like to read like that. So, the book in your hand is composed of four major sections:

I.   Knowing God's Desires
II. Overcoming Challenges

III. Blessing through Obedience

IV. Thriving by Thirsting for God

The nature of books also does not make it easy for me to make clear that these four major sections are not intended to be a linear progression with a dead end; rather, they are a circular rhythm of motion, much like a clock's hands. We navigate the journey of faith by seeking to know God's desires. This equips us to overcome the challenges we face. We experience blessing through our humble obedience. And no matter our circumstances, we thrive on the faith journey by thirsting for more of God and his desires. Again and again, we go around the cycle. It's a rhythm of commitment renewal. Another analogy that comes to mind is that of sunflowers. They face the east in the morning and wait for the sun to rise. Once the sun breaks the morning darkness, the sunflowers follow the sun all day until it sets. Then at night, programmed by their DNA, they return to the east, ready to receive the sun again. Oh, that this would be our forever posture! Longing for God above all else, enduring the heat of the day, staying fixed on him in obedience, and growing into fruitful people of God.

Guided by God's Desires

We all have a craving for control and certainty. We have desires for the future and our happiness. And as strong as these desires are, God's desires for us are even greater. He is sovereign over his creation, and he wants it to be good, very good. He makes his desires known to us in the Bible, but they are not presented as a quick fix, map, or formula. Commitment to God has a direction: toward the destination and way he chooses, not our own. This I learned the hard way. Learn from me what not to do.

For this reason, we will explore how control blinds us to God's desires and how his presence opens our eyes. We will discover that the faith journey is not a treasure hunt or quest in an action-adventure video game or movie. And we will see how the formulas we create most often let us down. I created my own quick-fix formula, and it nearly cost me my life.

I don't like to be the bearer of bad news, but along the journey we will experience opposition and obstacles. God has enemies, so anyone committed to Jesus is subject to attack. Suffering is guaranteed to all his children.[12] So it's not a matter of *if* we will struggle but *how* to overcome our obstacles. Also, suffering has a way of surfacing our deepest questions. It has a sobering effect on our controlled stupor.

Yet the questions that rise up are of great importance and well worth exploring. They reveal the deep longing in our heart and allow the Lord to meet us there with his perfect and healing love. Even if the struggle does not come from outside of us, sadly, we cause enough of it ourselves. We all make mistakes and will continue to do so. Some mistakes are so huge that they enslave us in shame. But God does not desire us to live in guilt or shame. This, too, we can overcome. I say this from experience. You'll know more about me than you probably wished when you bought this book. But I'm in good company with many biblical characters who also made a mess of things and experienced God's mercy. Maybe you need a bit of it yourself.

Blessed by God's Faithfulness

Commitment to God is costly. It costs us our agenda. Our ever-existence is secured by Jesus, for even when our earthly life is done, he promises us eternal life in him. But our agenda, our selfish ways, our pride, the desires of the flesh, whatever you want to call it, must die for God's purposes to be accomplished in and through us. We will explore this in more detail, but for now, it's a soothing balm to know that nothing is wasted with God. He gives us a heavenly mindset if we seek it. He designed us to walk this uncharted journey in community with others. So, whatever the cost, it is worth it. This promise is from Jesus, not from me. You'll see.

All of this does not mean that we will see exactly how things will work out or that we will not be fearful in the journey at times. Because he is the one in control and all-knowing, ambiguity is inevitable. We must learn to find peace in the fog of the journey. There is a way. Even our suffering, as we have discussed previously, can turn out to be a blessing of sorts. God is at work in everything. One of the great parts of this mysterious adventure is getting to see Jesus do his miracle of transformation in people's lives, including our own. Therefore, we must resist the temptation to pursue certainty on our own terms, for that kind of certainty hinders growth. Wanting more of God is the only way to live. Solomon said, "In the fear of the Lord one has strong confidence and his children have a refuge."[13] We're in good hands, my friend.

Walking in Spiritual Discipline

As I mentioned earlier, the key points of this book are offered as a rhythm. In other words, this book on "active surrender" is meant to trigger our commitment to Jesus—not to earn the love of Jesus, but to experience it to our core, to remain attached to the vine that gives us a fruitful life.[14] I know of no better way to remain committed than to practice commitment. Sometimes people say to me, "Inés, you are so close to God. I wish I had that." I'm not special. Believe me when I tell you that I don't always do it well, but I do work at remaining committed.

Spiritual practices help us activate our commitment by creating space to keep company with Jesus. For centuries, Christians have engaged in intentional practices, disciplines, and experiences to increase their awareness of God's presence in their lives and maintain a passionate flame of love, to stay on fire for Jesus. That is what I seek. I want this for you as well. At the end of each chapter, I have suggested a spiritual practice or two that goes along with the material presented. There are many other practices to discover. I hope this whets your appetite for them or encourages you to rediscover them anew. Also, as a companion to this book, I have compiled the spiritual practices in an easy-to-use guide that you can access on my website at inesfranklin.com.

I say it again: The journey of faith is mysterious. It is not always easy, but it is always worth it. Trusting in the Lord and following his will for our lives is the best decision we can make. My heart's prayer for you is that as you commit yourself to him, the joy of Jesus will be in you and that your joy may be complete.[15]

Thank you for being my companion on the journey of faith with Jesus. I hope that through this book, you will be encouraged and challenged in your own walk with the Lord.

Onward!

I.
KNOWING GOD'S DESIRES

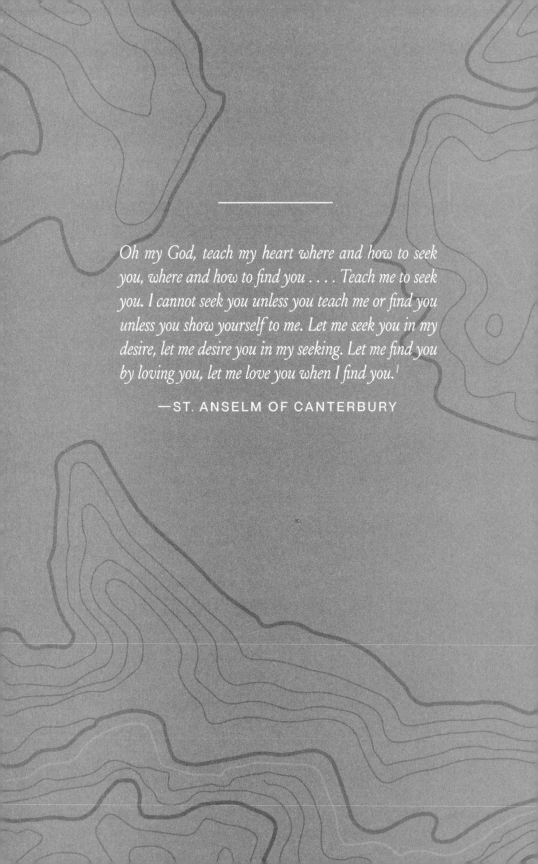

Oh my God, teach my heart where and how to seek you, where and how to find you . . . . Teach me to seek you. I cannot seek you unless you teach me or find you unless you show yourself to me. Let me seek you in my desire, let me desire you in my seeking. Let me find you by loving you, let me love you when I find you.[1]

—ST. ANSELM OF CANTERBURY

CHAPTER 1

SEEING THE INVISIBLE

KNOWING GOD'S DESIRES FOR YOU

The first time I heard about the Creator of everything—of all that we see and cannot see, the birds of the air, fish in the sea, sun, planets, mountains, ants, and rain, all the animals and people, air, gravity, and love—I imagined a bearded older man, dressed in a glowing white outfit and holding a magic wand, floating away in the dark universe. With my seven-year-old mind's eye, perhaps subconsciously avoiding divine authority, I drew small the Almighty God.

The idea of an all-powerful God who is sovereign over everything was alarming. Already I had deep scars from several obsessively controlling people in my life. I had a life-draining, deep-seated desire for certainty and control, to shape outcomes and life events to my liking.

But though I didn't know it, God was already offering me life-giving water from a deep well. The truth was that his authority held the key to peace. My sovereign God wanted me to seek, find, and know his good, perfect, and loving heart—and he would eventually open my eyes to see him, revealing to me his good desires.

I didn't know this. My desire for control hid it from me. But my Puerto Rican grandmother, my abuelita? She knew.

Abuelita knew that in the human soul there is a deep yearning that is satisfied only by the love of God. Her life was successful, but also tough. My abuelo (grandfather) ran a small construction company, farmed their land, and tended their cattle. From early morning to late at night, Abuelita helped him and took care of the household and children's needs. Their team effort and hard work paid off as they built their own beautiful home and had enough resources to be generous to others.

Even so, as the matriarch of thirteen children, Abuelita experienced the devastating loss of her first son, the terror of sending sons to war, and walked through many seasons of relational, financial, political, and health-related uncertainty. The many challenges she faced built her into a driven woman and a strong leader. She set lofty goals for herself and her family, and her determination helped her accomplish much!

But sometimes, when others did not behave the way she wanted them to, she became overly controlling, angry, frustrated, and disappointed. She knew God was in control, and that his path was peace, but she, too, struggled to cope with uncertainty. I used to watch her from a distance as she trimmed her roses and prayed out loud, seeking God's help. The fact that she knew to reach out to God showed that, despite her trust issues, she knew the right steps to take to find freedom from the fear that grips the control-obsessed human heart.

Blinded by Control

I come from a long line of control freaks. You do too. My sweet abuelita would say so; and if she were here, she'd point her shaky, arthritic finger at each of us for emphasis. All of us like to have control, some of us more than others. We want things to happen as we expect them to, people to behave in a certain manner, and life to function within our boundaries. We want our parents to be perfect, our spouses to know what we are thinking, our children to immediately do what we tell them, our boss to reward our accomplishments, and all manner of illnesses to skip over us. We all crave certainty.

It all started in a garden, the most beautiful and perfect garden ever to exist. Humanity was birthed in complete bliss and blessing, provided with everything needed for flourishing, joy, and peace, including an intimate, loving relationship and communion with the Creator. God "formed the man out of the dust from the ground and breathed the breath of life into his nostrils, and the man became a living being."[2] He created men and women in his image, in his likeness, and set them on a mission with God-given authority.[3] Then he planted a garden for humanity to enjoy walking in and working in with him. That joy, however, depended on Adam and Eve trusting God above all else and relying on his supreme power and authority.

But they didn't.

Adam and Eve gave into the temptation to surpass their status as "image bearers" and tried to reach out and snatch extra power and knowledge for themselves. Then "they knew they were naked," and their desire for control was exposed.[4] As their descendants, we've all been exposed, and we all "have sinned and fall short of the glory of God."[5]

Abuelita would agree with modern psychologists and behavioral scientists in their assessment that control feels good to us because it makes us believe that we have power over things, events, people, and, more importantly, the future. However, the more we try to control outcomes, the more likely we are to fall prey to what Dr. Ellen Langer termed the "illusion of control"—the belief we have more control over a situation than we actually do.[6]

The illusion of control is like being blind but thinking we're just in a dark room. It is a fake straight line. A straight line between two points usually indicates the most efficient way to travel, yes, but life, nature, and people rarely function that way. If we could go "as the crow flies," we would reach our destination without the twists and turns, bumps, or trauma of the not-so-straight road. Linear paths are faster, predictable, efficient, and orderly. We crave these attributes in our lives and assume taking a straight path is going to make us happy.

But we aren't crows, and we can't fly. So the linear path is mostly an illusion—and illusions can't make us happy. *Nothing unreal can make us happy.* Sure, many things happen in a semi-orderly fashion, and we do have *some* level of control over things, but not fully, not as much as we want.

A human is like a breath; his days are like a passing shadow.

—Psalm 144:4

The writer of Psalm 144 reminds us that our life is but a breath, fleeting and vulnerable. We have a lot less control than we realize or wish to admit. The worldwide experience of the COVID-19 pandemic was proof of this hard-to-accept reality. Even if we felt in control in many of the areas of our own lives (our health, relationships, financial security, and spiritual grounding), coping with the uncertainty of world events was sometimes overwhelming. Surveys show that there was a major increase in the number of adults who reported increased stress, fear, anxiety, depression, and insomnia.[7] Alcohol and drug abuse grew, and so did divorce and suicide risk. People tried to cope with their fears, get clarity about the future, and gain control over their lives, yet social tensions multiplied. Sadly, the more controlling we get, the more unhappy, stressed, and anxious we become.

Think about a time in your own life when someone was overly controlling toward you. How did it feel? Conversely, think of times you have been the overly controlling one. What did it cost you?

We might think it is better to be in control than to be under someone else's control, but both scenarios are harmful to us. Being overly controlling and becoming obsessed with desired outcomes not only hurts our physical and emotional health, but it also affects the health of our relationships, both with God and with others. It makes us blind to God's wonderful, loving, and blessed desires, and it keeps us from building intimacy with other people.

When we are apart from God, we face a nagging emptiness and hopelessness concerning our numerous struggles and limitations. It is God who holds all things together,[8] and "in him we live and move and have our being."[9]

His sovereign control is not like ours. He sees the big picture, while we have extremely limited access to it. His rule is good, very good, while history has proven that human authority is easily corrupted.

Only when you let go of your craving for ultimate control, and abandon your quests for a quick fix, are you able to fully experience the freedom and joy that God desires for you

All of this leads to an unavoidable conclusion—only when you let go of your craving for ultimate control, and abandon your quests for a quick fix, are you able to fully experience the freedom and joy that God desires for you. Indeed, God has many desires for you, and they are perfect.

And here is the good news: God's not hiding his desires for you; they are in plain sight.

Seeing with Faith

Abuelita believed that the entire faith journey is theological, a study of the nature of God. As C. S. Lewis so eloquently put it, "Theology means 'the science of God', and I think any man who wants to think about God at all would like to have the clearest and most accurate ideas about Him which are available."[10] At times it might feel like we're seeking to behold what is invisible, but we can't help but engage in theological reflection, seeking deeper connection and greater understanding.[11] As we do, we join the ongoing conversation that started long, long ago between humanity and the Creator. The conversation concerns everything related to religious life. "Not only ideas of God *per se*, but everything associated with faith, church, and ministry."[12]

But it is faith that gives us eyes to see the One who is above it all. To know the desires God has for us, we first must put our faith in him.

Abuelita's faith commitment to God was on full display during her life, and in hindsight, I know she was a great example for me to follow. She was a dedicated follower of Jesus, trusting him as the Savior who paid the penalty for our sins and secured eternal life for all who believe in him.[13] She served him faithfully and wanted us to do the same. She never missed an opportunity to declare her heartfelt desire for all her forty-five grandchildren to know God's heart. Her ambition for her descendants to have faith in God and dedicate their lives to seeking and serving him was no secret. I watched as she remained faithful to her Savior year after year, through all her struggles. She wasn't perfect, but she was faithful.

Faith like Abuelita's hardly ever treads a linear path. Think of your own faith journey. How linear and neat is it, really? Sometimes it helps to write it out: the ups and downs, wrong turns, successes, disappointments, times of growth, walls of struggle, moments of doubt or despair, accreting past sin, crashing into ditches of temptation, or the times when we quit. Perhaps take a moment to jot down a quick list of the big events in your faith journey, and then prayerfully reflect on them.

As we reflect on our own experience, and the experiences of those we know well, it's easy to see that no two faith journeys are the same. Abuelita's was unique because it was hers. Yours is unique because it is yours. Even if you cannot remember when or how yours started, even if it seems easygoing compared to other people's stories, it was not linear, and you know it. But that is what makes it wonderfully yours! The important thing is that faith in Christ is the only way for any of us to experience God's desires for our well-being and our eternal future.

Abuelita took her last breath just one month shy of her hundredth birthday. Her transition to eternal glory came in peace as she was surrounded by loved ones. The moment she died, she could see clearly what the rest of us can only imagine. I am convinced my abuelita, Isidora "Angela" Morales, heard those sought-after words, "Well done, good and faithful servant!"[14] These are words many of us wish to hear from God when we come into his presence. They come when we put our trust in Jesus as our Lord and Savior and surrender our lives to him.[15]

Abuelita could see what was invisible to me for the first forty years of my life. I just wasn't looking.

Sharing Desires Out of Love

Out of her deep love, Abuelita made her desires known to me. One of the ways she did that was by the names she gave me. Abuelita named me "Inés Soccoro," which meant, in essence, "pure help." Names were a way for Abuelita to express her faith.[16] With these names, she broadcasted her desire for me to become a woman dedicated to God's service—maybe a nun. She expressed her faith in the God who has the power to purify my sinful heart and equip me to help others. With these names, Abuelita sought to give me a glimpse of her desires—but also of God's desires for me.

I felt the pressure to make Abuelita's treasured dreams come true. She was convinced that her plan aligned with God's will, but she could not have imagined the very crooked path I would travel on my faith journey—and I will be sharing a lot more about my faith journey (not just Abuelita's!) in the later chapters of this book. For now, suffice it to say that for me to see what she could see, and what God wanted me to see, I had to embark on my own uncharted faith journey with God.

This is the case for all of us. Each of us must walk our own journey, and, like I said, it's not as linear as we tend to think.

Think of the many biblical characters whose names have great promise but whose lives did not follow a linear path. They lived one day after another, as we all do, but their journey did not follow a predictable trajectory. Aaron ("teacher") never taught. David ("well-beloved, dear") had a history of making mistakes that hurt his own beloved ones. Moses ("taken out, drawn forth") ran for his life after he killed an Egyptian. Tamar ("palm, symbolizing goodness") was the name of two unique women in the Bible whose stories were messy and tragic. While Abuelita's dream for me was beautiful, my life did not work out exactly as she wished. Her chosen name declared me "pure help" to this world, but I was born with a sinful nature—and I went on sinning, in ways neither one of us could have anticipated, before finally surrendering control of my life to Jesus. My nonlinear journey was marked by doubts, obsession with control, and forty years spent wandering in the wilderness.

But God, in his goodness and faithful love, still pursued me with his good desires.

And just as Abuelita did, God worked to make his good desires known to me.

Why? Because he loves me.

And he loves you too.

Not Control, but Commitment

Perhaps you struggle with doubts about your journey because you believe that God is too big, distant, or busy to care about you. Perhaps you think you are alone. Or maybe you struggle to interpret every circumstance of life, and therefore, your confidence and commitment get beat down. If you tend to compare your journey with others' and think God has better desires for others than for you, you're not alone. These are all common struggles that lead us to seek control of our circumstances and the faith journey itself. Yet, control is a trap that keeps you and me from enjoying the intimate relationship God is fervently seeking with us.

Abuelita knew that the answer to our control problem is to not just surrender our hearts and our problems to God—although we should—*but to double down in our commitment to Jesus.* To see God's desires for you unfold, you must dedicate your life to seeking a deeper relationship with him in the present, pursuing God as passionately as he pursues you, moment by moment.

Simply waving the white flag of surrender to God is not enough. Lifting our hands up in the air and assuming a passive posture is not what God invites us to do. Joshua would not have made it into the Promised Land if he had simply surrendered to God's plan. He had to be surrendered, yes. *But he was also dedicated to a trusting relationship with God in the present.* Joshua had to surrender and act. Both were necessary to have the strength and courage to gather the people, organize the army and the priests, and then join them in obedience as they circled around Jericho for seven days in silence and on the seventh day seven times, culminating with a shout and blasting of horns.[17] He didn't just *passively* surrender his will to God's; it was *active* trust that drove Joshua to take such bold steps. Day by day, Joshua's commitment to God was on display way before the walls of Jericho came tumbling down. Joshua could see what seemed invisible to others. He could see God's desires, God's heart.

You can too.

> *Control is a trap that keeps you and me from enjoying the intimate relationship God is fervently seeking with us*

Invisible No More

Many of us, even after we have entrusted our lives to Jesus as our Savior, struggle to surrender control. While our salvation is not at risk, our worship of God and our witness to others are obstructed by our lack of dedication to what we say we believe. The answer to your control problem is to make it a daily practice to keep your eyes open in the moment, faithfully committed to a relationship with Jesus no matter the outcome, trusting in his desires above your own, and holding all things with open hands. After all, one of the few things we can control is our attitude toward the present moment.

Keeping your eyes open in the moment allows you to see how God is at work at the macro and micro level. As Jesus said, "Don't worry about tomorrow, because tomorrow will worry about itself. Each day has enough trouble of its own."[18] Releasing control of tomorrow and living in the present can be challenging, especially if you're suffering, or if you are a person who likes to think way ahead and plan for unforeseen circumstances. That is why the purpose of this book is to offer you encouragement and spiritual practices to take you into deeper discipleship with Jesus as you walk step-by-step, day by day—sometimes breath by breath—with the help of the Holy Spirit.

The same God who walked with the people of Israel as they wandered in the wilderness wants to light our seasons of darkness and lead our brightest days

The first step in beholding the invisible is recognizing that you're not alone, never have been, and never will be. Scripture reveals that God is ever-present. This truth inspired Abuelita to keep her Bible always open and heavily marked with underlines and notes. With his presence and love, God wants to touch and transform your heart. 1 Corinthians 1:9 says, "God is faithful; you were called by him into fellowship with his Son, Jesus Christ our Lord." The Greek word for "fellowship" is *koinonia,* which means to have the closest possible intimate relationship with someone—in this case, God. This passage is calling us to the highest level of intimacy with God, to become one with him. He seeks to transform your desires, interests, and priorities to match his own so that you may become a person after God's own heart and live forever in unity with him. He seeks to conform you into the image of his Son.[19]

When we release our need for control and allow God to be in charge, we can trust God to lead us exactly where we need to go—even if the path is not always clear. Rather than live in the grip of fear from lack of control, our hearts can rejoice, following the example of David, who wrote in the midst of tremendous struggle, "God, I will sing a new song to you; I will play on a ten-stringed harp for you!"[20]

Not only is your loving God ever-present, but he leads you day and night, making his desires known to you—even if you are unaware of his presence. The same God who walked with the people of Israel as they wandered in the wilderness wants to light our seasons of darkness and lead our brightest days.

Seeing the Present

If we don't go for the quick fix, what are we supposed to do? Commit to following the Lord wherever—and however—he leads us.

The book of Exodus tells the story of Israel's departure from hundreds of years of slavery in Egypt toward a new land God was preparing for them to live in with freedom and purpose. It is clear when we read these passages that it is not by human planning, control, or purposeful direction that the people made it through their very difficult journey, but it was by God's leading.

The obvious, straightforward, and safe path along the Mediterranean coast was not how God moved the nation of Israel from the oppression of the Egyptians to the Promised Land of Canaan. God moved Israel around the desert in an unusual, roundabout, and uncharted route. God led them this way purposefully, perhaps to keep them from the temptation to return to Egypt. If it were up to them and within their control, they would have taken themselves back to slavery.[21] And if an outside observer could have watched them, that observer would have been tempted to believe that Israel was wandering about aimlessly in the wilderness. They seemed like runaway slaves without any hope of surviving—but they were actually a freed people on the road to joy and victory.

The way in which God led the people of Israel highlights the central point of the book of Exodus: Yahweh is the rightful Master over Israel and the world. I wish to encourage you today. No matter what is happening in your life right now, God is leading you to a better place! That's who he is. That's what he does, always!

> *The Lord is the one who will go before you. He will be with you; he will not leave you or abandon you. Do not be afraid or discouraged.*
>
> —Deuteronomy 31:8

God led his people on an uncharted journey of faith, in a "pillar of cloud" during the day, and in a "pillar of fire" at night.[22] These are powerful images! In the Bible, together or separately, fire and cloud represent the splendor, glory, mystery, and awe of God's presence. The language in Exodus 13:21 denotes that this sign was present in a continuous fashion. God gave them a visible form for them to follow as they moved through unknown and dangerous territory. God had a physical presence with his people so they could see and follow him. Likewise, Jesus was present with his disciples and called them to follow him.[23] And now, God is present in us through the Holy Spirit living within us.[24] The entire Bible depicts God as present, not distant, as some other religions believe.

In the Israelites' escape from Egypt, God led his people whether they wanted to follow him or not. He led them along the right path according to the right timing, even if they did not want his direction. He led them through the obstacles, his way.

Sometimes, God led them to stop and wait. Numbers 9 tells us, "When the cloud remained over the tabernacle a long time, the Israelites obeyed the Lord's order and did not set out," but "whenever the cloud lifted, they set out."[25] We're told that sometimes the pillar of cloud and fire remained above the tabernacle for only a day, other times for several days or months. The people did their best to settle but also remained flexible so they could move when God moved. I imagine they decorated their tents, grew some beans, and then, whoops!—they had to leave their bean farm behind and follow God because he decided it was time to go on.

It's easy for us to say, "I follow God. I trust him. I accept his direction all the time." But, if we're honest, when we think about it, how often do we ignore that still, small voice of God? Too often, we follow our internal rebel's yell of, "I don't give a rip! I'm going down this path!" Even if deep in our hearts we know God is saying, "No! Not that way!" We often let God direct, but follow partially. Thankfully, his mercies are new every morning, and his guidance never stops. God promises to lead you through all circumstances, and always in the right direction.

> *I will instruct you and show you the way to go; with my eye on you, I will give counsel.*
>
> —Psalm 32:8

The twelve disciples left everything to follow Jesus. They went everywhere he went; followed his every step. Even when Jesus took off to be alone, they went looking for him. Some people refused to follow Jesus, and some followed for a little while and then left, but the twelve apostles were convinced he was taking them in the right direction.

At one point, when many followers deserted Jesus, Jesus asked the Twelve if they also wanted to leave. But Simon Peter answered, "Lord, to whom will we go? You have the words of eternal life. We have come to believe and know that you are the Holy One of God."[26]

After three years of intensive instruction, Jesus still knew that there was much more he wanted to teach his disciples. But what he needed to teach, he chose to reveal after his resurrection, after atoning for the sins of believers, after proving his deity, and after the Father glorified him. Only then would the disciples be ready to receive the further revelation he had for them. He promised believers that they would receive that guidance from the Holy Spirit.

In the same way, we don't learn everything that God has for us right away. But we have something else in common with the disciples: We have the assurance that God is leading us in the right direction. Like them, we also have the Holy Spirit with us. He comforts us when things seem uncertain, and he leads us in the good ways that are certain to *him*. Where we are confused, he is not. He knows everything and loves us fully, so we can trust him completely.

In Ephesians 1, Scripture teaches that once you put your trust in Jesus, the Holy Spirit assures your salvation, gives you wisdom and revelation, and empowers you.[27] He purifies you, unites you with other believers, intercedes for you, and gives you spiritual gifts.[28] He declares every Christ-follower a child of God and seals us as his. But he also leads and guides us in and through the most important decisions we will ever make. He does this for us one step at a time. The

Holy Spirit powerfully transforms our minds, and desires for us to walk in step with him.[29]

Your *unique* journey matters to God so much that he makes his desires known. Just as Abuelita wanted me to know her desires for me, through my names, God wants you to know his desires for you, through the words of the Bible and by the power of the Holy Spirit.

The voice of God will give you the direction you seek and the peace to trust him with your future. May you hear it and respond as the prophet Samuel did. When he heard God's voice, and once he recognized who was speaking to him, Samuel responded, "Speak, for your servant is listening."[30]

Like Samuel, we all must say yes to God, not knowing what is ahead, with open eyes waiting eagerly for whatever he has planned next. This may sound simple, but it is not simplistic. It is a decision to give up our illusions of control. It is an act of courage and commitment.

And always remember, you're not alone—as I discovered in a very surprising way when I was seven years old. We'll talk about that, and more about what actively trusting God looks like, in the chapters to come.

SPIRITUAL PRACTICE: THE PRESENCE

Introduction to the Spiritual Disciplines

In the words of Dr. Dallas Willard, spiritual disciples are "activities of mind and body purposefully undertaken, to bring our personality and total being into effective cooperation with the divine order. They enable us more and more to live in a power that is, strictly speaking, beyond us."[31] Willard contends that "the rigors of discipline certainly lead to the easy yoke and the full joy of Christ."[32] Adele Alberg Calhoun compiled a comprehensive list of spiritual practices in her *Spiritual Disciplines Handbook*. "Practice" is defined as "performing an activity repeatedly or regularly in order to improve or maintain one's proficiency."[33] Calhoun asserts that spiritual disciplines have the power to transform us, refocus our scattered thoughts, and calm our anxiousness. I will showcase a few of the disciplines briefly at the end of each chapter and invite you to practice them. Often, I combine two practices because they complement each other, as well as the material in the chapter. You can do one or both. I also recommend that you read their books for more practices and details.

We have inherited many of these deepening practices from church tradition, from brothers and sisters who have walked this uncharted faith journey ahead of us. Calhoun says that "spiritual disciplines open us to God" and align our spirit to the Holy Spirit to deepen our relationship with our Creator.[34] Willard says that because we "cooperatively interact with God," the disciplines result in a "new overall quality of human existence."[35] The practices, whether done individually or in community, help us know Christ Jesus deeply and become like him because they open our hearts to join him with our everyday selves.

"Practicing the Presence" is designed to increase our "openness and awareness" of God's nearness and "experience every moment as a gift from our Creator."[36] We bring Jesus to mind for a specified time or throughout the day, centering our scattered thoughts on him. There are many benefits to this practice. It can take us into deeper union with Christ, help us let go of the need to perform for God, and help us experience each moment as sacred. Take time to jot down in a journal how the practice helps you grow in your journey.

The Process

This simple but profound exercise can be done anywhere, at any time. You don't need any special equipment or training. You can imagine yourself in God's presence (for example, sitting at his feet). Or you can picture God sitting, standing by, or walking with you as you do your daily activities. Since the Holy Spirit is inside you, ask him to help you sense his presence. Try to maintain a listening posture and an openness to receive. Just set aside a few minutes each day to focus on Jesus.

As you do, you may find your heart opening more and more to his love. If you're new to the practice, start with just a minute or two each day. Gradually increase the amount of time you spend as it feels comfortable. There's no need to force it; just let it happen naturally. You can also use objects to help you focus. You can put a symbol, cross, or a passage within your view, or light a candle. The physical presence of a symbolic object also helps bring God's presence to mind. You might find it helpful to set a timer so you don't have to keep track of time. Focus on whatever image of Jesus comes to mind. It could be from a painting or statue, or it could be your own mental image. Just let yourself be drawn into his presence. As you focus on Jesus, you may find your thoughts wandering. That's okay. Just gently bring your attention back to him whenever it happens. Remember, this practice is about building a relationship, not a performance.

When you're finished, take a few moments to reflect on your experience. What did you see? What did you learn?[37]

Prompting Scriptures

> "The Lord your God is among you, a warrior who saves. He will rejoice over you with gladness. He will be quiet in his love. He will delight in you with singing."
>
> —Zephaniah 3:17

Where can I go to escape your Spirit? Where can I flee from your presence? If I go up to heaven, you are there; if I make my bed in Sheol, you are there. If I fly on the wings of the dawn and settle down on the western horizon, even there your hand will lead me; your right hand will hold on to me. If I say, "Surely the darkness will hide me, and the light around me will be night"—even the darkness is not dark to you. The night shines like the day; darkness and light are alike to you.

—Psalm 139:7–12

"And remember, I [Jesus] am with you always, to the end of the age."

—Matthew 28:20

Draw near to God, and he will draw near to you.

—James 4:8

Let us draw near with a true heart in full assurance of faith.

—Hebrews 10:22

If a man once looked at the Atlantic from the beach, and then goes and looks at a map of the Atlantic, he also will be turning from something real to something less real . . . The map is admittedly only colored paper, but there are two things you have to remember about it. In the first place, it is based upon what hundreds and thousands of people have found out by sailing the real Atlantic. In that way it has behind it masses of experience just as real as the one you could have from the beach; only, while yours would be a single glimpse, the map fits all those different experiences together. In the second place, if you want to go anywhere, the map is absolutely necessary.

—C. S. LEWIS, *MERE CHRISTIANITY*

CHAPTER 2

INCOMPLETE MAPS

GIVING UP CONTROL AND
EMBRACING COMMITMENT

A week after I learned about the Creator of the universe, I heard him speak to me. It happened just as I was about to jump off the roof of my home, thinking it was a good way to leave this painful life and go to heaven. You see, I had sketched my own map for my faith journey, hoping to take myself that day from the dirt to the presence of the Almighty.

I was six or seven years old when Abuelita enrolled me in Roman Catholic catechism class. The lessons took place at the old Iglesia San Miguel Arcángel (Church of St. Michael the Archangel) located in the town plaza of Naranjito, Puerto Rico. A small group of children sat on the front wooden pews, trying not to move, as the dry wood made creaking sounds that echoed around the room. The air smelled of burning candles, and a large crucifix loomed above with a "sleeping," barely dressed Jesus held up by nails. It was a prime environment for my inquisitive mind.

At the first class, I listened with deep curiosity to the nun as she told us that God created everything: the trees, the animals, the birds, and the rain. But then, after a little while, as she elaborated on the details of the Genesis 1 creation narrative, her voice faded away, like the sound of a train gradually losing intensity as it leaves a station. My mind became preoccupied with a louder incoming and nagging question: *If God created everything, and there was nothing before he created it, where was he standing?*

I could stand it no more. My question blew out through my lips and broke the flow of the teacher's presentation. I heard my classmates' audible gasps and giggles, quickly followed by a moment of silence as we all stared at the nun's face. We watched her lips tighten and her brows come together with magnetic speed. For a moment, the only sound in the room came from the street, rolling in like fog through the high windows of the chapel. Then the silence was disrupted by the nun's stern voice as she proceeded to chastise me for my lack of faith. "You have no faith!" she said in Spanish, "You must ask God to forgive you for your unbelief!"

I know she said more, but I was too traumatized to remember the rest of her words. She sent me to the back of the church, her arm outstretched and her long index finger pointing to the dreaded last pew where great sinners often cried. I was instructed to pray in repentance—my question left unanswered.

When I came back the following week, the nun was teaching about heaven. I decided to sit at the back of the class, in the empty third pew, but then leaned forward as if trying to grab every word that came out of her mouth. She described the difference between this world and heaven, this existence and the next. My young brain recorded her every word. "In heaven, there is no more pain, no sorrow, no violence, no tears! In the beautiful place of heaven, God's majesty reigns, everything that is good is there, and nothing evil can ever enter for eternity."

And then I got distracted by another question: *If heaven is that good, and if we're headed there anyway, why do we stay here on earth?*

I ignored the ringing question in my head and bit my lower lip to keep the words locked inside. My eyes scanned the room to see if anyone else realized the good news, but they seemed oblivious to the ramifications of what was just declared. In my mind, I thought, "Well, you all can stay here. I'm going to heaven."

With that determination made, I turned my attention to how I would accomplish my goal.

From Point A to Point Z

What would tempt a seven-year-old girl to end her life and go to heaven after learning about God in a catechism class?

Incomplete maps. I was attempting to use my own map—my own interpretation of what was right and what was wrong, and how things should go. There was no room in my mind for any other human's opinion or experiences, much less God's.

As I look back, I remember the pain in my heart. My sense of paradise on earth was lost sometime after I turned one and my father left our family without returning even for short visits. We struggled to survive in deep poverty in a tiny, crudely built shack, one third of which served as a store to sell candy and the other two thirds as a bedroom for my then-pregnant mother and her six children. I already knew the sorrow of abandonment, the pain of hunger, and the terrifying fear of being separated from my mother and my siblings because she could not take care of us on her meager income.

The shame of poverty as we stood in line for government assistance was permanently inked in my mind. Grief for my mother's struggles (the stress of providing for so many kids, and the challenge of keeping them safe from the world and each other) stunted my emotional development. Going to heaven seemed a reasonable way to escape the already intolerable pain of life. My mom would have one less mouth to feed. I figured she'd be happy about that. (Boy, was I wrong!)

We live in a chronically anxious society that wants a quick fix to everything. We want things now. We pay a premium for products and demand same-day shipping. We are incensed at being forced to wait for the episodes of the next season of our favorite show to drop.

If our impatience were limited to shopping and entertainment, it would not be such a big deal. But this quick-fix mentality influences all aspects of our life, including how we engage with God and each other.

When traveling along twisting and winding roads, it is easy to get a bit anxious and a little bit sick, especially if you're the passenger and you don't have a lot of confidence in the driver. You do not know what is going to come around the corner. In the same way, in our spiritual journey, we can get anxious when we don't know what is up ahead.

Even when our lives are going well, and all is as it should be, we can experience fear.

We might be afraid that since all has gone well for a while, naturally something bad is bound to happen soon. We start to worry and have a little anxiety about the phone calls we might receive or what the doctor is going to say the next time we go for a checkup. Things can't stay good all the time, right?

Some of us are just pessimistic like that. But we can also feel that way if we are at a relational, financial, physical, or mental low point. Sometimes when we're in the middle of a challenging season, it can seem like the worst disaster possible with no end in sight. We can't help but wonder, "Is this going to get worse?"

Sadly, when we're constantly worried about what is next, whether the times are good or bad, we cannot be all God has called us to be. We cannot rest in the present.

But none of this is a surprise to God, and none of it is new to humanity.

God knows we are wired to seek certainty and want control, believing that knowing how the future will pan out will keep us safer today. We think that maybe if we can control the majority of things happening in our life, we won't suffer as much.

But if we knew the future, we would likely be more prone to despair, boredom, apathy, impatience, and a lack of peace. Think of the last time someone told you the entire plot of a movie before you watched it. Knowing too much ahead of time changes our expectations and the quality of the experience, not the outcome. God knows how our story will go, and he wants us to develop a heart for him, delighting in him, his Word, and his ways. We cannot manipulate God into giving us a detailed account of our future—not by our good deeds *or* by our evil acts. He loves us too much to do that. The way forward is to rely on our relationship with Jesus.

We cannot manipulate God into giving us a detailed account of our future—not by our good deeds or by our evil acts. He loves us too much to do that.

As we rely on him, we become more aware of our vulnerability and develop an increasing propensity for selfless service toward others.

Twists and Turns

The story of Jacob's son Joseph takes up an impressive amount of biblical real estate and contains many details about the ups and downs of his journey. If God had given Joseph a complete and detailed map of his faith journey, he likely would have tapped out early. His story is told in Genesis 37 and Genesis 39–50. For thirteen chapters we read of the many twists and turns and ups and downs of Joseph's life.

His story starts when he is seventeen years old, the second

youngest of twelve brothers. Normally the eldest son would be the one to be held in the highest honor, but Jacob, Joseph's father, does something remarkable. He favors a younger son with a *këthoneth*, or fancy coat. The description of the coat in Genesis 37:3 is a Hebrew word that is hard to translate. It is often translated as an "ornate robe" or a "coat of many colors," but it strictly means a coat of some sort with long sleeves or stripes. The point is that this coat was hard to miss. It had meaning and purpose. The coat would have given Joseph a level of authority over his older brothers, something they resented. The plot thickens when Joseph starts having dreams.

He had two dreams and made the mistake of sharing them with his family. In one dream, his brothers were bowing down to him. They didn't like it when Joseph told them that at all! Then, in the other dream, the sun, the moon, and the stars, which represented his parents and his ancestors, were also bowing down to him. Recounting his dreams did not make Joseph popular in the household!

Then, it gets even worse because Joseph's father, Jacob, sends Joseph to report on his brothers who were tending the flock. Would you like a brother like that? His brothers got so upset that they plotted to kill him. Joseph went from unmerited favor and having huge dreams to being so hated that his life was at risk. His brothers tore off his fancy coat and threw him in a cistern—a hole in the ground lined with rocks that fills with water in the rainy season so livestock can drink from it. This one was empty, but they left him at the bottom of it to die.

Then, one of the brothers had second thoughts and convinced the other brothers to spare Joseph's life. So they sold him for twenty shekels of silver to a caravan of Midianite merchants bound for Egypt.

Joseph was sent off to Egypt to an unknown future, and the brothers returned to Jacob with the "coat of colors," now stained with the blood of a goat they had killed to simulate his death. For

Joseph, his authority, his father's favor, and all of the dreams he may have had were stripped away with his coat. Gone! Now he and his shattered dreams were headed for Egypt, probably being dragged behind the caravan.

Has anybody ever shattered your dreams? Have the twists and turns of your life discouraged you to the point of wanting to give up?

That humid day in Puerto Rico, when I heard that heaven was within my grasp, I felt extremely vulnerable, and I didn't like it. I wanted the treasure of heaven and went on the hunt for it. I walked the less than two miles home with excitement. I had traveled that road many times before, yet it felt longer than ever that day. My pace was fast, and I switched to a sprint at times, beads of sweat dripping down my face as I pondered theological questions. I kept wondering, "Am I free to choose when I go to heaven? If so, can I go today, as soon as I get home?"

I climbed to the roof of my house with urgency, walked to the back corner, and looked down—into the deep ravine behind our house. It was filled with a huge pile of debris: plants, broken trees, and the trash my mom was constantly telling us not to dispose of there. It gave me pause. It seemed likely that I would need my body in heaven—probably best not to destroy it on the way there. So I walked to the other corner of the concrete roof. Looking down upon the flat ground below, I inched my feet to hang off the edge. I could feel the warm afternoon air come up through the hole of my one-pair-per-year government-issued black shoes. As if I could breathe the air through my shoes into my lungs, I took a really deep breath, lifted my arms toward the sun, closed my eyes against its brightness, tilted my body weight forward, and exclaimed, "*Aqui vengo, Dios.*" ("Here I come, God.")

Then I heard a loud voice say, "*Bajate!*" ("Get down!") and I drew back as if a force pulled me from behind. Climbing on the roof was strictly forbidden by my mother, and my older sisters enforced the rule. I quickly climbed off the roof, knowing that punishment was soon to follow. Ironically, I ran to the very spot where I would have fallen, and I curled up in a ball of tears, waiting for the discipline I deserved. After waiting for a minute or so, it was evident that no one was coming. I started to wonder whose voice I heard. Was it a family member, a neighbor, a man, a woman? Then this trickling thought landed on the runway of my mind: It was God's voice; neither a human man nor a human woman. It sounded loving yet firm, authoritative, and strangely comforting.

From the first to the last page of the Bible, we read about a God who speaks. Genesis 1 begins with God already present and speaking creation into being: "Then God said" and it was so. Revelation ends with Jesus making a promise as he says, "Yes, I am coming soon."[1] In between, there are many stories of God speaking audibly to people, from kings and rulers, old men and women, to shepherds, peasant teenagers, and even children.[2]

God spoke and he still speaks—sometimes through people, dreams, visions, thoughts, and even natural manifestations. He speaks to us today, sometimes audibly, to make his desires known. God does not speak to us as often as some people claim; but when he does, he never contradicts what the Bible says. Audible words we hear, if any, are in full agreement with what God has already said in Scripture.[3] He does not contradict himself.

For reasons only God can know, he chose to speak audibly to a seven-year-old poor girl who was about to make the gravest of mistakes.

Once I sensed that I had an audience with the Creator, I wasted no time. The complaints started flying out of my mouth with no filter or periods. Life is unfair, complicated, confusing, unpredictable, and full of violence, injustice, and suffering. I was groaning with the "whole creation"[4] and crying out for a complete map that I could follow. Then I heard these four statements:

> *"No puedes elegir cuando vas al cielo. Esa es mi elección solo."*
> *("You don't get to choose when you go to heaven. That is my*
> *choice alone.")*
> *"Tienes que aguántarte." ("You must wait, hold on, endure.")*
> *"Tengo un propósito." ("I have a purpose.")*
> *"Voy a estar contigo." ("I will be with you.")*

It was hard for me to interpret the "map" I felt I had just received, but I guarded these words in my heart for thirty-five years before I ever repeated them out loud to others.[5] Without ever reading the Bible and having learned very little about God, I knew that day that God is sovereign and in control of all things, ever-present and purposeful.

Sadly, I then rejected God and decided to make my own way in life. The map for my faith journey seemed incomplete and useless to me, but it has never been so to him. God went with me to all the places I went, including the darkest and ugliest spiritual caves.

I tried to make my own map rather than relying on God's, but my map failed me.

Yet still, God did not abandon me.

Think of the maps you have relied upon on your journey of faith. Did you create these maps, or did you inherit them from others? How have they failed you? If you are tempted to leave behind your maps or abandon the idea of maps altogether, remember the words of C. S. Lewis quoted at the beginning of this chapter: "If you want to go anywhere, the map is absolutely necessary." So, it's not the maps per se that are the problem; rather, we're trusting in incomplete maps. They may give us some direction, but they lead us nowhere good.

The Better Map

My conversation with the heavenly voice that day became a mysterious foundation for my faith journey. While I didn't get to go to heaven that day, I learned that God would always be with me and that he has desires for my life. Since then, I've learned that hearing what God desires does not have to be audible, mysterious, or dramatic. His invisible desires are in plain sight. The Bible reveals God's heart and desires for all of humanity. The writer of Hebrews makes that clear:

> *Long ago God spoke to our ancestors by the prophets at different times and in different ways. In these last days, he has spoken to us by his Son. God has appointed him heir of all things and made the universe through him. The Son is the radiance of God's glory and the exact expression of his nature, sustaining all things by his powerful word. After making purification for sins, he sat down at the right hand of the Majesty on high.*

—Hebrews 1:1–3

Unlike the often self-imposed twists and turns of my faith journey, Joseph experienced twists and turns not of his own making. Joseph was sold, falsely accused, charged, imprisoned, and forgotten. He went from unmerited favor and huge dreams to being hated. Yet, "The Lord was with Joseph,"[6] extending kindness, granting favor and success, always intending "to bring about the present result—the survival of many people."[7]

Our search for a "map" that will allow us to navigate our journey successfully can give us the illusion that there is some sign that we'll see in our lifetime that will assure us that we "got it right" and were in fact on the right path.

But God will not display our full journey for us ahead of time.

We will not receive an exhaustive map that provides every detail or reveals each landmark and waypoint along our journey. If we did, there is a pretty good chance that we would either be terrified about what is to come or develop an ego-centeredness, and both scenarios would divert us from God's ideal plan. Physical road maps allow us to operate with self-confidence, but when it comes to the journey of faith, incomplete human-made spiritual maps tempt us to believe God's guidance is unnecessary.

No matter the promises, human-made spiritual maps will, at some point, fail us. Only God's promise of transformation stands.[8]

His past promises are our map for the future.

God is the one who somehow makes all things work, and in the end, his good desires are better than anything any one of us could come up with on our own.

Joseph was given a dream and a promise—but not a clear explanation of every step of his journey. His true map was a better map: It was God's presence with him on his journey. He experienced God's faithfulness, and that was enough—more than enough.

When it comes to the journey of faith, the harder we search for our own way of getting there, the less we find, because what we're looking for was right in front of us all along.

The truth is that all of us, at one point or another, will struggle in our faith journey. You will struggle to trust the Lord. You will have questions and at times get confused. Others—sometimes even spiritual leaders or trusted pastors—will lead you in the wrong direction and/or wound your heart. But I implore you, in the words of the wise writer of the book of Proverbs, to "trust in the Lord with all your heart, and do not rely on your own understanding."[9] God is the one who somehow makes all things work, and in the end, his good desires are better than anything any one of us could come up with on our own.

Relinquish your crumpled map, release and let go of control, and follow him. His map may seem incomplete to you, but it is not to him. Jesus said to his disciples, "If anyone wants to follow after me, let him deny himself, take up his cross, and follow me."[10] You must let go of your desire to protect yourself, have your way, and be in control of your circumstances.

Don't be a crazy backseat driver who tries to steer the car or hit the brakes when God is the one behind the wheel.

Our faith is not a treasure hunt. The treasure is already ours in Jesus Christ.

There is a way to surrender more of ourselves daily and to know what God desires for us without a completely laid-out and detailed map, but it requires us to slow down—and sometimes stop—in order to refocus our search on him, and him alone.

We'll learn more about how to do that in the next few chapters.

SPIRITUAL PRACTICES: SIMPLICITY AND SLOWING

Jesus lived in simplicity. This is remarkable when you consider he is "God with us," and everything was created in, through, and by him.[11] Paul proclaims that Jesus, "existing in the form of God . . . emptied himself"[12] by taking the most modest of human postures, that of a humble servant. From the first moment of his life to his last breath on the cross, Jesus lived a life devoid of attachments outside of his dedication to the Father and his followers. When we practice simplicity, we detach ourselves from the tangles and complications of life and fix our eyes on Jesus. Simplicity creates space for God to take up more real estate in our minds and hold greater priority in our hearts and on our calendars. For this reason, I have coupled this practice with the spiritual discipline of slowing. You don't have to, but doing them together is a powerful combination.

Slowing helps us forgo the demand for immediacy and hurriedness. Jesus was not idle. He was always occupied with preaching, teaching, and healing. Yet, he always took the time to stop and be present with others. Even in his passion to complete the work he was sent to do, he showed restraint by saying, "my time has not yet arrived."[13] Slowing develops in us more dependence on God and more patience for ourselves and others. It helps us practice waiting and enables us to enjoy the present moment more fully.

Simplicity and slowing help us remember that our faith is not a treasure hunt. Again, the treasure is already ours in Jesus Christ.

The Process

Ways to enjoy simplicity include reorganizing our priorities for the day to make extra space to reflect on God, curtailing monetary purchases for a period of time, giving away possessions, enjoying a simple evening with friends without spending money, etc. You can also be more thoughtful in your use of words for a day, intentionally speaking less and listening more. As we open up to Christ by decluttering our lives and releasing the excesses we've collected over time, Jesus teaches us to abandon our tendency to covet, and open up to him and his desires for us—that we would be more generous and loving toward others. Like it did for Paul, this process helps us learn to be content in every season of life.[14]

The practice of slowing entails reducing the speed in any given area of our lives. Examine your activities. We can reduce our hours of work or the number of things we're trying to accomplish in one day. We can stop to rest or listen to a loved one. Slowing can be practiced easily, as we all move about in a hurried state most of the time. We can slow down in the way we breathe, walk, eat, speak, drive, and browse social media, just to name a few examples.

When you're finished, take a few moments to reflect on your experience. What did you see? What did you learn?

Prompting Scriptures

I know how to make do with little, and I know how to make do with a lot. In any and all circumstances I have learned the secret of being content—whether well fed or hungry, whether in abundance or in need.

—Philippians 4:12

If we have food and clothing, we will be content with these.

—1 Timothy 6:8

Then he said to his disciples, "Therefore I tell you, don't worry about your life, what you will eat; or about the body, what you will wear. For life is more than food and the body more than clothing."

—Luke 12:22–23

For the Lord God, the Holy One of Israel, has said: "You will be delivered by returning and resting; your strength will lie in quiet confidence. But you are not willing."

—Isaiah 30:15

Return to your rest, my soul, for the Lord has been good to you.

—Psalm 116:7

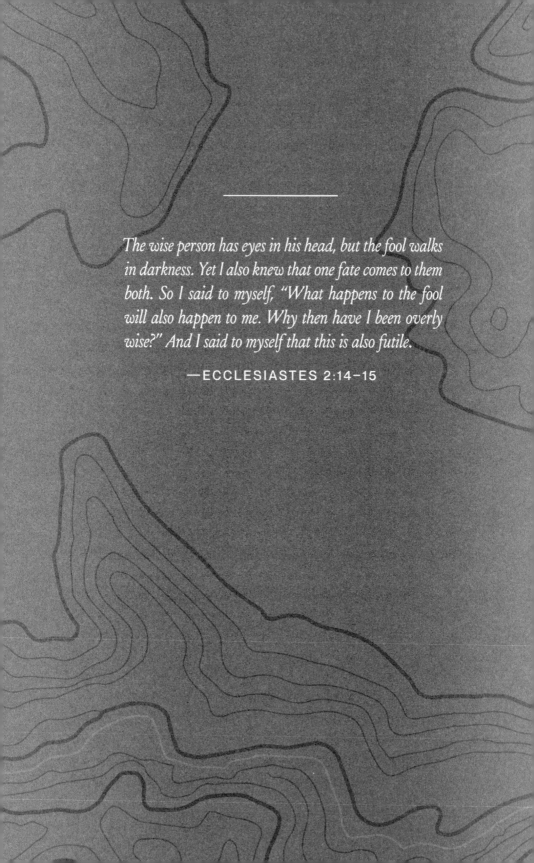

———

The wise person has eyes in his head, but the fool walks in darkness. Yet I also knew that one fate comes to them both. So I said to myself, "What happens to the fool will also happen to me. Why then have I been overly wise?" And I said to myself that this is also futile.

—ECCLESIASTES 2:14–15

CHAPTER 3

FAITH IS NOT A FORMULA

WALKING IN TRUST WITH JESUS

Despite God calling to me as a young girl, I didn't follow him faithfully until much later in my life. Well, Abuelita's prayers were finally answered when I surrendered my life to Jesus a month before my fortieth birthday.

For much of my life, I had acted according to my own will, wisdom, and desires. Once I came to faith, however, I decided to live the rest of my life according to God's will. Yet, for the first ten years of my faith walk with Jesus, I was buried under an old formula: "If I find the right way to live, then my life will be successful." That was my plan.

Now, before you think that's a good formula, understand that I was imposing my secular success model over my relationship with Jesus. I was saved, but I still wanted a linear journey of faith—one like a good economic chart, moving steadily up and to the right. I went on a search to understand how to discern the will of God, read dozens of books, and even went to seminary, but the formula of success was still my trap. I got caught up in searching for the perfect way to live my faith to avoid any more mistakes and to limit suffering in my life.

The Comforting Familiarity of Formulas

We live in a complex world, don't we? Both natural and human-created systems are complicated and not always predictable. And we humans often do not behave as we should, frequently acting impulsively. As a result, we are at times bewildered by the way things happen or work out. Life is both an exciting and vulnerable existence.

Our human way of responding to the unpredictability of life is to create solutions, set up systems, and draw up formulas that increase the predictability and security of desired outcomes. It makes sense. We find protection and comfort in knowing there are ways to navigate through complexity. It is no surprise, then, that a large percentage of bestselling books and online courses offer some sort of formula. Three steps to *this*. Three ways to accomplish *that*. From *this* to *that* in thirty days! Even on social media, the posts that offer us practical steps are the ones we tend to gravitate toward, dancing posts included. We want to know what to do and how to do it.

Formulas have the power of offering us clarity, but we can misuse them or corrupt them. Also, they often overpromise easy answers and strategies that do not always work, even when followed perfectly. In chapter 2, we talked about human-made maps: our fallible attempts to predict and plan out our lives. Maps are about what we *want* to happen or what we *think* will happen—they're about where we want to go. *Formulas* are how we try to get there. Once we realize we can't control our future (maps), we try instead to control how we meet that unknown future (formulas).

When our human-made spiritual formulas collapse beneath the weight of our expectations or ineptitude, our relationships with God and others in the faith community end up buried in the rubble

Corrupted formulas are especially damaging when it comes to our faith journey. People crave a formula to God that will guarantee success and prevent failure. When our human-made spiritual formulas collapse beneath the weight of our expectations or ineptitude, our relationships with God and others in the faith community end up buried in the rubble. For this reason, while we may not be able to give up our dependency on formulas entirely, it is wise to hold them more loosely. To do so, we may have to ask ourselves some difficult questions: What am I believing? What am I assuming? What are my expectations of God and people? What am I attaching to that is false and very likely going to let me down sooner or later?

As a pastor, my heart aches as I hear people express their corrupt formulas in casual conversations as though they are rock-solid truths. They do not always offer them in an "if . . . then" structure, but you can hear the formula behind their confident statements. Here are a few examples:

> *"Good people don't have moral failures as long as they regularly study the Bible." Not true. Even followers of Jesus battle with sinful urges and desires,[1] and all of us sin.[2]*

> *"If I am faithful, no one will ever hurt me." Lie. Even faithful believers will very likely experience persecution.[3]*

> *"I am God-blessed because I have not experienced serious sickness." God blesses his children in times of plenty and through afflictions.[4]*

> *"If I try to do all of the right things all the time, I will not suffer." Wishful thinking.[5]*

> *"My obedience to God will make my journey trouble free." The worst kind of lie. Jesus was perfectly obedient to the Father, yet he suffered greatly.*[6]

After reading those examples, maybe you're finding that your own heart is resonating with one or more of them. Take a moment to think through what formulas you've used in your own faith journey, whether it's one of the ones listed above or a different formula altogether.

The uncertainty of life, the feeling of being unprepared, the fear of making mistakes, or the abhorrence of missing out on the best outcome builds in us an attraction to formulas and a craving for a specific direction. But if there is one thing the journey of faith guarantees us, it is that we are going to get uncomfortable, and we will likely even suffer for our faith. If we're honest, we all want our faith journey to be easy. We secretly believe it should be smooth and fun, like a fast ride on a newly asphalted road. Yet God does not promise us this.

The writer of Ecclesiastes blasts right through our carefully built formulas when he exclaims, "I have seen all the things that are done under the sun and have found everything to be futile, a pursuit of the wind."[7] It does not matter where our formulas come from—our parents, pastor, church, teacher, spouse, or friends—because they are not always reliable, and they can derail us on our faith journey.

When our spiritual formulas fail us, we may question if we missed a step, have lost our way, or entered the wrong path long ago. We blame God, others, or shame ourselves for past mistakes. But what if the problem is the formula?

There is a chance that the formula we have been mining for gold will collapse and bury our faith so deep that it may not survive.

> *"For my thoughts are not your thoughts, and your ways are not my ways." This is the Lord's declaration. "For as heaven is high-*

*er than earth, so my ways are higher than your ways, and my
thoughts than your thoughts."*

—Isaiah 55:8–9

God is above it all, and his perspective is greater than ours. The Lord intends to bless and prosper his people.[8] It may be difficult for us to fully grasp how, why, and what he is doing as he executes his perfect plan. We may misunderstand and misapply even the specific formulas we find in the Bible (such as those in Proverbs, for instance), especially because we tend to take them out of context and read them as formulaic promises rather than godly wisdom that will serve us well in life. The answer is not to replace one faith formula for another, but to realize that faith is not a formula at all—it's a relationship with our Creator. We can trust him because he is 100 percent faithful and trustworthy. There are countless stories in the Bible that prove this to be true. I have also experienced it in my own life. With God, we will experience more mystery, awe, wonder, and unknown, but in Christ, we will also reach the eternal and good destination he has prepared for us, guaranteed.[9]

> *The answer is not to replace one faith formula for another, but to realize that faith is not a formula at all—it's a relationship with our Creator. We can trust him because he is 100 percent faithful and trustworthy.*

The journey of faith often requires us to sit in the unknown, endure struggles, feel the tension of complex theological truths, and wrestle with God and our doubts. We may feel like we are suffering in the dark, deep depth alone, like the trapped miners[10] in Chile, but we have reason to hope. Even if things are going smoothly right now, we're all but a crisis away from being knocked off balance, becoming afraid, and feeling vulnerable yet again. One way we tend to fight this discomfort is to seek formulas or a "sure way" out of our pain. Yet, not all formulas work, and most are likely to lead us further away from our destination.

I am convinced that on our journey of faith, we are guaranteed to get uncomfortable. We are going to have seasons where we will be stretched and challenged. Rather than searching for a formula to avoid those struggles, we must be prepared for them. A particular Bible story has been instrumental to me and my own faith journey as I've learned to survive without my old formulas: the story of the woman who met Jesus at a well.

Buried Under a Formula

As I've mentioned, I spent my first few years as a Christian trying to apply worldly formulas to my spiritual life. I thought that if I took logical steps, in good order, that I'd grow in my faith.

Instead of bringing me success, this approach tied me down. It made my spiritual world cramped and small.

My freedom came from a deeper study of the story in John 4 of the woman who met Jesus at the well. I read the story over and over for several months. Her story breaks all the religious formulas we tend to create. We don't have to slaughter lambs, make grand promises, or offer extraordinary sacrifices as a means of bargaining our way into the presence and pleasure of God.

We don't have to slaughter lambs, make grand promises, or offer extraordinary sacrifices as a means of bargaining our way into the presence and pleasure of God.

What Jesus offered her was not a formula but a relationship. He offers us the same.

When Jesus learned that the Pharisees had heard he was making and baptizing more disciples than John (though Jesus himself was not baptizing, but his disciples were), he left Judea and went again to Galilee. He had to travel through Samaria; so he came to a town of Samaria called Sychar near the property that Jacob had given his son Joseph. Jacob's well was there, and Jesus, worn out from his journey, sat down at the well. It was about noon.

A woman of Samaria came to draw water.

"Give me a drink," Jesus said to her, because his disciples had gone into town to buy food.

"How is it that you, a Jew, ask for a drink from me, a Samaritan woman?" she asked him. For Jews do not associate with Samaritans.

Jesus answered, "If you knew the gift of God, and who is saying to you, 'Give me a drink,' you would ask him, and he would give you living water."

—John 4:1–10

It is helpful to keep in mind the context of this story. The woman was a Samaritan. Back then, Jews and Samaritans did not associate with each other. They shared a common history but had parted ways after King Solomon's reign. At one time they were one nation, the twelve tribes of Israel, descended from the twelve sons of Jacob, whom God had renamed Israel. After the time of Solomon, the northern ten tribes broke off and formed the independent kingdom of Israel, centered around Samaria.

The two other tribes in the south, Judah and Benjamin, set up the kingdom of Judah, centered at Jerusalem. Both kingdoms repeatedly sinned and were plagued with corruption. God warned them again and again that because of their wicked ways they would be conquered by other nations. Both nations failed, but the northern tribes (Israel) did not manage to have even a single king that led according to God's desires. Their long line of wicked rulers caused the nation to fall into the hands of the Assyrians. Many Israelites gradually assimilated, intermarried, became half-Jewish and half-Gentile, and eventually were known as Samaritans.

The strife between Jews and Samaritans cut deep. The people of the north believed that they could worship in the north, and the people of the south believed that they must worship at the temple in Jerusalem. Jews believed that Samaritans were unfaithful, as they had mixed with other nations who worshipped pagan gods. They also had a different view of Scripture and disagreed on many fronts.

Jesus and the woman met at the well of Jacob, the father of the entire nation of Israel. There were so many formulas and rules shattered by this encounter. In the first century, men did not talk to women one-on-one in public, and they certainly did not carry on a whole conversation with them. Secondly, as the conversation between this woman and Jesus does carry on, we learn that she had been married multiple times and was currently living with a man who was not her husband. We don't know the reason for her circumstances. We don't even know if it was her fault or if it was sin that drove her story. But either way, in the patriarchal society of that time, she would have been treated—as we tend to say today—as "damaged goods." Either she was terribly unlucky, or she was an inadequate wife, or worse. She meets Jesus at the noon hour instead of the cooler hours of the day when other women came to fetch water, so she also seems to be estranged from the community in which she lives.

The woman said to him, "I know that the Messiah is coming"
(who is called Christ). "When he comes, he will explain every-
thing to us." Jesus told her, "I, the one speaking to you, am he."

—John 4:25–26

To this broken, unnamed outsider, Jesus reveals his messianic identity. She is the first person he reveals himself to in this way. He is the one she and her Samaritan people were expecting to come to "explain everything." Sadly, they too had the wrong formula. The Messiah was coming to do more than just explain everything.[11] He was coming to save God's people and conquer death.

As Jesus was speaking to her, the disciples who had been in town buying food showed up. As they did, they "were amazed" that Jesus was talking with a woman, a Samaritan, a divorcée with a messy story. They started questioning Jesus, and as they did, she slipped away. "Then the woman left her water jar, went into town, and told the people, 'Come, see a man who told me everything I ever did. Could this be the Messiah?' They left the town and made their way to him."[12]

The conversation with Jesus changed everything for this woman. Instead of hiding, she ran back to the town and told "the people," implying everyone, about Jesus. Her passion must have been contagious because they left everything and went to meet Jesus. A little bit later, in verse 39, we are told the result of this woman's courage: many Samaritans came to believe in Jesus because of her testimony.[13]

Relationship over Formula

Now, here is why this story fits with my point about faith formulas. Just before the woman's encounter with Jesus in John 4, there is a story in John 3 about a Pharisee named Nicodemus, a leader among the religious Jews who was also seeking to understand Jesus. What happens in John's gospel is that the woman's story and Nicodemus's story mirror one another. They show two formulas that are very, very different. Through these, we see how God works and what he values.

The "formula" that produces the right result is the one you would expect not to. Let me just give you a quick rundown of the differences between the story of Nicodemus, who comes to Jesus asking questions, and this woman, who wasn't even seeking Jesus.

To start, Jesus goes out of his way to meet her in the middle of the day. Nicodemus comes to see Jesus in the middle of the night.

The woman is unnamed and has no social standing or authority. She is poor and marginalized, most likely uneducated. She is a religious follower but not a religious leader. She is not orthodox because she is a Samaritan. Because of her marital situation, she would have been considered unclean and undesirable, separated from God. In fact, living with a man who is not her husband probably entailed a great deal of shame, which is why she came to the well at the hottest time of the day.

We are told the man's name is Nicodemus. He is a wealthy and important man, a religious leader, which means he would have been highly educated. In fact, he's a member of the Sanhedrin.[14] In that time, the Sanhedrin oversaw the religious laws. Because he is a Sadducee, he has to keep a pure life; he has to be correct and orthodox. He is a very devout Jewish believer. He is well-regarded; he's a man of stature. He is considered clean because he is obeying all the laws of the people of Israel.

Now, you would think a man with all this background would be a perfect person for Jesus to reveal himself to, because someone like Nicodemus would go and tell everyone about Jesus, and everyone would believe him because he had tremendous favor. People would have trusted whatever he had to say. It's one of those formulas, right? A person high in the church who possesses great authority, or someone who is very wealthy and has reached a certain level of education or opulence, is one whom people will be more likely to trust to have all the answers. They are the type of person others should get on their side.

If they're following a formula.

The woman at the well had no clue who Jesus was, but the well-educated man had heard about Jesus and about his teachings. He had heard about his miracles. Nicodemus tells Jesus, "We know you're a teacher. You come from God because no one could do the miracles you have done unless they were with God."[15] He seems to revere Jesus, but he approaches Jesus at night when no one else can see them talking.

Nicodemus comes in secret, and he comes confused. He does not understand who Jesus is, even after Jesus reveals himself to him and says those wonderful words we love to quote from him in John 3:16: "For God loved the world in this way: He gave his one and only Son, so that everyone who believes in him will not perish but have eternal life." Nicodemus *leaves* in the dark, not believing and still confused.

The woman meets Jesus at the brightest time of day: at the sixth hour, which is noon. She meets him in the open and she leaves not confused but clear about who Jesus is. Because of that clarity, she tells everyone.

Now, this is not the way people, including the disciples, expected the story to go. The Jewish people were expecting the Messiah to reveal himself to the religious leaders. In fact, anyone who claimed to be the Messiah was inspected by the religious leaders. Over the years, a lot of false messiahs were brought to the Pharisees for this purpose. It would be the Pharisees and other religious leaders who would say, "Yes, this is the Messiah."

The woman at the well would have been invisible, a zero in her culture, but Jesus saw her. He talked to her. He treated her like some-one worthy of his time, his energy, and his teaching—worthy of his discipleship. This encounter shows us the huge contrast—and a very different formula—from what we might naturally expect. Jesus comes to seek out the lost, to bring freedom to the lost—such as the Samaritan woman. He comes to bring hope to those who are hopeless, and his formula is not like ours.

I love the question the woman asks in verse 12 of chapter 4. She says, "Are you greater than our father Jacob?" She's asking the big questions: "Who are you, Jesus? Are you trustworthy?" Remember that Jacob was the man who had the twelve sons who started the nation of Israel. She is essentially asking, "Are you more reliable, are you more trustworthy than Jacob, who gave us this well?" It was a powerful well, a deep well that gave water and refreshed people. And Jesus did not hesitate. He offered her something better: a "well of water springing up in him for eternal life."[16]

Jesus comes to seek out the lost, to bring freedom to the lost—such as the Samaritan woman. He comes to bring hope to those who are hopeless, and his formula is not like ours

That's the way Jesus works. From this well where people could quench their physical thirst, Jesus reveals that he is going to quench the deep spiritual thirst that we all have. We know her confusion is understandable, but she wants clarification. She asks Jesus for more information. She declares that she wants some of the water he possesses, but again, she doesn't yet know the great gift he is offering.

What Jesus wants to give her (and you and me) is even greater than the water of this earth. Even after she kind of gets it, she doesn't. That's us. We get God to a point, but we don't understand him fully.

Now, there is a key difference between Nicodemus and this woman, and that is their response. Even though she didn't under-stand everything, she still sought what Jesus was offering her.

We can do that too. We don't have to understand *everything* in order to take hold of *something*. You've probably heard the phrase "Don't let the perfect be the enemy of the good." Well, that's only talking about our side of it—it's saying that just because you can't get it exactly right, you shouldn't give up on making progress. It's true as far as it goes, but it doesn't go far enough. We want our perfect formulas to lead to perfect results. But that's doing things backwards. Instead, take hold of the *Person* who is perfect—Jesus—and then make your good effort, with his help, to receive from him the good and perfect gifts he has to give you. Your efforts may be imperfect, but his response won't be.

Nicodemus asked, "How can these things be?"[17] Nicodemus had doubt. The woman, on the other hand, said, "Give me this water ..."[18] Then Jesus revealed himself to her. In fact, this is known to be one of the great "I am" statements that Jesus makes in John's gospel: "I, the one speaking to you, am he [the Messiah]."[19] She left the jar behind. Perhaps this was the most important possession she had, the most important object. This is how she would have brought water for her home, but she left it behind because, frankly, nothing was more important after she met Jesus and saw that he is the One.

She ran into town. I can imagine her running to town thinking, "How can this be? How can this be?" She was probably looking at her life and thinking, "Why would he talk to *me?* How can he care about *me?* I have done so many things. I have lived with so many lies. I am a Samaritan. I am a woman. How could the Messiah, the one who God sent, offer me grace?" But she believed and told others.

Leaving the Jar

In the spring of 2011, my husband, Jim, and I traveled to India. The purpose of our trip was to deliver wheelchairs to the disabled living in poverty without access to mobility. We were there with an organization we love called the Free Wheelchair Mission.[20] The partner who hosted us invited various members of our team to speak at the different events. He mainly wanted us to give a word of encouragement and let people know that friends in America were aware of their struggle and were trying to help out as best they could.

But one day our partner asked me to preach a sermon at one of the little towns we visited. He told me that there would be about eighty women, and all I had to do was share a little message with them. Now, I had felt called to be a Bible teacher for a long time, but I did not feel worthy of this call. I felt like there were certain things that had to happen in my life before I could do such an important work for Jesus. I was already studying in seminary, but I wasn't yet finished or confident. I felt very inadequate and unprepared for this invitation, but I decided that since it was a small group of women, maybe I could just tell them my story and get out of there quick before they threw stones at the woman who had been married and divorced multiple times. However, our partner wanted me to teach a story from the Bible as well, so I selected John 4.

When I arrived at the church, there were six hundred people crammed into the second story of a white building with open squares as windows that let the warm breeze in. The pastor escorted me to the front of the room, where a row of plastic chairs was aligned facing the expectant crowd. I sat there watching their faces as they studied mine. From my point of view, there were men sitting on the right side and women sitting on the left side. The pastor introduced me, and I took hold of the microphone as I stood with my knees shaking beneath my floor-length white skirt.

I started teaching the story of the woman at the well. The man translating was quick to capture my every word. We were showering the room with English and Hindi words. I remember hearing myself say to them, "God can use anyone. If he can use me, redeem me, he can redeem you. He can use you. He used this woman. His formula doesn't work like ours." I heard myself say this, and I realized in my mind, "Oh my goodness. I am preaching. I am teaching the Bible. This is what God told me I was going to do long ago, but I've been afraid to do so." I was holding on to certain formulas. I believed that to teach the Bible, you had to be a special kind of Christian man with a complete education.

But God just doesn't work that way. He tapped me on my shoulder, a woman with a story, a woman with a past, a woman who isn't all that articulate and isn't all that great of a speaker. He told me, "I'm going to use you." There I was in that little town in the south of India called *Victory Town*, teaching God's Word for the first time, feeling completely inadequate to do so.

When it was all over, there were beads of sweat drenching my long hair. People started to walk toward me. The first woman who stood before me was shorter than me. I'm not sure why I did it, but I put my two hands on her head, and I prayed for her mind as I also prayed for mine. All the other women saw me do that, and they wanted me to pray for them. Then it became a scene, with hundreds of people coming up for prayer. I would never have imagined in my wildest dreams that God would use me in that way. My formula did not see me doing that whatsoever, anywhere. That was just the first of many times that I've had a chance to preach God's Word. It is an example of how my own formulas just fell apart.

There are places where I'm not allowed to preach or teach the Bible because I'm a woman and because people have a formula for who gets to do that. I don't want to make a big theological statement here, but again, God chooses people. Jesus chose this woman. She is the one who went and told her village about him. Jesus didn't say to her, "You're not allowed to talk about it."

Nicodemus had the religious authority to talk about Jesus but didn't, whereas the woman at the well, who had no authority, told everyone. That's what I'm trying to do, just be a witness. I've had to let go of the formulas that I had in my mind or maybe that the world put upon me. You must do the same if you want to experience the freedom of walking with Jesus in relationship and go wherever he takes you.

India was a joyful time that helped me see the inadequacies of one of my human-made formulas. But grief can help us see this clearly too. My friend Alan was a faithful man of God and walked with Jesus in the most beautiful way. A few years before Jim and I met Alan, he went through a battle with cancer in his esophagus that nearly killed him. The treatment left him with a limited ability to produce saliva, so eating was a challenge. Alan was a tall and slim man with a great sense of humor. Just after we met him, Alan's son, a freshman in college, suddenly died. It was a devastating loss for our friend, and we walked with him in grief.

Years later, when it seemed like Alan was rebuilding his strength, he got a severe case of pneumonia and again almost died. He miraculously recovered from the pneumonia, but the intubation did additional damage to his already scarred esophagus. Alan received nutrition from a feeding tube for the rest of his life, up until he died a few years ago. After going through so much pain and sorrow, I wondered how Alan was able to hold on to his faith. One day I got the courage to ask him, and he said, "You know, Inés, this is not the formula; this is not the way I expected things. But I am committed to my relationship with Jesus."

The way forward is not a formula but a relationship with Jesus cultivated by a rhythm of connection

Alan was a man of God, a faithful man. He walked with Jesus until his last breath. He was generous with his time, his talents, his treasure, and yet life threw all kinds of terrible things his way. Nonetheless, Alan did not lose his faith. Alan did not let go of God. He still believed that God was 100 percent trustworthy. He knew that even when his own way of doing things failed, God did not.

The Rhythm of Faith

Today, Jesus is inviting you to be faithful with what you have in front of you. Chances are that he has already given you some clarity in this very moment to take the next step. Take a moment and think. What is it that you *know* about Jesus and about what he wants you to do? Just as he did with the woman at the well, he is holding out to you an offer of water, an offer of life.

My dear friend, what formula are you holding on to? What are your expectations and assumptions? What would it look like for you to put them aside and trust Jesus instead? I'm not promising that things will go great, but I'm declaring that Jesus will walk with you, and that is more than enough.

The way forward is not a formula but a relationship with Jesus cultivated by a *rhythm of connection*. Relationships don't follow strict, human-made rules, but good relationships have a rhythm to them. Like music has a beat that gets your feet tapping, love has a rhythm that keeps people in relationship moving in concert with one another.

In the same manner that we build relationships with people near to us, we can grow our relationship with Jesus. We can engage in meaningful time together (worship), frequent and daily conversation (prayer), confide our highlights and our low moments (praise and confession), and even have fun together (service).

All of these practices are part of the rhythm of relationship.

And so we must build our dependence on God, not on formulas. When we invite Jesus to transform our minds[21] and teach us to think through a heavenly mindset,[22] we can more easily let go of the need for formulas. We can hope in God because he is trustworthy (our formulas aren't). We can learn to be vessels to be filled by God.

As we do this, we learn that even the seasons of deep suffering are part of the journey of faith and that from them, the greatest blessings of our lives can come. In the next few chapters, we'll start talking about how to face obstacles, challenges, and suffering—not on our own, but walking in relationship with the One who loves us.

SPIRITUAL PRACTICE: WORSHIP

It is hard to surrender our life to God if we don't know how wonderful he is. Worship helps us pay attention to who he is and what he does. It reminds us of his greatness, goodness, beauty, and faithful love, just to name a few things. Whether we worship privately or in community, in words, music, ritual, generosity, or silence, we intentionally honor God and demonstrate our love and respect for him. This is why church services start with worship music. To receive the message from the Bible, we must set our hearts and minds to reflect on who it is that is speaking to us. He is the very focus of our faith and the giver of our faith.[23] Therefore, he deserves all of the honor, glory, and praise.

The Process

Worship is often associated with music and songs. Of course, that is a wonderful way to worship, but the practice of worship begins when we fully turn our attention to God, face our Creator, and, at least in our minds, behold his holiness, glory, and strength. We can sing a lot of songs, but if we're not postured toward God with our whole being, we are not truly worshiping. To worship God is to make him first, the focus of our adoration and reverence.

There are many ways to show God our reverence and adoration. We can be silent before him, sing songs, kneel, give generously, speak words of affirmation, and talk to others about him. We can do our work with excellence and humility as unto the Lord. In other words, worship is an attitude of the heart, a submissive posture that understands who God is to us. One of my favorite ways to worship is to list God's attributes. When I cannot think of words to say, I use the language of the Psalms. There is a lot of worship modeled for us in them, even in times of struggle.

When you're finished, take a few moments to reflect on your experience. What did you see? What did you learn?

Prompting Scriptures

God is spirit, and those who worship him must worship in Spirit and in truth.

—John 4:24

Doing what is righteous and just is more acceptable to the Lord than sacrifice.

—Proverbs 21:3

So I gaze on you in the sanctuary to see your strength and your glory. My lips will glorify you because your faithful love is better than life.

—Psalm 63:2–3

Love the Lord your God with all your heart, with all your soul, with all your mind, and with all your strength.

—Mark 12:30

Therefore, brothers and sisters, in view of the mercies of God, I urge you to present your bodies as a living sacrifice, holy and pleasing to God; this is your true worship. Do not be conformed to this age, but be transformed by the renewing of your mind, so that you may discern what is the good, pleasing, and perfect will of God.

—Romans 12:1–2

II.
OVERCOMING
CHALLENGES

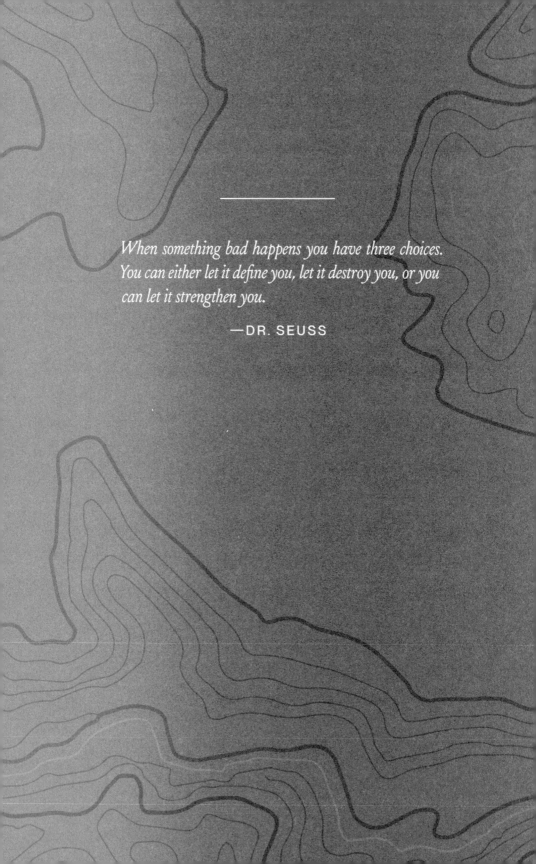

———

When something bad happens you have three choices.
You can either let it define you, let it destroy you, or you
can let it strengthen you.

—DR. SEUSS

CHAPTER 4

OBSTACLES ARE A GIVEN

CIRCLE THEM IN PRAYER

After hearing what I interpreted as the voice of God, I told no one—I knew that people who heard voices or tried to commit suicide were usually locked up and fed through a tiny window. How did I know this? My friend's grandmother lived in a concrete block bedroom with two steel-reinforced windows and a single heavy door kept shut by a huge lock. Her children had built the stand-alone structure behind their house and surrounded it by trees to ensure people would not hear her constant, nonsensical chattering and occasional desperate cries for freedom. Out of curiosity, my friend and I would walk back there and peek through her windows to see how a person with schizophrenia lived. Each time, she would scare us half to death as she came rushing to the window, her grey and frizzy hair unkempt, loudly begging us to open the door.

While spying on her was a bit of entertainment for two bored little girls, the sad reality of this woman's life did not escape our notice. Looking back, I now understand why I kept the roof-top experience to myself. The threat of a schizophrenia diagnosis and lifelong entrapment was a strong incentive to keep secret my mysterious encounter with the Creator of the universe. His message, calling me to endure in this life because he had a purpose, as well as his promise to always be with me, left unanswered my main question: What can a seven-year-old girl, on her own, make of the challenges and suffering in this world?

Years later, I heard a speaker at our church say, "Children are the best recorders of information, but they are the worst interpreters." While I cannot remember her name, I have never forgotten her statement. It certainly applied to me. After hearing God's voice, I no longer questioned his existence, and I believed that he was near and more powerful than anything in this world. But I certainly questioned his goodness! A good God who intended for me to live with him in the bliss of heaven would never force me to live in such a harsh world bursting with suffering, injustice, violence, and annoying siblings. A good God would do something about my family's lack of resources, help us get our unpainted house finished, and fix my father's alcoholism so he could live with us again. A good God would make my uncle stop beating my aunt. A good God would heal my brother's leukemia. I accepted God's existence but was doubtful of his goodness and love.

The prevalence of obstacles, challenges, and suffering on our journey of faith raises difficult theological and ethical issues. St. (or Pope) Gregory the Great,[1] a bishop of Rome in the sixth century, was a prolific writer who offered practical wisdom to followers of Jesus in his day. He was born in a time of deep struggle for Italy, when they experienced cycles of famine, a devastating plague, war, and invasion by the Lombards in AD 568. In his work *Moralia on Job,* Gregory presented his belief that all suffering always has a purpose. Some of our challenges correct wrong actions, others prevent future ones, and some seem to have no other purpose but to lead us "to love God more ardently for himself alone and so discover the ultimate peace and freedom."[2]

Gregory believed that when something bad happens to us, we are not to become helpless victims of inevitable fate. Rather, we are to learn to suffer patiently, like Job, in the hands of an all-knowing, all-powerful, all-loving, and good God. He taught that human sin is generally the root of all suffering, though not all suffering is a direct result of a specific sin. The main lesson in the book of Job is that only God has a full understanding of the reason and purpose of suffering in this world. It does not explain why Job or any of us suffer but makes clear that God is just and good. His very character necessitates God to always act justly and for the good of others.

In her book *Horrendous Evils and the Goodness of God*, Marilyn McCord Adams contends that all evil, even the most horrendous type, is "defeated by the goodness of God." She "holds open the possibility that genuinely unjust horrors might be defeated by not being turned into justice after all, but by being relevantly integrated into [an individual's life] to a great enough good."[3]

Those are two classic, solid takes on the challenge of understanding our all-powerful God in light of the existence of evil, and it is worth reading how faithful people before us have wrestled with this problem—because it is a problem that faces us all.

Not a single story of a person we know or find in the Bible works out in a linear fashion or is void of difficult experiences

It wasn't until I was in my forties, when I finally met Jesus, that I came to understand that the suffering of this world is not for lack of love in God, but that out of his goodness he helps us overcome even our greatest challenges. Our commitment to God does not achieve a faith journey devoid of obstacles; rather, it increases our yearning and sensitivity for God to redeem those same obstacles.

Not a single story of a person we know or find in the Bible works out in a linear fashion or is void of difficult experiences. The brokenness of this world will affect our journey of faith. These experiences can lead us to become doubtful, impatient, or frustrated with ourselves, others, and God. If we take on the victim mindset that obstacles *happen* to us, as if they have no redeeming purpose, we may be tempted to give up. If we believe that obstacles are cruel sharpening tools at the hand of the Creator, we will struggle to submit to his wisdom. Our relationship with God can start to resemble the one some of us have with our dentist: visit only when absolutely necessary and as a last resort.

But, if we believe that commitment to Jesus is saying yes to the entirety of the faith journey, knowing that God protects, guides, and heals us along the way, I am convinced that we can endure and live to see God's goodness on display. It is comforting to see how God can grow flowers of blessing from the mire of suffering—in Joseph's story[4] as well as in ours. May it inspire us to stay the course and trust the Lord even more.

Fight from the Inside Out

My mother, Luisa, worked very hard to give us a stable home. Most of my nine uncles and a few family friends helped build our six-hundred-square-foot home piece by piece. My mother sold pies, cookies, Puerto Rican pasteles, and other pre-cooked foods to raise money to pay for concrete, iron, metal louver windows, and whatever else was needed to give us a place to live and call our own.

Slowly but surely, my mother raised the funds for leveling the one-acre plot of land my grandfather gave her. Then she built the foundation, walls, windows, and the roof of the tiny two-bedroom home. Then she focused on fixing up the inside. She painted the walls, installed interior doors, and purchased basic appliances and minimal furniture. Perhaps motivated by the mounds of laundry her seven children produced, she skipped installing a hot water heater and instead stretched for a washing machine with a manual wringer. We used to think she ran out of steam at some point because the house was never finished with stucco and paint.

Until I moved to California, I lived in a concrete-grey house with exposed cement blocks and oozing mortar frozen hard into a rough texture. People knew not to lean up against our house. We kids were embarrassed by the look of our incomplete home—but not my mother. *She* knew that the inside was what made our house beautiful.

Spiritually speaking, we Christians should have the same mind-set that my mother did. Since obstacles, struggles, challenges, and suffering are a given on our faith journey (they are like the exposed concrete blocks and rough mortar), we should spend the greatest energy on building and protecting what is on the inside: our heart, mind, and soul.

With that in mind, let's look at how to face the first kind of obstacle that we will encounter: temptation from the enemy.

Opposition from Without

The Bible teaches us that Satan is the opposer of God's people and has been using the same tactics against us for millennia. He is a thief who comes to "steal and kill and destroy"[5] and is always "prowling around like a roaring lion, looking for anyone he can devour."[6] I'm not implying that all our struggles come from Satan. Other people can be hostile toward us, and often we act as our own worst enemies by doing things we know will harm us.

But the apostle Paul makes it clear in Ephesians 6 that Christians should expect to face strong opposition, not just from "flesh and blood," but we also battle "against the rulers, against the authorities, against the cosmic powers of this darkness, against evil, spiritual forces in the heavens."[7] Paul urges fellow Christians to "take up the full armor of God"[8] and "pray at all times in the Spirit."[9] Paul encourages Christians to protect themselves from the attacks of the enemy, which are never new. Paul himself experienced many hardships on his faith journey[10] and knew that his life would be fraught with "chains and afflictions,"[11] but he purposed to finish well with the help of the Lord Jesus[12] and pass on to others this important mindset: "But as for you, exercise self-control in everything, endure hardship, do the work of an evangelist, fulfill your ministry."[13]

In the beginning of its story, in the narrative of Genesis, the Bible reveals the power of temptation with these words of the serpent to Adam and Eve: "Did God really say . . . ?"[14] This doubt-inducing question is perhaps the most prolific tactic of the enemy. It opens the door for the delivery of a few well-constructed lies.

Even Jesus faced the attacks and lies of the enemy. In Matthew 4, immediately after Jesus is baptized, the Holy Spirit leads him to the desert "to be tempted." In Greek, the word for "tempted" is *peirázo*, and it also means "tested." Jesus faced a direct confrontation with the very enemy he came to destroy—Satan, Diablos, "the adversary." This wasn't so much a test with a pass or fail grade, but a test in the way you would try out a new automobile to demonstrate just how powerful it is. The tempter approached Jesus at his weakest moment, "after he had fasted forty days and forty nights" and "was hungry."[15]

First, the tempter goes straight to the core (deep hunger), asking Jesus, "If you are the Son of God, tell these stones to become bread." Satan is not questioning Jesus's identity. In fact, in the manner he asks the question, he actually acknowledges it. But he was tempting Jesus to *misuse* his identity, to use it for self-serving purposes. *Do it yourself,* he is urging. *Take matters into your own hands.*

You and I struggle with the same temptation. In times of struggle, we find it difficult to wait on God. Jesus responded by referring to Scripture, in this case to Deuteronomy 8:3, "Man must not live on bread alone but on every word that comes from the mouth of

God."[16] He points back to the time when God fed Israel *manna* in the harsh desert, giving them the perfect amount of food for each day.

We, too, can turn to God's promises when we are tempted. Our big brother Jesus showed us how to meet this test.

Secondly, the tempter tried to influence Jesus's perspective. He took Jesus "to the holy city, [and] had him stand on the pinnacle of the temple."[17] He said, "If you are the Son of God, throw yourself down."[18] Again, he's not challenging Jesus's sonship, but encouraging Jesus to use his authority to force the Father to prove his faithfulness. He strengthens his temptation by quoting Psalm 91:11–12 ("He will give his angels orders . . . they will support you . . . you will not strike your foot."). Demand. Again, Jesus responds by pointing back to the Scriptures: "Do not test the Lord your God as you tested him at Massah."[19] God's faithfulness is self-evident.

Jesus blazed the trail for us. When we are tempted to demand that things instantly go our way, we can instead rest in God's authority and sure provision.

Thirdly, the temptation that perhaps may have been the most appealing is left to the end. That's usually how the devil works. He takes Jesus to a high mountain, to a place where Jesus could see "all the kingdoms of the world and their splendor"[20] and then offers Jesus a shortcut to suffering. Compromise. "I will give you all these things if you will fall down and worship me."[21] Jesus could rule the earth without having to go through the suffering of the cross. The offer is both deceptive and impossible. The only way the kingdom and all its glory could be attained was through the shame of the cross. Rather than bowing down to Satan, Jesus displays his authority by commanding Satan to go away and by again quoting

> *Jesus blazed the trail for us. When we are tempted to demand that things instantly go our way, we can instead rest in God's authority and sure provision.*

Scripture: "Go away, Satan! For it is written: Worship the Lord your God, and serve only him."[22]

Have you ever been tempted to compromise? If it happened to Jesus, it will happen to us. Think about times you have faced the temptations that Jesus did: temptations to misuse the good things you've been given, to demand what you want immediately, or to compromise in your obedience to God. Take a moment to hold these experiences before the Lord, offering thankfulness, repentance, or your questions, as is appropriate.

The Good God Brings Out of Times of Temptation

In a time of struggle and unsurmountable challenges, Jesus trusted the Father. By refusing to feed himself, Jesus fed the hunger of humanity for all time. By resisting the request to force God to save him, Jesus saved the world. By his unwillingness to compromise the journey to the cross, eternal and abundant life is now available to all who put their trust in Jesus. The question for Jesus was not identity, but obedience. Everything the enemy tempted Jesus with was within his right according to his identity. The enemy does not go after our God-given identity—he has no power over it[23]—but his tactics tempt us to distrust God and misuse our identity. He cannot force us to disobey God, and he knows that, through Jesus, we will ultimately have victory over him.[24]

If you are a follower of Jesus, your identity has been fixed by him. According to Ephesians 1, you have been chosen "in him, before the foundation of the world, to be holy and blameless in love before him," predestined, adopted, redeemed, forgiven, given wisdom and understanding, given an inheritance and sealed by the promised Holy Spirit. According to Romans 8:16–17, you are a child of God, heir of God, coheir with Christ, "if indeed [you] suffer with him so that [you] may also be glorified with him." Your identity is secure in Christ.

But your identity does not relieve you from your eternal dependence on God, your Father. Even Jesus prayed to the Father regularly, alone and with his disciples. At another time of deep struggle, this time before his arrest, Jesus once again relies on the Father through prayer: "Father, if you are willing, take this cup away from me—nevertheless, not my will, but yours, be done."[25]

Neither Joseph, Paul, nor Jesus took on a victim mindset nor blamed God for their circumstances. They remained faithful and committed no matter what was before them. If there was a hint of entitlement in Joseph's or Paul's heart, the hardship served to soften it. Satan indeed tempted Jesus, but Jesus battled these challenges with the truth in Scripture. He could have done a miracle, but instead, he modeled for us how we, too, can respond to our challenges.

I want you to know that the greater your obstacles, the further you can count on God for guidance and support.

I want you to know that the greater your obstacles, the further you can count on God for guidance and support. The stronger your temptations, the more you can store up in your heart truths about God and your identity as weapons against doubt. The bigger the lies against you, the deeper you can walk in God's sovereignty, wisdom, and love as revealed to you in Scripture. Jesus chose to give you victory and is working in you from the inside out to make you more than a conqueror because he loves you.[26]

Breaking through Walls

A big part of being a successful athlete is identifying your wall and making a plan for knocking it down.[27]

—Jordan Metzl, MD

73

If you've ever run a marathon, you know that there is a point of exhaustion that overtakes your resolve to continue. It's called "hitting the wall," and it happens to runners regardless of fitness level, from "couch-to-5k-ers" to veteran ultramarathoners. Some runners describe this moment as if suddenly a brick wall popped up in the middle of their path and they hit it head-on. Unable to take another step, some runners collapse to the ground, others just stop running and stand there dazed at their inability to move. Every runner fears "the wall," the point when the body gets heavy, energy drains, and crossing the finish line begins to look impossible.

However, marathon runners have figured out how to get past this dreaded barrier. They have learned that to be ready for a long and arduous race, they must address their weak links (past injuries), take care of their gut (be well-nourished), be realistic (well prepared), and understand the power of the mind (rest). Of all of these, they have concluded that the hardest one to deal with is the last one: trouble in the mind. Discouragement is a huge obstacle, the tallest of walls.

Paul equated the faith journey to a "good fight" and a "race" in his letter to Timothy. He wrote, "I am already being poured out as a drink offering, and the time for my departure is close. I have fought the good fight, I have finished the race, I have kept the faith."[28] He fully expected to receive the "crown of righteousness" from Jesus for breaking through the many walls he faced.

The people of Israel were rebuilding the wall of Jerusalem when they hit the barrier of discouragement. Their enemies mocked them, saying:

> *"What are these pathetic Jews doing? Can they restore it by themselves? Will they offer sacrifices? Will they ever finish it? Can they bring these burnt stones back to life from the mounds of rubble?" Then Tobiah the Ammonite, who was beside him,*

said, "Indeed, even if a fox climbed up what they are building, he would break down their stone wall!"

—Nehemiah 4:2–3

Nehemiah's response to their taunting is instructive for you and me. His response was to pray an honest and vulnerable prayer to God, and then they all went back to work. This was a regular rhythm for Nehemiah: pray and work.

Nehemiah was surrounded by enemies. Negativity was coming at him from every direction. He had enemies in the north (Sanballat, the governor of Samaria), the west (Tobiah, the governor of Ammon), the south (Gesham, the Arab), and the east (the people of Ashdod). The weapon they all had in common was ridicule. What was their aim? To discourage, exhaust, wear out, and prompt the Israelites to quit.

Israel's enemies had one intention: "They won't realize it until we're among them and can kill them and stop the work."[29] That's the aim of the enemy against you and me: to destroy, to discourage, to stop us from doing the work of the Lord. What is another tactic of the enemy? To instill fear. The Israelites were constantly under the fear of attack, saying, "Everywhere you turn, they attack us."[30] Nehemiah and all the people of Israel dealt with this constant opposition as they were doing the work. They found a way to break past the fear. Fear paralyzes us, doesn't it? It keeps us from doing what God calls us to do.

Men were used to discourage Nehemiah and the Israelites, but make no mistake, all these enemies put together represent the real enemy that is against God's people. The work the good God is doing is opposed by Satan, together with his demons. There is an attempt constantly . . . *constantly* . . . against anything related to God. This is a reality we live with that we often forget, and the reason he's so effective at times is that his voice often matches our own. How many times do you do this? I say things to myself that are very negative. I've called myself some names. I've talked to myself, and I've said things about myself that, when I hear it coming from the outside, matches what's in my head and I believe it. I buy in because I think, "Yeah! That's exactly what I think of myself." But those are lies straight from hell.

The enemy knows our buttons; he knows our weaknesses. He is a roaring lion, and he doesn't come in quietly. He comes right at us. How many times have you heard his roaring in your life? If you haven't heard him lately, you might be in denial, but he's roaring. That's what he always does. I'm not sharing this with you because I want you to be afraid or become overly obsessed with this. I'm sharing this with you because we must all be aware of his tactics so we can seek God all the more.

Nehemiah was aware of these enemies, but what we're going to see now is what Nehemiah did with that reality. Did he obsess over it? Did he stop the work? Did he get discouraged? Did he let fear freeze his progress? Did he decide, "I can't do it"? No! We see different behavior from Nehemiah, and it teaches you and me what we are to do when we are discouraged by the obstacles, challenges, and even the suffering that comes our way.

Nehemiah prayed.

We totally undervalue prayer, don't we? You might be a prayer warrior. If so, awesome! But some of us can improve in this area, because as soon as things go wrong, our initial reaction is to get angry, discouraged, and whiny. As soon as opposition comes, prayer may not be the first place we go. It might come a few steps below, if not at the end of our rope. But prayer was the first place Nehemiah went. He cries out to God, "Listen, our God, for we are despised,"[31] and when they are opposed, he reports, "So we prayed to our God

..."[32] and then, when he again faces intimidation, he begs, "But now, my God, strengthen my hands."[33]

Nehemiah *constantly* went to prayer. Even before he started building the wall, he prayed for four months, asking God for wisdom. We see throughout the whole story of Nehemiah that prayer was an essential tool or strategy he used to deal with the enemy and his fears, and so should we.

Nehemiah remembered.

Memories have a way of shifting our minds. They bring the past together with the present and maybe even with the future. It's a beautiful thing that God gives us the ability to remember what we often forget. Often, in a time of struggle, we forget certain truths that are essential to get us through whatever challenge we're in. Nehemiah stood up before the nobles, officials, and the rest of the people and commanded them, "Don't be afraid of them. Remember the great and awe-inspiring Lord, and fight ..."[34] What did Nehemiah offer the people as encouragement? A memory.

Years before this, according to 1 Samuel, the Israelites were overpowered by the Philistines[35] and defeated in the war. They cried out to God, and God came through. In their next battle, after crying out to God, they completely wiped out the Philistines.[36] Samuel the priest (their leader) built a pillar and called it *Ebenezer* (meaning "stone of help") to encourage Israel to always remember—because they were prone to forget how God had provided for them in the past.[37] We all are. But our God never changes!

Perhaps you are fighting a battle right now. You are reading this book and are completely worn out. You don't even know how you got here. Perhaps you are feeling overwhelmed and deeply discouraged. Again, I wish I could give you a hug and sit down with you to hear your story and pray with you. But here is something I can offer:

Remember.

Remember the Lord who has already been great and awesome in your life.

Remember how he has been there for you.

Remember what Jesus did for you.

I am convinced that if there's only one thing you can think of that God has done for you—although I'm sure he has done more than that—I am confident that actively remembering it will change the state of your mind.

I am convinced that if there's only one thing you can think of that God has done for you—although I'm sure he has done more than that—I am confident that actively remembering it will change the state of your mind. Contemplate the details of that memory, and let the Holy Spirit transform your mind.

Nehemiah trusted.

To me, this is where Nehemiah really paints for us a picture of what grounded him no matter the challenges he faced. This was not a practice; it was activated trust and unwavering commitment.

> *From that day on, half of my men did the work while the other half held spears, shields, bows, and armor. The officers supported all the people of Judah, who were rebuilding the wall. The laborers who carried the loads worked with one hand and held a weapon with the other. Each of the builders had his sword strapped around his waist while he was building, and the one who sounded the ram's horn was beside me. Then I said to the nobles, the officials, and the rest of the people, "The work is enormous and spread out, and we are separated far from one another along the wall. Wherever you hear the sound of the ram's horn, rally to us there. Our God will fight for us!" So we continued the work, while half of the men were holding spears from daybreak until the stars came out.*

—Nehemiah 4:16–21

In church, we often talk or sing songs about surrendering to the Lord. We take on physical postures to demonstrate our surrender: arms way up, getting on our knees, or lying on the ground. Don't get me wrong here, I think surrender is an important component of trusting God and the journey of faith. But trust is more than surrender. *Trust is active surrender.* Nehemiah did not sit back and wait for the Lord to build the wall. He trusted God, surrendered the outcome, surrendered control of the future, and got to work—staying at work until it was finished.

When the challenges got the toughest and Nehemiah needed every person on the job, what did he do? He cut his resources in half. Half the men became warriors watching out for the enemy. The other half were laborers who carried materials with one hand and a sword with the other, which meant they could not carry as much. Nehemiah trusted God enough to reduce his workforce substantially! He trusted God to help finish the project—while they worked.

What a refreshing way to trust God! Sometimes, my tendency is to power up, do more, and figure out a way to increase my capacity. That's when I need to surrender. Nehemiah reduced. But, then in my "surrendered" state, I can also become disconnected, inactive, and frozen—and that's when I need to get active. Nehemiah worked from "daybreak until the stars came out."[38] Nehemiah trusted God with the outcome.

> *I think surrender is an important component of trusting God and the journey of faith. But trust is more than surrender. Trust is active surrender.*

If you're exhausted, if you're worn out, ready to quit, or are frozen at that wall, then chances are you're going at it on your own strength. God wants you to trust him. God wants you to do this, whatever he's calling you to do, on his strength and by his power.

There is a man named Dennis Kimetto, from Kenya, who, in 2014, ran the marathon in Berlin in a world-record time of two hours, two minutes, and fifty-seven seconds. Several YouTube videos are available for viewing his technique. When I look at him running, I think of the words in Hebrews 12:3, "For consider him who endured such hostility from sinners against himself, so that you won't grow weary and give up." Dennis runs so smoothly, calmly, consistently, and confidently, with no weight overcoming him! That's what God wants for us. He wants us to keep our eyes fixed on him to take us to the finish line.

Nehemiah got to see the work to completion in record time: "The wall was completed in fifty-two days . . . When all our enemies heard this, all the surrounding nations were intimidated and lost their confidence, for they realized that this task had been accomplished by our God."[39]

What a great feeling that must have been! However, just because you may have completed one "marathon" with or for God doesn't mean there isn't going to be another. Sometimes the finish line is a door to the next thing God has for us. Nehemiah completed the task, and just like that world-record run was not Dennis's last marathon (he's still running them as of the time of this writing), this finished task wasn't Nehemiah's last race either. The people of Israel returned to the land of Israel, and Nehemiah went on to the next assignment God had for him.

At the finish line, on the other side of you finishing the work God has called you to do, God is glorified. The world gets to see who God is. Time and time again we see in the Old Testament God proclaiming, "Then they will know that I am the Lord." Nothing is more beautiful than a Christian who runs the race well through opposition and challenges, praying always, remembering, and trusting who God is and what he has done. On the other side of the finish line is a promise that God will be revealed, and his glory will be displayed through us.

Do you want to finish your race well? Somewhere down the line, you'll see the benefit of the fruit of your labor.

Years ago, I set out to run a marathon, but I was never able to complete it. For ten years I ran 5Ks and 10Ks and half marathons. I was working toward a marathon and made it to running eighteen miles when my left hip locked up. I found out I have a degenerate hip and torn labrum, and if I did not stop running, I was going to need a hip replacement. I had a few surgeries to repair the labrum, but my doctor told me, "You're done with running, Inés. You need to walk. You need to do yoga or swimming or something else." To me, that was the worst news and I got depressed.

To relieve my sadness, I took all the running bibs, those numbers you see runners wearing at races, and made a decoupage oil painting of a runner. It turned out beautiful—at least I think so. The painting hangs in my garage, and I see it every day and remember how the Lord met me in my hardship. As I was painting the runner, I felt God encouraging me: "Inés, you're still a runner. You're still a runner for me." Now I remember that my running is my journey of faith, and I run as Paul did, "in such a way to win the prize,"[40] trusting in the Lord through all of the challenges, obstacles, and even the suffering. Abuelita did not get to see the fruit of most of her prayers, but she, too, finished the race well. I imagine her together with the cloud of witnesses mentioned in Hebrews 11, watching over me and you.

You are a runner for Jesus Christ; his witness and his name are written all over you. Don't ever forget that!

Now that we've looked at how to keep going in the midst of temptation and trials, in the next chapter we'll take a look at what to do when we get disoriented—when we start to have questions about where we're going and why.

SPIRITUAL PRACTICE: PRAYER

Prayer—a conversation with God—is an essential aspect of our faith journey. There are many ways to pray that help us keep it fresh and effective. In prayer, we can ask God to give us eyes to see how he is at work despite our obstacles. In prayer, we can submit to the Spirit to strengthen our resolve to remain committed and transform our hearts to be more like Jesus. Prayer with others can help us hear how God works and reminds us that he does not change. Jesus modeled a life of prayer and called his disciples to pray regularly. He offered the Lord's Prayer as a simple example of prayer, but he also modeled long prayers, as in John 17. Paul did the same, modeling both short, simple prayers, and long, complex prayers. Prayer is powerful, and God hears all of our prayers even if he does not answer them in our timing or according to our desires.

The Process

Space does not allow me to list the many wonderful ways to pray. But since prayer is a conversation with God, we can have it any time and in any manner we wish. We can pray in times of trouble or moments of happiness. We can pray alone or with others. We can pray in the silence of our minds, out loud, or in writing. We can even sing our prayers. We can pray for ourselves and for others. We can pray boldly, as Mark Batterson encourages us to in his book *The Circle Maker*. The bigger the obstacle, the more we should pray. Batterson writes that "bold prayers honor God, and God honors bold prayers."[41]

But prayers can be laments as well. We can take our complaints, anger, frustration, disappointment, and deep pain to God. Crying out to God for help is prayer. Also, prayer can be a practice of remembering all the ways in which God has helped you and provided for your needs. You can pray while you lie down, sit down, go on a walk, or run around the block. Another suggestion is to create a prayer wall. For example, mine is a corkboard with pinned written prayers and photos that hangs just above my dog's food and water bowls, so I look at it twice a day. As Noelle eats, I pray. We can use a journal to keep track of our prayer requests and see how God answers them. I could go on, but it'd be better to just stop and pray.

When you're finished, take a few moments to reflect on your experience. What did you see? What did you learn?

Prompting Scriptures

> *The prayer of a righteous person is very powerful in its effect.*
>
> —James 5:16

Pray at all times in the Spirit with every prayer and request, and stay alert with all perseverance and intercession for all the saints.

—Ephesians 6:18

Rejoice always, pray constantly, give thanks in everything; for this is God's will for you in Christ Jesus.

—1 Thessalonians 5:16–18

When I think of you as I lie on my bed, I meditate on you during the night watches because you are my helper; I will rejoice in the shadow of your wings.

— Psalm 63:6–7

*To struggle with one's faith is often the surest sign
we actually have one.*[1]

—A.J. SWOBODA

CHAPTER 5

QUESTIONS ARE ESSENTIAL

THEY REVEAL YOUR HEART

For her tenth birthday, I took my daughter Kayleigh to Knott's Berry Farm with a few of her friends. I am not a fan of roller coasters, but Kayleigh insisted I try a few of them. Seeking cool-mom status in the eyes of her friends, I, of course, acquiesced. She talked me into riding the Supreme Scream attraction, claiming that it would be as close as I would ever get to experiencing the thrill of bungee jumping. She got that right. I never understood how people enjoy bungee jumping. Still don't. I should have known better than to go along. The name of this ride is accurately descriptive. This thing shot us up at high speed to 252 feet and then "power-blasted" us back down in three seconds at fifty miles per hour. That would have been terrifying enough for me. But, as with bungee jumping, after just a few seconds of pause at the bottom—not enough time to even finish an awkward chortle—we bounced back up at least halfway and shot back down to a hard stop.

At the start, I enthusiastically planted my rear end on the roller-coaster cart and strapped the harness, believing something good was going to come out of it. But the ride juggled my brain so much that I left the ride shaking and confused, not knowing which way was up or down. Knott's labels this ride at the highest "thrill level." It was not a thrill for me. Rather than excitement, joy, delight, and amusement, I walked away completely disoriented, wondering if I had lost my mind or suffered a stroke. It took me over an hour to recover, but thankfully I came out of the experience all the wiser about my personal low tolerance for bungee jumping or any look-alike rides.

Disorientation on Our Faith Journey

At times, life can feel like a Supreme Scream ride: disorienting, with sudden ups and downs. In his commentary on the Psalms, Walter Brueggemann rightly notes that life has "equilibrium, coherence, and symmetry," but it is also "marked by disequilibrium, incoherence and unrelieved asymmetry."[2] We enjoy human connection, productivity, and health, but also face broken relationships, medical diagnoses, and losses of all types. No matter how much we try to banish or deny this reality, our experience of this world will never be completely smooth and comfortable. Brueggemann contends that this is the reason why the Psalms include songs of optimism as well as a large number of laments. They both help us stay in touch with the realities of life.

This might come as a surprise, but the Christian spiritual journey is no different. We will experience the "mountain top" of growth, clarity, and pleasing consistency on our walk with Jesus. But we will also go through what Eugene Peterson called "the badlands" of spiritual life, those seasons of dryness that lack interest, excitement, or meaning. Somewhere along our journey of faith, our experience of life, the world, church, or God can get utterly disrupted, leaving us feeling spiritually disoriented—as I felt after my forty-five-second thrill ride.

As I shared in chapter 2, my own faith journey started out with a heap of unwelcomed and unanswered questions. I was a curious little girl asking big questions about God, but sadly I was shamed for asking them. In that first catechism class, my disorientation began just as the seed of God-given faith was sprouting. Before that day, I had mostly accepted that life was random, unfair, and operated according to the theory of "survival of the fittest." Perhaps this mindset came from my position in the family, number six of seven children raised by a single mother. I intended to be a survivor, believing this life was all there is, and that it was up to me to make it worthwhile. Yet there I was, fully captivated by the nun's teaching on the existence of the Creator of all things.

Unfortunately, she perceived my innocent question ("If God created everything, and there was nothing before he created it, where was he standing?") as a sign of doubt; and her response was to shame me in front of others. I'm not sure who was more disoriented at that moment, me or her. The demand that I repent for my lack of faith led to a bigger question for me: "Why would a loving God be offended by my questions?"

Too many of us have been raised to believe that some questions should never be asked about God, the journey of faith, or the Bible. Has this happened to you? Have you been shamed for your faith disorientation? If so, I am sorry. Once I shared this experience in an interview with Pastor Mike Erre. He paused the discussion with these words, "What a catastrophe, and in microcosm, such a representation of some of the heavy-handedness of faith communities that have existed and held to beliefs in ways that make them almost intolerable and self-defeating. Wow! To be shamed for asking a really thoughtful, logical question . . . What that communicated is there was no place to be intelligent; there was no place to be thoughtful; there was no place to be open."[3]

Mike validated my experience and reminded me that God does not shame us for asking questions. Shame for asking thoughtful questions is cancer to our commitment to faith. It increases doubt and silences our curiosity. Despite the hostile reception we might get when we ask questions, they are our way to assess the truth.

Questions are essential because they are relational—questions are not just for conjuring proof or evidence, but for building understanding and intimacy.

Sometimes, faith disorientation happens because of our choices, when we rebel against God, swan-dive into sin, or hang out with others who are antagonistic to our faith or who sow confusion and doubt. Other times, disorientation happens to us and takes us by surprise through the actions or inactions of a person, a group of people, or by life's circumstances. Then there are those times when the very ground beneath our faith is yanked away by the moral failure of a leader we once highly respected, a church's toxic culture inflicting wounds, or a terrible injustice being perpetrated by people who are supposed to be Christ-like.

God does not shame us for asking questions.

Other times, faith disorientation comes upon us slowly, by layers of confidence peeled off, or layers of doubt imposed, but we are so entangled in it that we do not know how to escape it. No matter how we enter faith disorientation, we will be tempted to respond by giving up, checking out, or, conversely, by tightening our control over things we cannot control, such as other people, circumstances, and God. When the place we once thought was safe becomes a hazard, understandably, out of a survival instinct, we take matters into our own hands.

Pilots in training are warned about "spatial disorientation," which can happen under a variety of flight conditions. Abrupt movements or changes in climb can affect a pilot's sensory organs for gravity and linear acceleration.[4] Even on a beautiful and clear day, conditions can change rapidly and obscure the visual cues a pilot uses to maintain orientation. Pilots deprived of natural, visual references (e.g., clouds, fog, haze, darkness, terrain, the horizon), can mistake their position and motion relative to the earth.

The human senses that help a pilot maintain balance and know "which end is up" become completely unreliable when there is no visual point of reference. Therefore, a pilot cannot discern if he is still going in the direction he planned, has deviated, or if he is flying straight toward the ground. It's believed that John F. Kennedy Jr. crashed because of spatial disorientation. Even for experienced pilots, this fatal risk is present, which is why all pilots are trained to fly not by their own sense of control but also by referencing their flight instruments. Pilots need an external point of reference to survive when they are disoriented. Christians do too.

God's Response to Our Disorientation

When you're disoriented, God is not. God knows everything, and even he asks questions. By studying Scripture and examining the questions that God asks, we are reminded that one of the unique things about our journey of faith is revealed by the questions we ask, and the questions God asks us.

"Where are you?"[5]

The first question God asks Adam and Eve is such an important one. When we're struggling, when life is hard, we ask a similar question, but we ask it of God. How many times have you asked God, "Where are you?" This is the same question God asked in the Garden when Adam and Eve were hiding. He did not ask because he was unaware of their location. Proverbs 15:3 reminds us that the "eyes of the Lord are everywhere, observing the wicked and the good."

But by his question, God invites Adam and Eve to come out of hiding and return to relationship. They disobeyed God's instruction by eating from the Tree of the Knowledge of Good and Evil and, in their shame, went into hiding. But God pursued them with an expression of love: a question. The Father knows exactly where you are amid your faith disorientation, and what has taken you there. He comes after you. His love demands nothing less. If he is willing and able to undergo extreme efforts to save us from our sin, he is certainly willing to rescue us from our state of confusion.

In the book of Judges, seven times we read stories of Israel doing "evil in the Lord's sight." Reading this book can be distressing, as we see the extent of our human rebellion. The very things God warned the Israelites not to do, they did—and worse. God's expectations were simple, "Do not fear [or revere] the gods of the Amorites;"[6] that is, the gods of other nations.

The Father knows exactly where you are amid your faith disorientation, and what has taken you there. He comes after you. His love demands nothing less.

God saved Israel from the oppression of the Egyptians. He promised to be Israel's God, and they would be his people. Their covenant relationship demanded mutual faithfulness. God, in his love, would warn Israel again and again when they were not living up to their side of the covenant, but Israel ignored God's messengers and his warnings. As we read the book of Judges, we see the nation of Israel stuck in a downward cycle of rebellion, judgment, repentance, salvation, further rebellion, and so on. Each time Israel got in trouble, they cried out to God in humility, and God sent them help. One such time was in the time of Gideon.

In Judges 6, the Israelites again did "evil in the sight of the Lord," and ignored all his warnings and calls to repentance, so God handed them over to their enemies. The Midianites oppressed the nation of Israel by repeatedly stealing their food and destroying their crops. The Israelites, terrified by the cruelty of the Midianites, went up to the mountains and hid in caves to survive.

Gideon, an Israelite man, was threshing wheat in a winepress. A winepress was a large vat carved out of rock and was usually located where grapes were available. The grapes were thrown in the vat and trampled underfoot until the juice flowed into a catch basin below.

Threshing wheat, however, was the process of beating the stalks of wheat on a stone floor with a sledgehammer—outdoors, so the wind would blow away the unwanted particles. In other words, you wouldn't really want to thresh wheat in a sheltered location like a winepress, because the wind couldn't help you there.

So Gideon was doing his best to survive under the conditions of distress his nation was suffering. That is when the angel of the Lord came and engaged in conversation with Gideon.

> *The angel of the Lord came, and he sat under the oak that was in Ophrah, which belonged to Joash, the Abiezrite. His son Gideon was threshing wheat in the winepress in order to hide it from the Midianites. Then the angel of the Lord appeared to him and said, "The Lord is with you, valiant warrior."*

> *Gideon said to him, "Please, my lord, if the Lord is with us, why has all this happened? And where are all his wonders that our ancestors told us about? They said, 'Hasn't the Lord brought us out of Egypt?' But now the Lord has abandoned us and handed us over to Midian."*

> —Judges 6:11–13

The first thing the angel does is declare God's presence and confidence in Gideon. "The Lord is with you, valiant warrior."[7] It's hard to picture a "valiant warrior" standing tall, confident, and seemingly invincible when all we see described is a man likely hiding in a cave,[8] threshing wheat in a winepress. (No offense intended, Gideon.)

In his response, Gideon ignores the compliment and brushes over it like it was meant for someone else. How many times do we do this? God speaks powerful truths to us through Scripture, the Holy Spirit, in prayer, or through other people, and we let it drop to the ground. It's akin to someone extending us a handshake and we leave them awkwardly standing there, arm stretched toward us, while we pepper them with questions. I'm thinking there was probably a bit of an attitude coming through Gideon's questions.

Maybe I'm hearing my own Puerto Rican edge, which comes up any time I'm feeling mocked. Gideon is in such difficult circumstances, it's hard for him to believe that God, if present, would allow such calamity. "If the Lord is with us, why has all this happened?"[9] He's even questioning the history he has learned, the stories he inherited from his ancestors.

God speaks powerful truths to us through Scripture, the Holy Spirit, in prayer, or through other people

Disorientation.

And then—and this is easy to miss when reading—not the angel, but "the Lord" responds to Gideon. He tells him, "Go in the strength you have and deliver Israel from the grasp of Midian. I am sending you!"[10] In my own words, "Gideon, you are part of the solution to the problem, and I will be with you." The words Gideon heard demonstrate consistency in the way God speaks to his people and are like God's promise to Moses in Exodus 3:12 and Joshua in Joshua 1:5.

Again, Gideon responds with a question, "Please, Lord, how can I deliver Israel?"[11] Gideon was hyperaware of his inability to come up against such a powerful enemy, especially considering his family was the smallest of his clan, and he was the youngest in his family.

Doubt.

The Lord puts his name on the line: "I will be with you ... You will strike Midian down as if it were one man."[12] What a promise. Gideon would not fight the enemy alone. He was promised the presence of the same Lord who rescued the Israelites from the mighty nation of Egypt through signs and wonders! Gideon was guaranteed success.

That should do it, right? No. Gideon responds, "If I have found favor with you, give me a sign that you are speaking with me."[13] Okay, at this point Gideon is not making sense. "If? If?" In the same fashion some people yell at characters in a horror movie ("He's behind you! Turn around! Run away! Lock the door!"), I'm over here hollering at Gideon, "Dude! The Lord *is* speaking!" What more proof does he need to hear God's voice than already hearing the voice of God? But that's just Gideon, right?

Disbelief.

I encourage you to read the rest of the story on your own and see how the Lord responds to Gideon's continuing questions and requests for confirmation with kindness and patience. Gideon is not chastised for his disorientation. He is not shamed for his questions. He's not sent to repent for his doubts. He's not silenced in his sadness. He's not abandoned in his disbelief. God asks questions and he also welcomes our questions! He is with us in our disorientation. Jesus promised us, his disciples, "Remember, I am with you always, to the end of the age."[14] Not, "I *will* be with you," but "I *am* with you." He told his disciples to go in the strength they had and promised to go with them. When we don't know which way is up or down, which direction we're headed toward, or what we're supposed to do, we must remember that the Lord is the one who calls us, and he goes with us.

Pay attention to the questions God asks you. What is he asking you right now?

Pay attention to the questions God asks you. What is he asking you right now? Perhaps you need to put the book down and spend a few minutes reflecting or journaling. If nothing comes up right away, pray for the Lord to prompt you. Here are a few of the powerful questions God asks in Scripture. Perhaps he is asking you one of these today:

"Where are you?"[15]
"What have you done?"[16]
"What is that in your hand?"[17]
"What are you doing here?"[18]
"Why do you call me good?"[19]
"But you . . . who do you say that I am?"[20]
"What will benefit [you] if [you gain] the whole world yet [lose your] life?"[21]
"What will [you] give in exchange for [your] life?"[22]
"Do you think that I came here to bring peace on the earth?"[23]
"What is your life?"[24]
"Where were you when I established the earth?"[25]
"Who will I send? Who will go for us?"[26]

There is a chance that one or more of these questions resonated with your heart as you read them. What is God targeting in your heart? God's questions reveal his good and perfect desires for you. He might be calling you back to his loving arms because you have distanced yourself from him. In his loving way, he might be pointing out an area of your life where sin has taken hold, inviting you to confess it to him and trust him to transform your heart by the power of the Holy Spirit. Remember, "There is now no condemnation for those in Christ Jesus."[27]

Sometimes, we get completely lost on our faith journey and find ourselves in places we know we should not be. If that is your situation, know that God follows you there, as he did with Jonah and Elijah, and calls you to look around and see if this is where you want to stay. Jesus will carry the weight of our burdens if we call out to him and walk alongside him. "Come to me, all of you who are weary and burdened, and I will give you rest."[28]

Perhaps you have been struggling to understand who Jesus is, especially if people who say they are Christians are presenting him in ways that make him unattractive, judgmental, or confusing. Jesus wants you to know him. The best way to know Jesus is to read about him in the Bible. Read the four gospels (Mark, Matthew, Luke, and John). Hear his voice yourself. He assures us that his "sheep hear my voice, I know them, and they follow me."[29]

Jesus gave his life to save you from the power of sin (bondage), the consequence of sin (death), and the effect of sin (hopelessness). If you're like me, you spend an inordinate amount of time trying hard and fighting an uphill battle to remain free, stay alive, and experience happiness. We sacrifice so much to gain these victories, but Jesus sacrificed it all for us to experience them through him. Remember his words: "I have come so that [you] may have life and have it in abundance."[30]

Jesus reminded his followers that there is only One upon whom we can build our ultimate safety: himself. "The Lord will protect your coming and going both now and forever."[31] This does not mean you will not experience suffering in this life. We all do. I will talk about this hard reality a bit more in a later chapter. But Job comes to mind when we think that suffering does not happen to people who trust in God and are doing all the right things. To Job, in all his confusion, deep agony, and frustration, God offered the gift of his presence. The One who established the universe by the power of his word is with you too. Read Psalms 8, 19, and 139, or Job 38–39 to remind yourself of God's majesty.

Lastly, God calls his followers to hear his words and act on them.[32] He chooses people, broken and flawed, like you and me, to do the work. Jesus said you are to be his witness in your community, city, country, and beyond, by the power of the Holy Spirit, which has come to you as you put your faith in Jesus as your Savior.[33] And as Paul puts it, you are an ambassador for Christ, "since God is making his appeal through [you]."[34] I'm here only scratching the surface of the many proofs the Bible provides us that asking thoughtful questions to and about God is a function of faith and not a sign of doubt.

We must train similar to the way pilots train. First, they are trained to fly planes during clear days when they can clearly see the horizon and reference points (VFR). If they want to further their training and increase the scope of conditions they can fly in, even when the weather is bad, they must learn to fly trusting only the cockpit instrumentation. For this training, pilots have hoods placed over their heads so they cannot see anything but the interior instrumentation. Imagine how terrifying! If the pilot does not understand the instruments or know how to interpret them, there's no way she can be trusted to fly the plane. That's probably one reason why there are fewer pilots than Uber drivers.

Thankfully, God gives us several reliable and trustworthy "instruments" to help us navigate our path.

Faith disorientation can also feel terrifying, whether you are new to the faith journey or have been walking with Jesus for a long time. Anytime you feel disoriented, the Holy Trinity will help you stay the course. Thankfully, God gives us several reliable and trustworthy "instruments" to help us navigate our path.

The following are four ways you can experience God's guidance.

1. The Holy Spirit. Once you put your trust in Jesus as Lord and Savior, the Holy Spirit comes to dwell in you and does a lot for you.[35] He leads you to all truth[36] and comforts you. He confirms your status as God's child[37] and makes you holy.[38] He inspires and helps you overcome,[39] teaches,[40] empowers, and equips you.[41] He guides you,[42] intercedes for you,[43] and convicts you when you sin.[44] In Paul's letter to the churches in Galatia, we read that the Spirit is at war with our sinful nature ("the flesh") and seeks to produce fruit in us so that we may reflect Christ Jesus to the hurting world.[45]

*If you love me, you will keep my commands. And I will ask the
Father, and he will give you another Counselor to be with you
forever. He is the Spirit of truth. The world is unable to receive
him because it doesn't see him or know him. But you do know
him, because he remains with you and will be in you.*

—John 14:15–17

Jesus left you his presence. He left you his guidance. Are you
sensitive to his voice? Are you willing to listen to his instruction?
Do you seek him?

2. The Word of God. Psalm 119 is the longest psalm in the Psalter, and
it is located at the center of our Bible. It has 176 verses organized as
an acrostic, according to the Hebrew alphabet, which is composed
of twenty-two letters. The entire psalm is about God's good instruction. God's instruction (the Torah) is at the center, reminding us that
the "primal mode of faithfulness and knowing God is obedience."[46]

Psalm 119 calls us to treasure God's instruction because it keeps
us from sinning.[47] Verse 105 says, "Your word is a lamp for my feet
and a light on my path." But this psalm is not the only writing to
elevate the importance of the Scriptures. Hebrews 4:12 says, "For
the word of God is living and effective and sharper than any dou-
ble-edged sword, penetrating as far as the separation of soul and
spirit, joints and marrow. It is able to judge the thoughts and intentions of the heart." It is from the Word of God that we understand
who God is. We get to learn more about God and about ourselves
when we read the Bible. You cannot trust a God you don't know or
understand. Read the Bible regularly (not here and there, as we tend
to do). Listen to it and meditate upon it.

When my husband and I go on a car ride, I'm usually the naviga-
tor. One time we drove from Southern California to Canada, which

was fun. When we started the trip, I was ready to go pro with my map app. I entered the destination and turned off the voice of the app. I sound better. "In one and a half miles we will turn right ... In one hundred feet, turn left." I gave Jim the correct directions along the way, but he refused to fully trust me. He kept looking at the GPS map, zooming it in and out to make sure I was giving him the right information.

God wants to guide us. He wants to give us direction and rest

Isn't that just like us on our spiritual journey? God wants to guide us. He wants to give us direction and rest, but we are the control freaks who give him directions from the back seat. I'm the worst of all. I want to navigate. But by delighting in the Scriptures, God will navigate our lives toward the good. He is better at it.

3. Prayer. I said it before, and I will say it again. Prayer is so important! Prayer brings us comfort. Prayer soothes our soul. But ultimately, prayer is a conversation with God, and it does not have to be fancy. When Peter took that first step off the boat and, after walking some, started to sink, his prayer was not eloquent. He took his eyes off Jesus, the storm swirling around him, and just as he was going to lose it and sink, Peter cried out, "Lord, save me!"[48]

A prayer doesn't have to be wordy or pretty.[49] From your heart, whatever you need to say to the Lord, just say it. Prayer is your opportunity to speak to the Lord and hear from him. It's powerful how prayer changes our faith. It changes our hearts. It even changes our journey. Paul tells us, "Pray constantly."[50] John tells us to pray in confidence, knowing "that he hears whatever we ask."[51] Ask God to help you when your faith gets disoriented. He who hears you is faithful.

4. Reach out to others. God wants us to rely on him, but he also commands us to "carry one another's burdens."[52] Sometimes we must go on what I call *borrowed faith*, where our faith may be weak, but we can gain hope from the faith of another person. Paul, and even Jesus, requested the prayers of others.[53] Of course, we ought to be very careful about choosing whom we give such a privilege, and ask God for guidance in making the selection. But it is important to have people in our lives—godly people who give us sound wisdom and are willing to hold us accountable, pray for us, guide us, and who help us think out loud. In fact, Scripture says in Proverbs 11:14, "Without guidance, a people will fall, but with many counselors there is deliverance." And Proverbs 15:22 says, "Plans fail when there is no counsel, but with many advisers they succeed."

Our disorientation and questions are distressing to us, but they are not a surprise to God. He has prepared for them, and we can trust him to meet us in the midst of them.

The Holy Spirit (his presence), the Bible, prayer, and wise counsel are the "instruments" God gives us to navigate in good weather and bad. Like the pilots who trust their instruments, we will be kept from crashing. These instruments are especially needed in our times of disorientation. If you put your trust in these tools, even if you cannot see where you are going, God promises to keep your path straight. "Trust in the Lord with all your heart, and do not rely on your own understanding; in all your ways know him, and he will make your paths straight."[54]

This is God's promise, and he will keep it.

But what about the times when we mess up? What do we do when we know we have not been walking that straight path? We'll take a look at that in the next chapter.

SPIRITUAL PRACTICES: SPIRITUAL DIRECTION AND DISCERNMENT

Spiritual direction and discernment are ways to help us recognize the voice of God. He speaks to us primarily through the Bible, but also by the power of the Holy Spirit—both to our spirit and sometimes through people and circumstances. For discernment, we should always look to the Bible as our ultimate authority. We should study it and seek the help of godly counsel whenever we are confused. The Holy Spirit never contradicts Scripture or leads us into sinful activity. The Spirit might bring a verse to mind or illuminate a verse during our reading that speaks to our current situation or struggle. Taking time to listen to God daily is important for growing in wisdom and gaining a heavenly perspective. Rather than seeking our own answers, self-mapping out our lives, or making decisions from a worldly perspective, we can trust that God will guide us faithfully toward the good.

Spiritual direction is a wonderful way to present our questions to God and process out loud the questions we feel God is asking us. We can pay special attention to our relationship with the Lord and share that experience with a trusted and prayerful guide. It's also important to open up to a person who is dedicated to assisting us in discerning God's activity in our life. When we do, it can bring additional perspective and insight.

The Process

Both practices are guided by reading and studying the Scriptures. They entail listening, sharing, and living what we are hearing from God. There are many practical ways to do this, such as joining a small group of Christians in a Bible study or setting up meetings with an accountability and discernment partner. Engaging the services of a trained spiritual director for one session, or regularly, is an effective way to dive deeper into a certain area of our lives. Also, attending a spiritual direction retreat like the one offered by many retreat centers can be a wonderful discernment experience. Sometimes the way to discern is to be silent before the Lord and listen, so we may choose to attend a silent retreat for a weekend. If you want spiritual direction but don't know whom to ask, pray to the Lord to give you insight. You can also ask your church if there are spiritual directors currently serving your local congregation.

Prompting Scriptures

> *The secret counsel of the Lord is for those who fear him,*
> *and he reveals his covenant to them.*
>
> —Psalm 25:14

Now if any of you lacks wisdom, he should ask God—who gives to all generously and ungrudgingly—and it will be given to him.

—James 1:5

Dear friends, do not believe every spirit, but test the spirits to see if they are from God, because many false prophets have gone out into the world.

—1 John 4:1

When the Spirit of truth comes, he will guide you into all the truth. For he will not speak on his own, but he will speak whatever he hears. He will also declare to you what is to come.

—John 16:13

Nothing sets a person so much out of the devil's reach as humility.[1]

—JONATHAN EDWARDS

CHAPTER 6

RECOVERING FROM WRONG TURNS

LEARN IN HUMILITY

Linkin Park's song "What I've Become" is a song of penitence and a cry for mercy. It communicates a person's desire to change as he looks back at his life and does not like what he sees. He admits that he has flaws and vows not to make the same mistakes again. He expresses guilt and seeks to engage in reparative acts. He concludes that the answer to his past mistakes is to "erase" himself so that he may start over, no matter the cost. His ultimate solution is to forgive himself. His conclusion is that mercy comes from his own heart.

The song laments a reality of human nature: We all make mistakes and long for mercy. We all wish we could finally stop doing wrong and secure a better tomorrow. We all desire to be forgiven and attain self-forgiveness. Naturally, the song's message struck a chord of deep human desire and succeeded on the music charts in over twenty countries, even making it to the top ten in some of them. Our desire to recover from human failure is universal. The consequences of our actions last longer than we'd like.

None of us has the "perfect" story, not even those people in church whose lives seem straightforward and relatively drama-free. So, of course, it is tempting to want to erase the history of our past wrongdoing. But even when it feels like that's worked, it only lasts until the next blunder, most likely bigger than or a repeat of something we've done before. This mindset cannot secure us a better future. If this was our only strategy for dealing with our past mistakes and guilt, we'd be stuck singing that Linkin Park song over and over again.

As Christians, we believe that the fundamental problem in this world is sin in the human heart (e.g., selfishness, self-centeredness, pride, greed, perversion). We feel the painful sting of sin no matter its measure, whether committed by us or others, inadvertently or on purpose. In the book of 1 John, sin is defined as rebellion against God's law or instruction.[2] The apostle Paul writes that "all have sinned and fall short of the glory of God."[3] The ways of sin go against the pure ways of God. "There is no sin in him."[4] Only Jesus was perfect in life, without sin.[5] As Paul describes it, we struggle to do what is right, "For I do not understand what I am doing, because I do not practice what I want to do, but I do what I hate."[6] Even devoted followers of Jesus will struggle with sin along the faith journey, sometimes in minor and easily recoverable ways and sometimes in disastrous ways.

God can help us recover even from our worst mistakes.

One of the challenges to owning our unique Christian faith journey is that our story contains mistakes, sins, and failures. The Bible calls us to confess our sins and repent. The way through isn't to live in shame for past wrongdoings or times when we acted against God's will, for that disregards God's gift of grace through Jesus and the power of the Holy Spirit to transform us.[7] It's even pointless to develop a hyperawareness of our sinful nature, traversing life stricken by fear of making mistakes, tightening our fists in control, and constructing elaborate boundary lines, as though the Spirit can't do his work in us.[8] God calls us not to shame, but to salvation through Jesus Christ:

> *For God loved the world in this way: He gave his one and only Son, so that everyone who believes in him will not perish but have eternal life. For God did not send his Son into the world to condemn the world, but to save the world through him.*
>
> —John 3:16–17

The beauty of redemption through Jesus, with the penalty of our sin paid on the cross, is that we are free to remember our history so we can learn, grow in humility, turn from our wicked ways, and help others do the same. That is where true change can occur. None of us is obligated to share publicly the details of our twists and turns, mistakes, and wrongdoing, but when we choose to share our story with one person or a whole group of people, we're in essence telling God's meta-story. It is why we have a special connection with the stories of people in the Bible. Most of us can relate our faith journey to that of a biblical character or two. I have a lot in common with the story of the woman who met Jesus at the well and King David's colossal failure.

We All Mess Up

It would be easier for me to tell you a shortened version, a cleaned-up copy. But from the moment I accepted Jesus as my Lord and Savior, a month before my fortieth birthday, God impressed upon my heart his desire that I share my faith journey openly and publicly. Not out of guilt or to earn his favor, but to celebrate his goodness and put the love of Jesus on full display. I offer it here to you as an example of what God can do when we fully surrender to him. It is a story of how God can help us recover even from our worst mistakes.

When I look back at my faith journey, which started when I was seven years old and took a sharp turn the day I heard God's voice, I celebrate some great stuff, but I also lament my sins against God and people. By my late thirties, I had accomplished business success, had three beautiful children, owned a home in a nice neighborhood, and had many friends. Generally, I have been a good person in many ways. But along the way, I also aborted two children, was divorced twice, and at my lowest point, had an affair with my boss. Our affair obliterated his twenty-four-year marriage and crushed the hearts of his wife and two daughters. I thought I would never do any of those things. My name, Inés Socorro, was given to me by Abuelita with the intention that I would be a "pure help" to others. She had dreams for me. I believed her and wanted the same. But our dreams went up in smoke. None of this happened overnight.

In 1979, my mother, "Mami," moved us to Southern California, looking for a better life and a fresh start. She was inspired by my older brother Pedro, who lived in Hollywood after he ended his service with the US Marines. Puerto Ricans more often moved to New York, New Jersey, or Florida—places on the East Coast where they could catch a short return flight to the island and visit loved ones. A commonwealth territory of the United States, Puerto Rico has a culture that is distinct, traditional, family-driven, and communal. We tend to stay close to one another. But Mami was all about the American Dream and had a spirit of independence and entrepreneurship.

My younger brother Javier and I flew from San Juan to Los Angeles in a plane filled mostly with businesspeople. It was Javier's fifteenth birthday, which I remember distinctly because the airline stewardess allowed us each to drink a Coors beer in celebration. We joined Mami and my older sister Maritza, who were already living with Pedro and his family. Eight of us lived together in a one-bedroom apartment until the four of us raised the funds for a place of our own. Mami taught us to be survivors because that's what she was.

At her command, we immediately looked for work every day after school. With our broken English, we would pour out our rehearsed speech to the store manager. It went something like this: "I need a job. I can clean, mop, and work hard." In a few weeks, the four of us had jobs. Mami worked as an accountant. Javier and Maritza worked at a movie theater doing all kinds of tasks. I got a job at a local pharmacy cleaning shelves and stocking merchandise. Every penny we earned went to Mami. There was no time for or interest in church or the things of God. I was in over my head in the sea of life, trying to survive. Then Mami announced it to us. We were all expected to move out on our own once we turned eighteen and graduated from high school. I had little time to get proficient in English and adjust to Southern California's individualistic culture but moved out to the San Fernando Valley the day after my graduation at the Hollywood Bowl.

There was no time for or interest in church or the things of God. I was in over my head in the sea of life, trying to survive.

Abuelita preferred that I marry a nice Christian boy, a Roman Catholic, so we would encourage each other to grow in our faith. She wrote me many letters telling me so. But a year after moving out of Mami's apartment, still a naive nineteen-year-old, I married a young man I met at a local shoe store. He was of Jewish descent, and we were both agnostic and indifferent toward any religion. He was a wounded man struggling to control his anger and manage our finances. I was a wounded woman unable to set healthy boundaries in relationships.

After four turbulent years of marriage, and the birth of our son Chad, I sought a divorce. The failed marriage brought me shame, especially since I had disappointed Abuelita in so many ways. But I referred to my first marriage as a "mulligan," analogizing it to the golf practice that allows a golfer to hit the ball a second time at the tee if the first swing is a disaster. I believed in that well-worn adage, "Everyone deserves a second chance!" Within a couple of years, I married again, this time hoping it would last for the rest of my life. At least Abuelita was happy that he was raised a Roman Catholic. I didn't have the courage to tell her that he too was agnostic. We had two daughters together (Kayleigh and Melissa) and pursued our business careers.

Being the sixth of seven children raised by a single mother, I suppose most of my ambition was fueled by a fear of being poor again. I also struggled with feeling invisible, since I grew up with no father and a very busy mom. When I performed well, people noticed me, and that made me feel secure. My job position, salary, home, marriage, children, and people's opinion of me became the key measures of my wholeness.

As wonderful as these things are, they are not reliable. We cannot fully control them, and at some point, they will let us down or we will mess them up. In my late thirties, my self-constructed success tower came crashing down when my second marriage also ended in divorce after fifteen years, and my son Chad became addicted to drugs. I shut down my art school business, put our house up for sale, and became a single mother of three children from two different marriages. It was a huge blow, but I was not done trying. I was not impressed with my track record, but I was a survivor. Sadly, I was also blind to the damage my pursuit of happiness was doing to my family and myself. This stubborn determination led me to make even more mistakes that eventually led to the lowest point of my life, what I now call my King David moment.

Even the Best Can Fail, Colossally

The name David means "beloved." The name Bathsheba means "oath." The beloved one (the one loved by God), David the King of Judah, broke an oath by sending for and "sleeping" with Bathsheba, the wife of Uriah the Hethite, and conceiving a son.[9] King David was hand-selected by God to deliver Israel from enemy nations intent on destroying God's people. Uriah was a trusted soldier in David's army. David's failure happened on a night when he remained in Jerusalem, when all his fighting men were gone to battle. It was spring, the best time of the year to fight, for the weather was favorable, bringing neither extreme heat nor deep cold. But for some reason, the king stayed back and enjoyed the comfort and safety of his palace.

> *Every human wrongdoing follows the cycle of temptation unless we choose to stop at any one point.*

One beautiful spring night, David struggled with sleep and went walking around on the palace roof. The king's house was higher than most of the other structures in the city. From his high place, David could see the homes below. That night the king spotted "a woman bathing—a very beautiful woman."[10] David sent for the woman—Bathsheba, wife of one of his soldiers—and slept with her, and his wrongdoing was then compounded by his attempts to hide it. Everything he did from the moment he decided to bring a married woman into his bedroom (which I assume was against her will, for no woman could deny the demands of a king), was a disaster.

Every human wrongdoing follows the cycle of temptation unless we choose to stop at any one point. The first step in the cycle of temptation is for us to become aware of the object of our desires. We see it and want it. We could stop there, as 1 Corinthians 10:13 tells us that God provides us a way out of our temptations. But often, we don't.

David saw Bathsheba, was attracted to her *and* sent for her. I equate this moment of David's temptation to skydiving. The goal of skydiving is to go up very high on a plane and then jump to the ground using a parachute to land safely. There is only one direction in parachuting. Down. The moment of "seeing" in temptation is like standing at the open door of a plane just before one is about to jump off for the thrill. You "see" the ground and set your aim to get there. You know the risk, the potential for disaster, and have a foretaste of the promised joy. That's a good moment to decide not to jump. The parachute could fail. You don't have wings. There is no way to save yourself once you jump. Unless the equipment works perfectly, you will crash. No matter how hard you try, you cannot flap your arms hard enough. You can't fly.

David isolated himself. There he was with no one to hold him accountable, no one to say, "David, what you're looking at is going to lead you in the wrong direction." David did not have a parachute. He wasn't even seeking God. There, in his total isolation, he took the next step. Dietrich Bonhoeffer offers this sobering truth:

> Sin demands to have a man by himself. It withdraws him from the community. The more isolated a person is, the more destructive will be the power of sin over him, and the more deeply he becomes involved in it, the more disastrous is his isolation. Sin wants to remain unknown. It shuns the light.[11]

We are weakest when we are isolated, but sometimes we're also weak when we are gathered with the wrong people. Using the skydiving illustration again, if you're standing on the edge of that plane and friends are encouraging you to jump, there is a good chance you will go with the flow, all the way down. The men who worked for David were not able to hold him accountable. They took their orders and followed them as good servants to a king. David's elaborate plan to hide his wrongdoing grew to bringing Bathsheba's husband home from the battlefield, getting him drunk, and encouraging him to go home to be with his wife—that way, no one would know it was David who'd gotten her pregnant.

If Uriah the Hethite had not been such a dedicated servant, he might have slept with his wife and no one would know what David did—that is except God, who knows everything. When that plan failed, David took it a step further and created an elaborate scheme to have Uriah the Hethite killed. Pregnant Bathsheba was left a widow, and David took her in, perhaps projecting himself as a good and compassionate king. David did not confess his wrongdoing to God or anyone else. That would have been the end of the story. But God sent the prophet Nathan to confront David, and all his wrongdoing was fully exposed.

> *Why then have you despised the Lord's command by doing what I consider evil? You struck down Uriah the Hethite with the sword and took his wife as your own wife—you murdered him with the Ammonite's sword.*

—2 Samuel 12:9

God presented David with the awful consequences of his compounding sins, which included the death of the child he conceived with Bathsheba. David's response to Nathan's confrontation was to repent. God's response to repentance is forgiveness.

> *David responded to Nathan, "I have sinned against the Lord." Then Nathan replied to David, "And the Lord has taken away your sin; you will not die."*

—2 Samuel 12:13

As a reflection of this experience, David wrote two psalms. Psalm 51 reveals David's truly repentant heart: "Against you—you alone—I have sinned and done this evil in your sight. So you are right when you pass sentence; you are blameless when you judge."[12] Psalm 32 reveals David's gratitude for God's forgiveness: "How joyful is the one whose transgression is forgiven, whose sin is covered!"[13]

Remarkably, despite the real, painful, and long-lasting consequences of his actions, King David ultimately recovered from this colossal wrongdoing by restoring his relationship with his God. David's story demonstrates to us that while we may not be able to eliminate the consequences of our actions, there are two ways we can recover from our mistakes.

Take the First Exit

The best way to recover from wrong turns is to stop the progression at every opportunity. God, in his grace, constantly offers us a way out of sin. David had many "off-ramps" he could have taken. He could have gone back inside his house after seeing the beautiful woman. He could have sought appropriate companionship. He could have called for the prophet Nathan to come and pray for him instead of sending men to fetch Bathsheba. The king had the power to call anyone he wished to his presence. He could have confessed to Nathan the moment he made the first huge mistake and many times after. Confession is like throwing retardant on a burning fire.

When I look back at my biggest mistakes, I can see a whole lot of off-ramps I chose not to take. Like David, I just kept going, piling up more consequences in my life. Going back for me is not an exercise of second-guessing myself, for there is nothing I can change about the past. But I can learn about my tendency to ignore the warning flags and alarm bells, or what conditions make me more susceptible to weakness before temptation.

Jim and I worked together for many years. We are both ambitious, and so we found that we could get a lot done together. We had a lot of fun, too, as our personalities are well matched. For years, our relationship was professional but grounded in friendship and mutual respect. Everything changed when I got divorced, which also happened to be at a time when Jim's marriage was in trouble. We were both weak at that time and ignored all the warning signs. Suddenly, our personality sparks had a different effect on our broken hearts. The numerous conversations, meetings, lunches, and dinners increased our feelings for each other. There were many opportunities to stop and avoid what came.

Confession is like throwing retardant on a burning fire.

I never intended to commit adultery with a married man. He never intended to fail his wife or hurt his children. But our relationship evolved because we continued to share time together and opened our hearts to each other. The burning fire of passion then got louder than the still, small voice of God telling us not to sin. Jim decided to divorce his wife, and we started our plans for marriage amid great turmoil. Now that my track record included adultery, I entered a season of emotional and spiritual crisis. My road to happiness had reached a dead end, and my prize for arriving there through destructive sin was overwhelming shame.

Maybe you've never fallen like this. Maybe you read David's story and my story, and you think, "Gosh! You guys are really a mess!" I don't disagree. But perhaps this message is especially for you. Perhaps it's a warning and reminder not to go down the drain as I did or as David did or as many of our brothers and sisters have. Whether we have fallen a little bit, some, or have swan-dived into sin, it feels unpleasant, and we know we don't want to do it again. We want to live a life that is flourishing under the grace of Jesus Christ, daily dependent on him to help us recover from our wrong turns. Thankfully, he offers us recovery through repentance.

Tell the Whole Truth

True humility comes when before God we see ourselves as nothing, have put aside self, and let God be all.[14]

—Andrew Murray

The second way to recover from our wrongdoing is to repent as soon as possible and completely humble ourselves before a loving God who is eager to forgive and seeks to conform us "to the image of his Son."[15] Again, in the words of David, "Many pains come to the wicked, but the one who trusts in the Lord will have faithful love surrounding him."[16]

While we wish we could go back in time and change things, both Jim and I have found a way through the mess we made. Just before Jim and I got married, Jim suggested we start attending church. Considering the mess we had made, and the desperate state of our hearts, that was a very wise idea, and I'm convinced God put it in his heart. After attending many churches over several months, we decided on a church to attend regularly.

I started reading the Bible for the first time. Using a chronological version of the Bible, one day I read Exodus 20 and Deuteronomy 5 back-to-back. I read the Ten Commandments for the first time, twice! And then it hit me: I had broken every single one of them. I know this sounds like hyperbole. It is not. It will make more sense after you read the next chapter. I now understand the bell curve God uses to measure our "goodness." In comparison to God's holiness and the goodness he intends for each of us, we all fall short.

When I first read Paul's words that "all have sinned and fall short of the glory of God" in Romans 3:23, they did not bring me any comfort, for they simply stated the facts. I was just another sinner, now aware that the wage of my sin is death. But the next verse made all the difference, because it said all "are justified freely by his grace through the redemption that is in Christ Jesus."[17] There is a penalty due for my sins. A just God must do something about evil, including the evil that I had done and the evil that still lives in me. There is a cost for my sins, and someone had to pay. Jesus took the penalty I deserved, the death I deserved ("for the wages of sin is death"[18]), so that I may have the life he deserves.
Redemption is the restoration of shalom, peace with God. Redemption is the sweetest of gifts, the costliest. Redemption is the way we recover from our wrongdoing.

> *Redemption is the sweetest of gifts, the costliest. Redemption is the way we recover from our wrongdoing.*

Because I am redeemed, I no longer live for myself, but for him who died for me and was raised again.[19] It means that my purpose is changed. My highest joy is to confess that I am a sinner saved by grace. My reliance on performance is slowly being chipped away by a loving God who reminds me daily that I am now and forever a child of God.

God redeemed my life and my marriage to Jim in the most remarkable way. I do not recommend that anyone follow my footsteps, for despite the gift of grace, the consequences and scars do not go away. However, our family is slowly healing from the many wounds inflicted by the way we started our relationship. We have many new friends and a community that celebrates with us a God that is full of grace. God has used us in many areas of ministry at our church and para-church ministries, and I have had the privilege to preach and teach the Bible around the world.

My story and David's story are living proof that God is full of grace, mercy, and love. I pray your story is too. Through Jesus, we have redemption and new life, even if we have messed up in the worst of ways. But also, our stories are a reminder that sin is disruptive, painful, and costly in the long term. In the next chapter we will talk about what we do with one part of the fallout of our sin: shame. There is beauty, restoration, and healing possible through Jesus, who conquered the most powerful, terrifying weapon against us: death. Because of this, we can be "more than conquerors through him,"[20] embracing our full unique story, with the good and the bad, and offering it to him to use in his larger story of faithful love.

SPIRITUAL PRACTICES: TRUTH-TELLING AND CONFESSION/SELF-EXAMINATION

Confession is perhaps one of the most misunderstood spiritual practices. We instinctively know that it's good for the soul, but we are often afraid to do it. Perhaps it is because we believe that confession entails putting ourselves before God to get a good beating. Without the righteousness of Jesus, we would get more than that. But because of Jesus, we can come before the throne of God with all our mess. Confession is an honest conversation with the Lord, the One who already knows what we have done and still loves us. It is an opportunity to give God the bad that is in us so he can fill us with the good that is in him. Confession is about receiving God's mercy and walking in the forgiveness already secured for us by Jesus.

When we confess to God, we acknowledge our very real need for his grace and refocus our hearts on his will. For a Christian, a person who has been redeemed by the sacrifice of Jesus on the cross, confession can be a space to learn about our temptations, habits, and tendencies. The debt for our sins is already paid for, but our sanctification grows through confession. And if you ever wonder if you have sinned, read the Ten Commandments[21] or the Sermon on the Mount.[22] None of us lives up to the holiness the Lord sets forth in these passages.

Telling the truth helps us remain in the present reality, free of the effect of shame and guilt, which wants us to hide and make up more lies to protect ourselves from the consequences of our sin. Truth-telling helps us live out God's goodness and see him at work even when we make mistakes.

The Process

Confession and truth-telling require intentionality. The world and our sinful nature don't encourage us to engage in these important spiritual practices. For this reason, we must set aside time for confession and create intentional space to open our deepest self to God. This may mean scheduling a meeting with a pastor, a trusted friend, or your spouse and asking them to listen and pray with you. You can also invite them to help you identify some habits or blind spots that you might be missing. It is a vulnerable and courageous act, but it is beautiful and fruitful if done with the right person. A confession is an act of worship, for doing so acknowledges, as David did in Psalm 51, that all our wrongdoing is ultimately against God, the one who is holy and sovereign. So we can confess in self-guided prayer during the worship experience at church or after the service, alone or with individuals we trust.

Truth-telling is not just a one-time action or a rhythm;

it's a lifestyle. It entails avoiding speaking falsehoods and exaggerations, greying the facts, rationalizing, or minimizing the truth for self-gain. We must keep from cheating of any kind, slandering, or gossiping. This can feel overwhelming when you think about it. The more you pay attention to your words, the more you will realize that we all struggle to be truthful. James said that the tongue is "a fire . . . a world of unrighteousness."[23] Yikes! Therefore, truth-telling needs to be practiced often. Apologize when you tell a lie and ask God to help you grow in this area. Be open to the convicting work of the Holy Spirit and choose to tell the truth even when it is hard. Start small and see the freedom it brings.

Prompting Scriptures

He erased the certificate of debt, with its obligations, that was against us and opposed to us, and has taken it away by nailing it to the cross.

—Colossians 2:14

For I am conscious of my rebellion, and my sin is always before me. Against you—you alone—I have sinned and done this evil in your sight. So you are right when you pass sentence; you are blameless when you judge.

—Psalm 51:3–4 (read the entire psalm)

*How joyful is the one whose transgression is forgiven,
whose sin is covered!*

—Psalm 32:1

*Therefore, confess your sins to one another and pray
for one another, so that you may be healed.*

—James 5:16

*But let your "yes" mean "yes," and your "no" mean
"no." Anything more than this is from the evil one.*

—Matthew 5:37

*Whoever speaks the truth declares what is right, but
a false witness speaks deceit.*

—Proverbs 12:17

We are all sinners alike. Only that the sins of the holy are not counted but covered; and the sins of the unholy are not covered but counted.

—MARTIN LUTHER

Only a very noble being can feel shame. The reason is simple: a creature meant to be a little less than God is likely to feel a deep dissatisfaction with herself if she falls a notch below the splendid human being she is meant to be.[1]

—DR. LEWIS B. SMEDES

CHAPTER 7

SHAME WILL ENSLAVE YOU

WALK THE PATH IN FREEDOM

Shame is a human emotion, and there are two types. The first reminds us that we are flawed people, that we are not living up to the persons we know we ought to be. Dr. Lewis Smedes calls this "healthy shame." Other people point out that healthy shame is a response to guilt or regret that focuses on what we *did*, not *who* we are. It signals that there is something we need to work on or pay attention to, something that needs to be made right. It is uncomfortable, but it drives us to seek change so that we may become more of our true selves. When it fits this description, a little bit of "healthy shame" is not so bad—provided it is a source of motivation and not discouragement.

However, there is a type of unhealthy shame that makes false claims about our identity. In the words of Dr. Brené Brown, it is the shame that says, "You are bad."[2] It is rooted in contempt because it makes us feel unlovable. At its worst, unhealthy shame, even if self-imposed, forces us into hiding. And it keeps us there with a steady diet of lies and accusations. It exaggerates our faults to the point that we cannot make a distinction between minor misdemeanors or major felonies.[3]

Unhealthy shame has no basis in reality. It "saps our creative powers and kills our joy."[4] Research shows that chronic shame is "highly correlated with addiction, depression, violence, aggression, bullying, suicide, and eating disorders."[5] Unhealthy shame has the power to enslave us in a cage of unreasonable expectations, deep insecurity, hypocrisy, or performance anxiety. It is a shame that can make us sick. It may come from all types of sources, even religion, but it is a godless shame.

Godless Shame Attacks *Who* You Are

I was in seventh grade when our teacher asked us to write a paper about an unusual relationship. She encouraged us to use our imagination to stretch the boundaries of connection. I wrote about a beautiful friendship between a giraffe and a red ant. They overcame fear, ridicule, and the practical challenges of their size and communication differences. My teacher loved the story and rewarded me by marking my paper with a big red A+ on the front page. A few days later, I happened to be volunteering in her classroom doing general cleanup after school. The task at hand that day was to wipe clean the huge chalkboards that covered the front classroom wall.

Unhealthy shame has the power to enslave us in a cage of unreasonable expectations, deep insecurity, hypocrisy, or performance anxiety. It is a shame that can make us sick. It may come from all types of sources, even religion, but it is a godless shame.

My teacher was sitting at a student table speaking with another seventh-grade teacher about the curriculum and their students. I had my back toward them but could hear their lively conversation. My attention increased when I heard my teacher share about a student's excellent response to one of the lessons. They were talking about my paper! I must have been doing some sort of joy dance or stood up straighter as I cleaned. Something in me changed from the inside out and they noticed. The celebration music in my head stopped abruptly when I heard my teacher call out my name with a hint of contempt. As soon as I turned to look at her, all I caught was the one word she used to describe me, "Egoísta!" (egoist). It was not just the word, but also the way she said it and how she looked at me that communicated her disapproval.

My face turned bright red, and I immediately left the classroom in tears, half the board still uncleaned. Her words cut deep into my heart. I went from joyful to utterly shamed. I was damaged, a bragger. The teacher had declared it. After that incident, I struggled with celebrating my successes without the fear of coming across as a show-off. I still fight the tendency to be hypercritical toward myself. I tend to find fault with everything I do, and fear that what I create is never good enough. With every one of my wrongdoings, the accuser who accuses us "before our God day and night"[6] added weight to my shame's holding power. That is what unhealthy shame does. It declares us broken beyond repair. Shame enslaved me for many years before I learned the way out.

What about you? Can you remember a time when shame stole your joy and forced you—literally or figuratively—to run away and hide? Think of the earliest memory of shame you have, and then think of the most recent. Shame is an experience that has colored our lives from the beginning, isn't it?

But it wasn't always so.

You Were Made in God's Image and His Likeness

The first time the Bible mentions shame, it is to declare there is none. In the Bible, the most common Hebrew word for shame is *bôš* (pronounced *bosh*). It means to be "ashamed, insulted, dishonored, disgraced or humiliated."[7] It first appears in Genesis 2:25: "Both the man and his wife were naked, yet felt **no shame**" (emphasis added).

In the creation narrative, we are given a picture of humanity free from the painful effects of shaming. Human identity was established and firmly secured by the Creator: "Let us make man in our image, according to our likeness."[8] God spoke his creation into being, including the dignity of every human.

The human feeling of shame comes after "the fall"—after Adam and Eve disobey God's command and go into hiding: "Then the eyes of both of them were opened, and they knew they were **naked**"[9] (emphasis added). This was more than embarrassment about their bodies; their nakedness extended to the soul.

They become aware of their "absolute nakedness," physical and spiritual, having been discovered for their wrongdoing and for accepting the serpent's false definition of their identity. The serpent set out to attack God's creation, threatening humanity's freedom and its ability to flourish. He provoked doubt in the woman and tempted her to be "more." He claimed that once they ate from the tree, their "eyes [would] be opened and [they would] be like God, knowing good and evil."[10]

Their eyes were indeed opened, but they did not like what they saw. They followed the trail to shame and were consumed by the drive to hide it, sewing "fig leaves together"[11] as a covering, and hiding "from the Lord God among the trees of the garden."[12] Thereafter, the Bible is full of stories of people who sin and experience shame. People like you and me.

God created men and women to be spiritual and moral beings. Unlike the rest of creation, humans are created to be in a unique relationship with God and, therefore, also have a unique capacity to rebel against their Creator.[13] All of us have rebelled. No human is righteous, not even one. All have sinned.[14] Sin severs our relationship with God and introduces us to shame, but our image-bearing status remains unchanged. Sin does not take away our God-given value. God never abandoned his people, nor his plans to restore humanity to himself.

Costly Grace

In the ancient world of the biblical narrative, "healthy" shame served an important social function. It was connected to one's public reputation, and the fear of dishonor was an effective motivator to prevent certain behaviors. Also in the Bible, we read stories of undeserved shame. The poor, the widows, and the sick were treated as though they were cursed by God. But the ultimate expression of "unhealthy shame" in the Bible was the one projected at Jesus. Although shame was used in an attempt to discredit Jesus's identity, Jesus used it to pour out God's grace.

The religious leaders and others carried out destructive shame techniques to denounce Jesus because he was "making himself equal to God."[15] Jesus did things only the Almighty could do, such as healing the blind, bringing people back from the dead, and forgiving sins.[16] He spoke of himself as the only way to salvation from sin.[17] He made himself equal to the great I AM, explaining that he himself existed before Abraham,[18] and he spoke of the Creator as his Father.[19] His opponents spit on him, struck him in the face and head, stripped him of his clothes, ridiculed him, insulted him, and then crucified him.[20] Jesus endured the worst of shame to provide life and freedom to those who believe in him. "For the joy that lay before him, he endured the cross, despising the shame, and sat down at the right hand of the throne of God."[21]

Although shame was used in an attempt to discredit Jesus's identity, Jesus used it to pour out God's grace.

True freedom and healing from shame come by the gift of God's costly grace, which Jesus secured through his suffering. Jesus came to restore "shalom" (peace, wholeness) to humanity, removing the ultimate source of shame, and "covering" sin so people can freely live as new creations.[22]

The effect of "costly grace" is beautifully described by the German Lutheran pastor, theologian, and martyr, Dietrich Bonhoeffer:

> *Costly grace is the gospel which must be sought again and again and again, the gift which must be asked for, the door at which a man must knock. Such grace is costly because it calls us to follow, and it is grace because it calls us to follow Jesus Christ. It is costly because it costs a man his life, and it is grace because it gives a man the only true life. It is costly because it condemns sin, and grace because it justifies the sinner. Above all, it is costly because it cost God the life of his Son: "Ye were bought at a price," and what has cost God much cannot be cheap for us. Above all, it is grace because God did not reckon his Son too dear a price to pay for our life, but delivered him up for us. Costly grace is the Incarnation of God.[23]*

When we accept the gift of "costly grace," unhealthy shame has no right to live in our hearts, unless we invite it. Just as Israel needed to leave their slavery to Egypt behind and follow God to the promised land, we must leave our shame behind and follow Jesus in freedom. If we're not clear about our new identity, unhealthy shame will weaken our ability to surrender our all to God, and we will willingly carry unnecessary and obstructive baggage and limit our ability to glorify God.

When we accept the gift of "costly grace," unhealthy shame has no right to live in our hearts, unless we invite it.

Our freedom comes when we walk in *active surrender.* An active way of surrendering is more than stopping a particular behavior; it is stepping forward into a new behavior. It is more than raising the white flag and saying, "God, I am at the end of my rope. I give up. You take it from here. I'm just gonna watch." That's surrender—and surrender is good, but it is *not* all that God desires for us. *Active* surrender is picking up God's plan and desires. It is leaning into what God is calling you to be and do in the present. It is letting go, day by day, of your expectations of what the future will hold *and* grabbing hold of the promises God makes and fulfills in his timing and his way.

We've talked about active trust or active surrender a few times now. How are you beginning to see what active surrender might look like in your life? Where are places you might have practiced it in the past? Where are places you think God might be calling you to practice it going forward?

> *To actively surrender, you must drop "unhealthy shame" at the foot of the cross and pick up "costly grace."*

Unhealthy shame and active surrender are at odds with each other. They cannot coexist. You can surrender due to shame. But to actively surrender, you must drop "unhealthy shame" at the foot of the cross *and* pick up "costly grace."

Unshackling Shame

When we see a Christian walking in active surrender, we tend to describe it as courage. It takes strength and courage to let go and let God, no matter the circumstances we face. It takes active surrender to admit our weaknesses, flaws, failures, and our utter dependence on God. Perhaps that is why Moses encouraged the Israelites as they were about to enter the Promised Land with a command to battle for it: "Be strong and courageous; don't be terrified or afraid of them. For the Lord your God is the one who will go with you; he will not leave you or abandon you."[24] To unshackle yourself from "unhealthy shame," you must fight against the temptation to go back into slavery by admitting that you are vulnerable and prone to foolishness. You must take a good look at your "ugly self" and offer it to Jesus. His hands are wide open.

As I write this chapter, my social media feed is flooded with posts about the recent ruling by the Supreme Court of the United States (SCOTUS). On June 24, 2022, SCOTUS overturned the 1973 landmark legal decision which held a woman's right to an abortion as a federal right protected by the Fourteenth Amendment to the Constitution and thus was a legally protected procedure across the United States. As of the time of this writing, abortion is no longer a federal constitutional right. Each state now has the responsibility to decide whether abortions are allowed within its borders and under what conditions. Emotions run high over this ruling and subject. News outlets and social interactions are peppered with arguments from both sides. Images and words take our breath away as people express their raw emotions and passionate perspectives.

In the meantime, in the silence of my writing room, I am thinking of my two babies, Micah and Angel.

I named them at an abortion recovery class. The pastor in charge of this beautiful program was unable to attend the last session of the class, and he asked me to fill in for him. He had heard my story and thought I would be an especially empathetic pastor to the participants who were about to do the most difficult part of the course. The goal of the last class is to help the parent(s) release their unborn, aborted children to the Lord, and to rest in God's grace, mercy, and love through Jesus.

At first, I complained to the recovery pastor, reminding him that I had never been through a recovery class of this type. I had not yet myself processed the two abortions I underwent as a young adult. And although I did not share this with him, I lived with deep, unhealthy shame as well as sadness about my actions. However, he insisted I could pastor these people on this important day. Fueled by his encouragement, I went.

My role was to tell my story, name my children, and join others as we released a single balloon with a name tag for each child. Each class participant had family members with them for this important day. In small groups, they spread out around the church chapel and found a place to cry, embrace, and release their babies. I was alone and lost my pastoral composure as my two white balloons ascended into the sky and disappeared behind clouds. A woman saw me sobbing and came to my rescue, helping me find my composure to finish the session in prayer.

Micah (or Michaela) was conceived when I was eighteen years old, the first time I had sex with my boyfriend. Deep shame. I could not tell my mother, and I certainly was not about to tell my siblings. My boyfriend told me an abortion was the only option and that we were too young to be parents. My mother was oblivious to my plan when I asked her for the one hundred and fifty dollars I needed for the procedure.

Angel (or Angela) was conceived when I was twenty-three years old, less than a year after my first divorce, when I was still dating my soon-to-be second husband. He was out of town when I found out, and I knew he would not be happy, so I took care of it before he found out. He was so sad when I told him. Deeper shame. It saddens me that both children were conceived with men I later married. My son and my daughters have siblings they never met. My older sister cried when she found out. Through a well of tears, she told me that she would have gladly raised my children. Other than her son, she was unable to get pregnant again, and her heart ached for more children. Abortion was not my only option.

Shame compounds. Sadness is still in my heart. It is impossible to talk about this and not feel my heart break into a million little pieces yet again. So what did I do? What do I do? All that awful, humiliating shame that says, "You are bad," I give it to Jesus. By his *costly grace*, I am no longer condemned.[25]

Were it not for Jesus, I would never tell you this story. My preference is to hide and cover up my pain. I did that for years. But I didn't just surrender my babies to Jesus, I actively surrendered my life. The Lord prompted me to share my story publicly many years ago. But first, I spent a lot of time in prayer, sought wise counsel, journaled, and talked to my family and friends. Not every person needs to tell the details of their story as I have here. But I pray that by my sharing

By his costly grace, I am no longer condemned.

how I reflected in my ugliest, you will be encouraged to surrender unhealthy shame and walk the faith journey in freedom. Jesus wants this freedom for you. But even if you struggle to do so today, know that he is pursuing you daily. Jesus is like the man in his parable who leaves the ninety-nine sheep in search of his one lost sheep, and he keeps looking until he finds it and brings it back on his shoulders, rejoicing.[26]

> *So now, little children, remain in him so that when he appears we may have confidence and not be ashamed before him at his coming.*
>
> —1 John 2:28

Shame Doesn't Have the Last Word

Peter's story demonstrates how shame can take us off course and enslave us for a while. However, it never has the power to remove us from the faith journey because Jesus will not allow it. Simon Peter was a disciple of Jesus, but he was more than that. He was in the small inner circle of Jesus's ministry. Peter, John, and James were hand-selected by Jesus to experience his life's highest high (the transfiguration), and lowest low (the Garden of Gethsemane). Peter was a trusted friend Jesus prayed for and depended upon. Peter left everything to follow Jesus. He was once a fisherman, but he left his nets and boat behind to learn from Jesus, to be and do as Jesus was and did.

After three years of following Jesus, witnessing his miracles, and experiencing his teaching and love, Peter was an insider, a man of faith in Jesus. Peter was always the one to ask the first question or blurt out the answer before anyone else. Peter was so committed that when he heard Jesus talk about his upcoming death, Peter vowed to protect Jesus and never abandon him. He was willing to die! Jesus knew that though Peter had good intentions, when the time came, he would be unable to follow through. To Peter's shock, Jesus predicted that Peter would deny him three times.[27]

When Jesus was arrested, Peter was the first to act, but Jesus commanded him to stop:

> Then Simon Peter, who had a sword, drew it, struck the high priest's servant, and cut off his right ear. (The servant's name was Malchus.) At that, Jesus said to Peter, "Put your sword away! Am I not to drink the cup the Father has given me?"
>
> —John 18:10–11

This must have been a huge blow to Peter, because the next thing that happens in John's gospel, after Jesus is arrested, is that Peter denies Jesus three times,[28] just as Jesus predicted.

Shame.

Peter stayed outside by the door while Jesus was being questioned. A servant girl spotted him and said, "You aren't one of this man's disciples too, are you?"[29]

Peter responded, "I'm not." Sometime later, Peter is "standing and warming himself," while Jesus is being slapped and bound, when a few come to Peter and challenge him, "You aren't one of his disciples too, are you?" [30] "No!" The third time, "a relative of the man whose ear Peter had cut off said, 'Didn't I see you with him in the garden?'"[31] and again Peter denied Jesus.

Deep shame.

After the death, burial, and resurrection of Jesus, Peter was with the Lord again. Jesus revealed himself to the disciples several times, and on the third appearance, he addresses Peter's shame. Peter and a few disciples are together when Peter decides to go fishing. The other disciples join him, and they all spend the night trying to catch fish. I can imagine Peter sitting on the boat thinking about denying Jesus after seeing Jesus's resurrection, after seeing that Jesus is who he said he is, after seeing that Jesus is calling him to go out and do these wonderful things in his name.

Compounding shame.

If I were Peter, I would be thinking, "I don't have what it takes. Clearly, I failed when I was most needed." Peter's shame leads him to isolate and separate. He goes fishing. He returns to his prior work, but this time he is unable to succeed at it. There are no "fish" in the sea of shame.

The beautiful thing we see in Peter's story is that Jesus comes to him, to seek him. Peter was sought by a loving God who did not want him to live in shame. This reminds me of Genesis 3 when Adam and Eve failed and went into hiding. God pursued them. He called them out of hiding, "Where are you?"[32] They did not search for God. Peter did not search for Jesus. God came close. Jesus came close. He came to rescue us from our shame and lead us on the path of freedom.

God came close. Jesus came close. He came to rescue us from our shame and lead us on the path of freedom.

Jesus appears to the disciples in a friendly way, calling them "friends," and invites them again to trust him by doing a miracle before their eyes. They catch 153 fish instantly. Peter, upon realizing it is Jesus, jumps in the water and joins Jesus on the shore for breakfast. After enjoying the meal, Jesus confronts Peter with an invitation to actively surrender his life once again. Three times Peter denied Jesus. This is the third time Jesus has appeared to the disciples. And three times Jesus asks Peter to declare his love:

> [Jesus] asked him the third time, "Simon, son of John, do you love me?" Peter was grieved that he asked him the third time, "Do you love me?" He said, "Lord, you know everything; you know that I love you." "Feed my sheep," Jesus said.
>
> —John 21:17

"Feed my lambs." "Shepherd my sheep." "Feed my sheep."
Do not be enslaved by your failures.
Don't be enslaved by shame.
Be whom Jesus calls you to be.
Jesus will search for you and go with you.

Jesus does not want us to compare ourselves to anyone else; rather, he wants us to live out our unique faith journey. Our faith journey is between us and God. Our experience of shame is no deterrent to the Creator who made us in his image and sent his Son to rescue us from our sins. No matter how loud the enemy's accusations get in our minds, we can admit to God what we have done, seek his forgiveness, and he will set us free from unhealthy shame. To stay committed on our journey of faith, we must keep shame nailed on the cross of Jesus and choose to walk in freedom.

Walking in Freedom

After my second divorce, I decided not to remarry again. It became clear that I, as the common denominator of the two marriages, was the problem. When I decided to accept Jim's offer to return to work as a marketing director at his company now that I was a single mom, my girlfriend warned me not to go back. I had quit my job at Jim's company after working seven years as the business manager. My marriage to my second husband was in crisis, and I wanted to remove the stress that my working twelve-hour days was bringing to our household. But, after three years of trying and some counseling, we divorced for other reasons.

My girlfriend watched me navigate all of this and was convinced my relationship with Jim could turn into something more. At first, I was offended, but then I wanted to prove her wrong, and prove to myself that I would never do that. But my character was indeed weak, my challenges were overwhelming, and within a year, our relationship changed just as she had predicted. Jim and I tried to fight our emotions, to break off our non-work-related meetings. We failed and a whole lot of people got hurt.

Shame has the power to reshape the way we live and prevent us from enjoying the fullness of life Jesus came to give us.

My coworkers were convinced we had been carrying on an affair for years. They were wrong, but I now understood the basis for their assumption. They probably saw what my friend could see: We got along very well from the moment we met, and we were two very broken people. Jim's relationship with his partner in business was forever altered. Jim's daughters and his wife of twenty-four years were crushed.

Overwhelming shame.

Shame has the power to reshape the way we live and prevent us from enjoying the fullness of life Jesus came to give us. It is a powerful force intended to break the proud heart, but it can enslave the humble heart if we don't let Jesus help us. Jesus intends for our lives to be fruitful, meaning they will be a witness to others about his love and goodness. There is too much at stake for us to live enslaved by shame.

Jim and I started our relationship on the foundation of an affair, and consequently, we dealt with deep shame for many years. Even after committing our lives to following Jesus, we allowed shame to affect our ability to walk in the freedom God had already secured for us.

Six years after we committed our lives to Jesus, we traveled with our church on a trip to Israel. We each brought with us a heavy bag of unhealthy shame. It turns out that we had been carrying the bags for a long time, to the point that our pastor, Kenton Beshore, could notice. When we visited the Sea of Galilee and heard our pastor teach the story of Peter, we were moved to tears.

Pastor Kenton pointed to us and asked if we loved Jesus enough to leave our shame behind that day. He challenged us to accept the invitations we had rejected to serve the Lord in capacities we did not feel fit to serve in. I was invited to teach the Bible. Jim was invited to join the elder board. We were both actively resisting saying yes because we were locked up in unhealthy shame. Pastor Kenton told all of us to pick up a rock from the shore, imagine our shame on the rock and then throw it in the Sea.

There is too much at stake for us to live enslaved by shame.

Soaked in tears, Jim and I went looking for a very large rock. The little pebbles along the shore were too small to carry our U-Haul load of shame. But after a while, we gave up the search. We gave up the prison. We gave up the unhealthy shame and threw two little rocks as far as we could. I watched mine bounce across the surface of the water: like my shame, it resisted the order to disappear. And just like Peter, we turned around and decided to follow Jesus from that point forward, shame-free.

Jim and I have learned that there is a big difference between being enslaved by shame and the appropriate act of carrying sadness and corrective guilt for the painful consequences of our wrongdo-ing. Shame often seeks to enslave me again. When it does, I remind myself of the costly grace that set me free on Calvary and pursued me at the Sea of Galilee.

What unhealthy shame is enslaving you? What ugly part of you are you unwilling to unpack and cover with grace? What stories do you need to revisit, at least in your mind or with a trusted confidant, so you can pray them into the nail-wounded hands of Jesus? Grat-itude for costly grace is the key to freedom from shame. The more you understand his grace, the more you can dispel the lies of shame. Gratitude leads to worship, and worship leads to gratitude.

Anytime you feel burdened by shame, I pray you will remem-ber Peter, confess your brokenness to God, turn once again toward gratitude in following him, and actively surrender to whatever he invites you to do.

I pray Jesus will help you remember who you are in Christ. You can read Ephesians 1 and take in Paul's affirmation of your new iden-tity, especially in those moments when you feel attacked by someone else, by your own words, or by the accusations of the enemy and the spiritual world, as Paul says in Ephesians 6. Remember the words of Jesus: "A thief comes only to steal and kill and destroy. I have come so that they may have life and have it in abundance."[33] When any-thing or anyone tries to discourage you, remember that because you have put your faith in Jesus, you are blessed, called, set aside, adopted, redeemed, given wisdom, and so much more.

In the next chapter, we'll take a look at how comparison and expectations can also trap us. But for now, remember that it is God's heartfelt desire for you to experience joy ("rejoice"), connection ("pray"), and gratitude ("give thanks"), as Paul wrote in 1 Thessa-lonians 5:16–18. Out of God's kind heart, out of his loving posture toward you, he invites you to rejoice, pray, and give thanks all the time for his gift of "costly grace." He's not hovering over you waiting for you to fail at this. But he is looking over you in anticipation of every moment you will do it, because he knows it is good for you—really good for you—to combat the chains of shame. Let me put it this way: Each time you delight in your Creator, experience a single moment of connection with him, or feel grateful for anything he has done for you, you are walking in freedom. For freedom you have been saved.

SPIRITUAL PRACTICE: GRATITUDE

Thankfulness is our faith in action. It is an act of worship when we acknowledge the generosity of God in our lives. It is a loving response to his unfailing love. Gratitude is one of my favorite practices because it has the power to change our entire well-being. Gratitude affects our sense of optimism, connection to others, and self-esteem, enhancing our physical energy and health. The effects of gratitude are not only good for us, but they can be long-lasting and contagious to others around us as well.

Conversely, a lack of gratitude darkens our hearts. Without gratitude, our hearts get filled with envy and selfish ambition. Left to our own devices, we want everything, including what others have. We seek power, possession, and even people as things. All of this brings disorder to our lives. Shame can enslave us to ingratitude because it cheapens the price Jesus already paid for our sins. The key out of the shame shackles is expressing our gratitude for God's amazing grace at every opportunity, reflecting on the events at Calvary, and remembering what he did for us. Gratitude brings healing to the mind and heart, which is why Paul calls us to "give thanks in all circumstances." It is good for us. It is right.

The Process
There are many fun and engaging ways to practice gratitude.

My favorite is keeping a gratitude jar handy next to paper and a pen. Throughout the year, Jim and I put every thank-you card we receive from others into that jar, as well our own notes about the things we are grateful for. We read the cards and notes around the first day of the following year and rejoice at all that God has done in our lives. You can also write your gratitude items in a journal or in the margins of your Bible. Start the day by reflecting on the abundance in your life. Count your blessings—literally. Say thank you at every opportunity to people and to God.

Prompting Scriptures

For you were called to be free, brothers and sisters; only don't use this freedom as an opportunity for the flesh, but serve one another through love.

—Galatians 5:13

Rejoice always, pray constantly, give thanks in everything; for this is God's will for you in Christ Jesus.

—1 Thessalonians 5:16–18

Enter his gates with thanksgiving and his courts with praise. Give thanks to him and bless his name.

—Psalm 100:4

Give thanks to the Lord, for he is good. His faithful love endures forever.

—Psalm 136:1

Let the word of Christ dwell richly among you, in all wisdom teaching and admonishing one another through psalms, hymns, and spiritual songs, singing to God with gratitude in your hearts. And whatever you do, in word or in deed, do everything in the name of the Lord Jesus, giving thanks to God the Father through him.

—Colossians 3:16–17

III.
BLESSING
THROUGH
OBEDIENCE

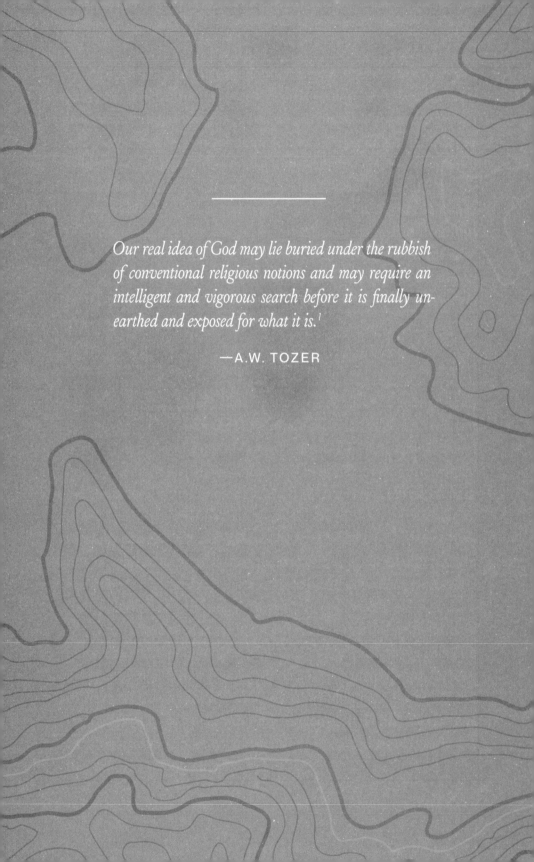

Our real idea of God may lie buried under the rubbish of conventional religious notions and may require an intelligent and vigorous search before it is finally unearthed and exposed for what it is.[1]

—A.W. TOZER

CHAPTER 8

WHAT NOT TO PACK

COMPARISONS AND EXPECTATIONS

I love mazes—the act of finding a route through a puzzle from start to finish. Years ago, I went to a harvest carnival and entered their corn maze, which was constructed of very tall corn stalks—taller than me. Once I walked in, it was impossible to see the people walking ahead of me in the maze or through the dense stalks of corn. The only way out was forward, hopefully in the right direction, or backward the way I came. In the beginning, I was confident that I could figure it out. But somewhere along the journey, I got lost and stopped at a turn that seemed likely to take me back to the beginning.

My pride didn't want me to go back to the beginning. But there were only two choices: take the turn that *looked* like it was going to maybe take me back to the entrance, or turn around and follow the path that would definitely lead me to the entrance. There was nowhere else to go. I decided to take the turn, and sure enough, I ended up back at the beginning, which I did not like. I considered quitting altogether.

After pouting for a few minutes, one of my friends popped out from where I had just exited. We looked at each other, had a good laugh, and decided to go back into the maze together. This time, we entered the maze with more information and in good company. We were doing it together, sharing about our prior experiences, and enjoying the adventure. We made it to the exit after lots of twists and a few wrong turns, but all the wiser.

The Trap in the Maze

In a way, the Christian journey of faith resembles walking through a maze with the Designer. But it is different in that, while every person is walking toward the same end goal with Jesus (eternal life in him), we are not all traveling the exact same "maze" design. Each of us has our own custom route, patterns, and branches that lead to the finish line. Every one of us walks a unique and complex faith journey.

Our relationship with God is personal and cannot look like anyone else's or follow an exact, pre-set pattern. We have a lot in common with others, including key defining moments and spiritual stages, but each of us walks our own independent labyrinth with our Creator. Sadly, we spend too much time comparing ourselves and our faith to others or obsessing about how our journey should go. These bad habits result in limiting not only the peace and joy of our unique walk with God but also the effectiveness of our witness to our broken world.

Every one of us walks a unique and complex faith journey.

Comparison Can Lead to a Dead End

Comparison in itself is not wrong. It is part of how we measure the things of this world, including ourselves, and determine their greater or lesser value. Even John the Baptist compared himself to Jesus when he said one was coming "who is . . . more powerful than I."[2] That's just stating the facts. But when done with improper intentions or wrongful objectives (i.e., to evaluate your dignity or worth), comparison leads to bitter discontent. Most of the time we are drawing conclusions with inaccurate or incomplete information. Using others as a benchmark for your own worth or the effectiveness of your faith journey will damage your sense of self. These are things only God can accurately measure.

When we study the stories of people in the Bible, many of whom God called, walked with, and used for his purposes, we don't see two that look alike. Wonderful people, broken people, and imperfect people like you and me are used by God for his purposes. Each person brings a God-given will and personality to their journey. Each life is made up of countless different pieces: people, places, events, experiences, and circumstances.

We have a lot in common with others, including key defining moments and spiritual stages, but each of us walks our own independent labyrinth with our Creator.

Our journey is further nuanced by our personal connections that contribute to our individuality. In his expositions of Ecclesiastes, author David Gibson observes that "most of the seasons of our lives are taken up with navigating the different stages of our relationships and the effects they have on us."[3] Also, because we all operate within the constraints and mysteries of time, our journey encompasses so many different seasons. The preacher in Ecclesiastes summarized life well: "There is an occasion for everything, and a time for every activity under heaven."[4] While our journeys will include the twenty-eight items listed in Ecclesiastes 3:2–8 (i.e., birth, death, planting, uprooting, weeping, healing, loving, etc.), none of us will experience them in the same order, intensity, or length of time. No two people are the same. No two faith journeys are the same.

Do you compare your faith journey to that of others? You're not alone. We all tend to do this. Here is the hard truth: Part of the reason we compare ourselves to others is that we seek to gain control over events, people, and our future. We would love to experience the fantastical exploits and mountain-top experiences of faith that people like Moses, Deborah, and Paul lived—minus the suffering, of course. We want to have a fruitful faith journey like the apostle John, Billy Graham, Mother Teresa, or our favorite Christian superstar leader.

We struggle to learn to live in our own journey, all the way, for as much as possible in the little stuff, the single breaths, the present moment. So, we make decisions on our faith journey, often checking them against the decisions of others, hoping we can accomplish for ourselves a larger-than-life faith with the least amount of effort. But here is the thing: If we're getting there by comparing ourselves to others, in the end, even if we reach our grand achievement, we will find ourselves disappointed and confused. It happened to the great prophet Elijah at Mount Carmel[5] after his expression of great faith in Yahweh, the one true God.

In the presence of 450 prophets of Baal (the supreme of pagan gods), God demonstrated his almighty power by consuming the water-soaked sacrifice Elijah offered with fire. Baal and his prophets were completely defeated. Then Elijah prayed for the drought to end, and a downpour occurred. Everyone recognized Yahweh's might and Elijah as his prophet. It was Elijah's larger-than-life faith moment. However, to our surprise, Elijah went into a depression immediately afterward.

His life was threatened by the Phoenician princess Jezebel, who was very angry about her prophets being slaughtered. She vowed to end Elijah's life. Elijah successfully confronted and defied 450 pagan prophets, but one woman sent him running and made him give up on life. I don't know what made Elijah think there'd be no more suffering to endure after his God-sized mountain-top experience, but his behavior proves my point. Mountain-top experiences or larger-than-life faith moments are not the priority of our faith journey. A growing relationship with God is.

After his mountain-top experience, Elijah feared for his life and desired to stop being a prophet. He quit and ran away. Have you ever quit on God? Have you ever tried to hide from him? I did on the day I heard his voice in my childhood. Ironically, like Elijah, I quit right after the moment I now recognize as my mountain-top experience, hearing God's voice audibly. Like Elijah, I decided to hide because I was disappointed with how things turned out. I was upset that I could not go to heaven on my terms and timing, and that I had to endure this life for some God-ordained purpose. But I quickly learned that God pursues us whenever and wherever we run.

> *Mountain-top experiences or larger-than-life faith moments are not the priority of our faith journey. A growing relationship with God is.*

As you may recall, I grew up in a very small home. Eight of us lived crammed in a two-bedroom, 600-square-foot house. My three sisters and I slept in one room, our three brothers slept in the other room, and my mother used a pullout couch to sleep in the living room. The arrangement was hard on her, so she eventually saved enough money to build a 200-square-foot lean-to addition. Her funds were barely enough to pour the concrete foundation, set a concrete block wall around the perimeter, and construct wood walls to create a bedroom, walk-in closet, and utility room. The ceiling of that entire section was made of corrugated aluminum panels nailed to the wooden frame. My mom's closet was my hiding place. I would often run into the dark, small room, curl up behind the door and look up to the ceiling for the eyes of God.

The carpenter my mom hired, probably one of my uncles, made a few mistakes when nailing the aluminum sheets—you could tell because there were several tiny holes where there should have been none. Both light and rain would pour into my mom's closet through the pinholes. Two of those holes were just above the back of her wooden closet door. That's where I would often hide when I got upset, smelling the musty odor of dust and mold, and looking up at the thin beams of sun or moonlight that shined through. There I sensed the "eyes of God" looking down at me.

No creature is hidden from him, but all things are naked and exposed to the eyes of him to whom we must give an account.

—Hebrews 4:13

If I say, "Surely the darkness will hide me, and the light around me will be night"—even the darkness is not dark to you. The night shines like the day; darkness and light are alike to you.

—Psalm 139:11–12

The eyes of God are always upon you. The writer of Hebrews and the psalmist declare it. There is no place you can go where he does not pursue you—no place too high and no place too low. God pursued and met Elijah at that low moment, providing him protection, provision, and encouragement. God followed him to another mountain, Mount Horeb, and to a cave there. Yahweh asked the depressed prophet, "What are you doing here, Elijah?"[6] Twice Elijah responded with a list of complaints and a declaration that he was the only prophet left. He seemed to think all his furious zeal and devoted efforts for Yahweh were in vain.

We will contribute to the content of our story, but we are not the main author. God is.

He was wrong. Elijah had an incomplete set of facts and had

disconnected himself from the source of his real strength: Yahweh. Nevertheless, God miraculously met with Elijah where he was and gave him instructions on what to do next. God commanded Elijah to reverse his retreat and continue his prophetic calling. He still had things to do.

God has things for us to do. Like Elijah, we must learn to live our own faith journey, depending on God every

God has things for us to do.

day in the high moments, low moments, and everything in between. When we learn to embrace our own journey moment by moment, we will find ourselves staring at the faith journey that has been staring back at us all along—the beautiful, unique faith journey God is building himself.

> *The truth of it is, we breathe in a world of mystery: No two sunsets have ever painted the sky the same. And of all the snowflakes that have ever fallen to the earth since the beginning of time, 10 followed by 34 zeros, no two have ever even once been identical. And every one of our stories are infinitely unique, and singular miracles that bear a glory all of their own.[7]*
>
> —Ann Voskamp

Only God has the perfect vision of our faith journey because he's above it all and outside of time. He understands how every little piece of our journey will work together in the future. We may have an idea of how we want our journey to go, and how we hope our life will turn out, but there is much we cannot control. We will contribute to the content of our story, but we are not the main author. God is. He works through our entire journey in every circumstance to transform us into the likeness of Jesus so that we may be one with him.[8]

The blessing you have been promised still lies ahead. In the meantime, you learn and practice trusting God with the details of your unique faith journey. Remember, when God called you to follow him, he did not invite you to manipulate the outcome or control the future by pointing to another person and assuming they are better or worse than you. So, if you're like me, you need the motivation to let go of comparison again and again. That motivation comes when we deal with another bad habit: expecting our faith journey to work out in a preset pattern.

Letting Go of Our Expectations

When we build an expectation that our faith journey will work out predictably, we will inevitably be disappointed. There are certain aspects we can anticipate but much that we cannot know until it happens, or until we have some hindsight. It is good to have an expectation for the future that God has promised his people, which includes "plans for your well-being, not for disaster, to give you a future and a hope."[9] He has promised to guide us when we're confused,[10] to help us when we're tempted,[11] to strengthen us and protect us from the evil one,[12] to help us in times of trouble,[13] to reward us for our service and generosity,[14] and to secure our eternal destiny[15] ... just to name a few of his promises!

But chances are, your faith journey does not look exactly the way you expected. Perhaps you are surprised at how God has changed you over time. Maybe you are dumbfounded at the incredible experiences you are having that you never saw coming. You are serving people you would not have associated with in the past—and loving it. You are vulnerable with your whole life to a small group of people whom you did not choose and who were previously strangers. You are generous when in the past you would have held back in fear. You are walking in places you would never have dreamed about entering before. You might be thinking, "How did I get *here*?"

Conversely, you might not be as advanced in your biblical knowledge, as good at loving people, or as mature in your faith as you had hoped to be by now. This is the universal condition for all of us believers. We are all a "work in progress," echoing the words of Paul when he said, "Not that I have already reached the goal or am already perfect."[16] This struggle may have you feeling stuck and unsure if you are going in the right direction. You might be frustrated by the sense that often you seem to be traveling backward, in zigzags, or circles, making little forward progress. You might be thinking, "How can I get *there*?"

> *When God says, "I will never leave you or abandon you," he means it.*

Stop for a moment and reflect on your own journey. What has turned out the way you expected? What hasn't? Are you happy with where you are, or are there aspects of your faith journey that are currently leaving you unsatisfied?

Either way, God is at work in your journey. Faithfulness is an immutable attribute of God, and he cannot act inconsistently with any aspect of his perfect character. Unlike people, God is not fraught with fear, weakness, loss of interest, or frustration. When God says, "I will never leave you or abandon you," he means it.[17] You may need to look back, perhaps as far as the beginning, to reassess where you came from, what's embedded, and how your journey has been formed thus far.

A Unique Journey of Faith

The satire of the prophet Jonah reminds us that there is no place we have been where God has not been at work in our faith journey. Jonah's story is told in four easy-to-read chapters that teach us a lot about God, about us, and about God's commitment to walking with us on our faith journey. It's not like the other books of the prophets, as it is not so much about the message God wants to be delivered (only one sentence), as it is about the man God sent to deliver it. I don't recommend we live as Jonah, for he seemed a very unhappy man. But even through him, we have a beautiful display and example of how God works in and through our unique journeys.

Jonah was not a good prophet. He challenged God's kindness toward the evil people of Nineveh and refused to participate in giving them an opportunity to repent. God commanded Jonah to deliver a warning message to the people of Nineveh. But the moment Jonah received the "word of the Lord," Jonah "got up to flee to Tarshish," which was far away, in the opposite direction of where God told Jonah to go.[18] Jonah believed he could run away from the Lord's presence. He boarded a ship full of pagan sailors, hid inside of it, and fell asleep. But God sent a massive storm that was so terrifying that the experienced sailors concluded it was delivered by a divine force acting against a person onboard.

After throwing dice to make out the culprit's identity, Jonah was singled out. They confronted the prophet, and Jonah admitted his connection to the God who created the seas and controls the storms. Jonah then confessed, "I worship the Lord."[19] The men were terrified! As the storm continued to get worse, Jonah advised the men that they should throw him overboard. Jonah was so intent on running away from God that he sought death as a solution. Jonah refused to repent, but the pagans prayed to the Lord for their lives and offered him sacrifices in commitment to him.

Then God did the unimaginable: He saved Jonah's life by sending a huge fish to swallow him. From the belly of the fish, the darkest place, the most desperate place, Jonah called out to God, and God heard his voice. Out of deep gratitude for God not abandoning him, Jonah promised to be faithful to God's command. Once again, God commissioned him,[20] and Jonah delivered the message, "In forty days Nineveh will be demolished!"[21]

He didn't even give them the complete message or tell them who was sending it. But upon hearing the truncated message, the king of Nineveh, all the people in the city, and even the animals repented! God did not destroy Nineveh, and once again, Jonah became upset ("displeased" and "furious"[22]) and complained about God's compassionate heart. Ironically, Jonah's name, *Yārad*, means "dove," which is a symbol of peace. The story ends with Jonah once again wanting to die and God protecting him, reminding him and us just how much God loves every human created in his image.[23]

In Jonah's story, we see the interplay between our will, our agency to make decisions, and God's sovereign faithfulness and love. God has a plan and a desire to accomplish it. What is remarkable is that he chooses to work with people who don't always want to do what he invites them to do. Yet, God walks with us, he tries to guide us and correct us so that, in the end, we reach the destination, the accomplishment, with him. Jonah had to go backward to go forward. He had to see the past pattern of God's unrelenting faithfulness to grow in gratitude and move forward.

Let us not run from God. Let us run to God. Let us run with God.

Even when Jonah rebelled, ran away, got in trouble, and was seriously stuck, God traveled with him. And God wasted nothing! Along Jonah's unique journey, God saved the pagan sailors, the king, and the people (and even the animals!) of Nineveh.

When you and I look back to our past, to our experiences, joys, hurts, and struggles, we can see God's hand upon us even then. Let us not run from God. Let us run to God. Let us run with God. Let us run where he calls us to run. If he's tapping you on your shoulder, let him take you where he wants to take you.

A year after I gave my life to Jesus, I sensed God calling me to teach and write about him, but I rejected the idea. I thought I was the last person God would use in his kingdom for anything other than mopping floors. I didn't think God would waste the intense house-keeping training my Mami put me through. Then God surprised me. Through a para-church organization, I had an opportunity to go on some mission trips to Peru. On my first trip, the pastor hosting us asked me to lead a prayer and translate the conversations between our American team and the Spanish-speaking Peruvians.

I was extremely hesitant to comply. It wasn't just that I felt inad-equate to pray, but I also did not want to speak Spanish. When I moved to California at the age of sixteen, I stopped speaking Spanish, hoping to eliminate my thick accent and avoid being discriminated against. That fear was grounded in multiple painful experiences. But the pastor insisted that I step in because he had an important meet-ing to attend.

This is one of many examples in my life where I had to step back and remember who I am and who God is. I had given up speaking Spanish because I felt like it was harming me. People were treating me as less-than because I was a Spanish-speaking person. But God took me back there and invited me to let him use it for his purposes. I was deeply blessed once I started translating and praying. God took me back to my past in order to bless my future. I have since preached in Spanish several times. Only God!

Here is another story. My friend Tanya shared with me that there was a season when she was feeling disconnected from God—and she was also feeling very guilty about it. Like Jonah, she knew where God wanted her to go: He was calling her to a more intimate rela-tionship with him. But she didn't know how to get there. She told me, "I have a Bible sitting here, and I think God is upset with me." She was stuck comparing her faith journey to that of others and felt that God was disappointed with her progress. Even as she knew God was calling her, she was afraid she was losing her connection to him.

One day she went for a walk on the beach, and God met her

there intimately in a beautiful moment. She experienced God's love, his perfect love. She shared with me that it was the closest she had felt to God in a long time. God reminded her that he walked with her everywhere and all the time. He showed her that the Bible was his gift to help her know him, rely on his promises, and understand her true identity. She was shown that her relationship with God was always there, no matter where she went. He wasn't just present on Sunday when she went to church. It did not matter where she went; her journey with God was beautiful because God was in it.

Tanya had to leave behind her fears of being rejected by God and embrace the truth that his perfect love was for her. Her journey, unlike Jonah's, was one she *wanted* to take. But the unexpected part was that she needed to receive God's own help to have the faith to stay the course on her own faith journey. Jonah ran away; Tanya was frozen in fear. Both reactions were ones that required God's help to correct. Now when Tanya reads the Bible, she says she does it with joy and not out of guilt.

What's your situation? Where have you run from God? In what way is he calling you to turn back to him? What is God calling you to walk back and re-examine? What is he wanting you to leave behind? What is God asking you to pick back up as you join him in his work? Remember that he gives us the power to choose, but still, he is there, always with us, guiding us again and again toward his perfect plan. Our journey is a beautiful mystery between our own will and God's sovereign will, his power, his ruling, and his ability to do the things that we can't do.

Comparing our own faith journey to that of others will lead us to expect—and even demand!—things of God that may not be his will for us. But rest assured that he *does* have a plan for you, and that he will be faithful to walk beside you every step of the way. You may need to turn back (if you've run away), or just start walking again (if you're frozen in place), or pick up again something you've put down (if God calls you to reactivate old gifts for his purposes).

Once again, trusting God is *active* surrender. We must constantly shift from control to commitment, and his faithfulness will help us let go of unfruitful comparisons and expectations. His sovereignty is at work saving others while, at the same time, he is saving us.

In the next chapter, we'll look a little bit deeper at how to let go of the things that we hold on to so tightly, so that we can have open hands to receive the new good things that God wants to give us. But for now, remember that the past is the past, and you cannot change it. But you *can* re-examine it to see the hand of God and his faithfulness along the way.

He does not waste anything!

SPIRITUAL PRACTICES: EXAMEN AND JOURNALING

God is at work in our lives every moment, every day, for eternity. Often, we are unaware of what he is doing for us, around us, and through us. The practice of examen (also known as "examination of conscience") has been around for centuries. Saint Ignatius of Loyola (AD 1491–1556) included this practice in his *Spiritual Exercises.* The purpose of this practice is to pay attention to how God is moving. It opens the mind to review the day through the lens of God's activity. We reflect on the beautiful and painful parts of the day through a set of questions we ask ourselves. I have connected this practice to the spiritual exercise of journaling because both invite us to write things that are often kept in our minds and hearts, perhaps even outside of our awareness until we think of them.

The examen practice does not require journaling, but I believe it has more fruit when we keep track of the daily movement of the Spirit in our lives. We can look back when we journal either through the guided questions of examen or our own journaling structure and see how God has grown us and remained faithful in our lives.

The Process
A spiritual journal can be many things to you, but when it

comes to faith, at its core, it's a place to explore your deepest thoughts and feelings about your relationship with God. It is a place to keep a written record of how God has been at work in your life and how your relationship has developed. Like any other relationship, it can be very close at times and feel distant at others. God never leaves us, but maybe we don't notice him. Also, we are all prone to wander.

Journaling can give your mind clarity and focus, your heart calm and peace, and allow your intuition to have a voice. Choose a journal that is right for you and that brings you joy when you pick it up. There is no right or wrong way to do this. Choose a quiet place and spend a few minutes in prayer or worship before you start to center your thoughts on Jesus. Start writing, and write as long or often as you wish. Decide where you will store the journal, and make sure to put it in a secure place if you do not wish others to read it. Review what you have written in the past regularly.

You can alternate between free-form journaling or writing through the examen questions. Below are the questions[24] offered by Calhoun in her *Spiritual Disciplines* book:

- For what moment today am I most grateful? For what moment today am I least grateful?
- When did I give and receive the most love today? When did I give and receive the least love today?

- What was the most life-giving part of my day? What was the most life-thwarting part of my day?
- When today did I have the deepest sense of connection with God, others, and myself? When today did I have the least sense of connection?
- Where was I aware of living out the fruit of the Spirit? Where was there an absence of the fruit of the Spirit?
- Where did I experience "desolation"? Where did I find "consolation"?

Prompting Scriptures

Remember what happened long ago, for I am God, and there is no other; I am God, and no one is like me.

—Isaiah 46:9

I lift my eyes to you, the one enthroned in heaven. Like a servant's eyes on his master's hand, like a servant girl's eyes on her mistress's hand, so our eyes are on the Lord our God until he shows us favor.

—Psalm 123:1–2

Search me, God, and know my heart; test me and know my concerns. See if there is any offensive way in me; lead me in the everlasting way.

—Psalm 139:23–24

Finally brothers and sisters, whatever is true, whatever is honorable, whatever is just, whatever is pure, whatever is lovely, whatever is commendable—if there is any moral excellence and if there is anything praiseworthy—dwell on these things.

—Philippians 4:8

Make your ways known to me, Lord; teach me your paths.

—Psalm 25:4

"Do you have eyes and not see; do you have ears and not hear? And do you not remember? When I broke the five loaves for the five thousand, how many baskets full of leftovers did you collect?" "Twelve," they told him.

—Mark 8:18–19

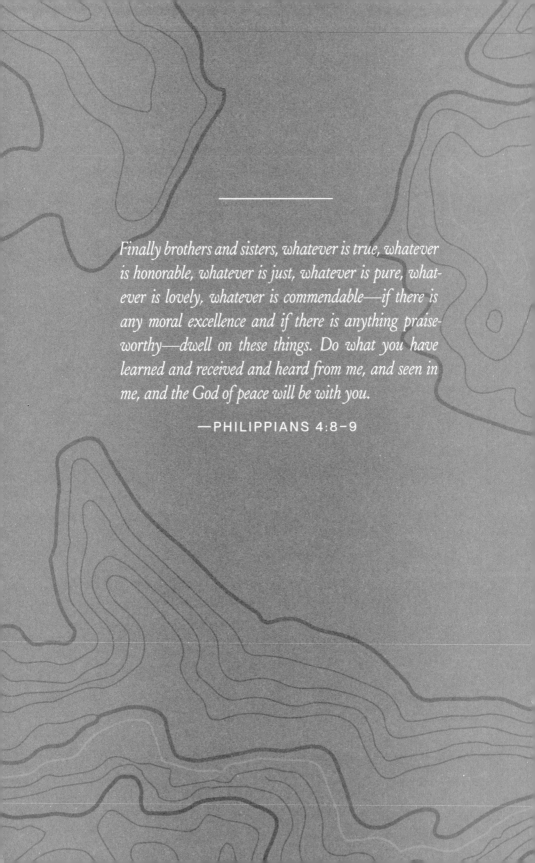

Finally brothers and sisters, whatever is true, whatever is honorable, whatever is just, whatever is pure, whatever is lovely, whatever is commendable—if there is any moral excellence and if there is anything praiseworthy—dwell on these things. Do what you have learned and received and heard from me, and seen in me, and the God of peace will be with you.

—PHILIPPIANS 4:8–9

CHAPTER 9

A HEAVENLY MINDSET

LEAVING EVEN THE GOOD FOR THE BETTER

I wonder if you've seen the illustration that is often shared via social media of Jesus holding a big stuffed brown bear behind his back with his left hand, while extending his right hand to a little girl.[1] She is shyly looking down at a little stuffed brown bear in her hands, unwilling to let it go. The caption reads, "Trust me, I have something better for you."

This can be misunderstood as a promise of prosperity if we offer Jesus what is "in our hands," but I read it as a good reminder that Jesus does indeed have something better to offer us than a life that is self-serving. Because we are created in the image of God, we are designed to love people. We are most ourselves when we, in love, give generously of ourselves for the benefit of others. But are we willing to follow God even when he asks us to do difficult things?

Following those we trust and admire is a core human survival strategy now made public by the power of social media. Our motivations to follow fall into two categories: rational and irrational. Our rational motivations make logical sense: we follow people because we hope to gain good things by doing so—and we're afraid that if we don't, we'll miss out on what following them can give us.

Our irrational motivations are often hidden from us. We subconsciously project emotions onto our relationships with leaders, feeling more attached to them and involved with them than we really are. Sigmund Freud, the founder of psychoanalysis, called this unconscious projection "transference."[2]

Either way, rational or irrational, our motivations for following are primarily self-serving.

It is by grace that Jesus calls us to walk with him, and without his grace and truth we would be unable to stick with it. Following Jesus is a costly journey, a sacrificial one, and the opposite of self-serving.

Following Jesus is a costly journey, a sacrificial one, and the opposite of self-serving.

It only appears straightforward and obvious. Nothing obscure, technical, or complicated about following a good teacher and servant leader who is faithful, sinless, and ever-present, right? Both our rational and irrational motivations are good with that. Yet, the Son of God calls us to do as he did: sacrifice self for the good of others. And he commands our total surrender, complete submission, and unwavering commitment.

He does not settle for being second place in our lives; rather, he expects us to be willing to give up anything and everything, including our family bonds, careers, wealth, and even our lives. Jesus said, "If anyone wants to follow after me, let him deny himself, take up his cross daily, and follow me. For whoever wants to save his life will lose it, but whoever loses his life because of me will save it."[3] Jesus does not call lukewarm disciples. He gave it all for us and expects us to give ourselves fully to him. In the words of Dietrich Bonhoeffer, "When Christ calls a man, He bids him come and die."[4] His divine call is for all Christians to leave their nets and follow;[5] committed, all in, repentant, with a "fearful spirit and a broken heart,"[6] desiring to please him above all else.

But we cannot do this when our own hearts are half-in, half-out. Such hesitation reveals our self-willed life and our preference for choosing our own path. To the extent we maintain any control over our own lives, we are not following Jesus faithfully and are likely deceiving ourselves and others. Following Jesus calls us to shed our obsession with self-preservation and be willing to leave behind all manner of things, at times good things.

Holding Even the Good Gifts with Open Hands

Years ago, I resigned from a beautiful role of pastoring a growing and thriving congregation to write this book. After seven years serving at the Mariners Church chapel, teaching sermons nearly every Sunday, God called me out of that assignment. The clarity for this change of direction started with my word for the year. Do you choose a word for the year? It has been my practice since I became a believer to prayerfully choose a word and a passage each year as anchors for my prayer time. I recommend it, as it has enriched my prayer time and connection with the Lord.

> *Following Jesus calls us to shed our obsession with self-preservation and be willing to leave behind all manner of things, at times good things.*

Just having one word has helped me ask better questions of the Lord, practice surrender, and enhance my study of the Scriptures. So far, I have prayed through nineteen words.[7] For 2019, my word was *listen*, inspired by Proverbs 4:20–21, which says, "My son, pay attention to my words; *listen closely* to my sayings. Don't lose sight of them; keep them within your heart" (emphasis added). I was so excited about this word and committed to saying less during my prayer time and listening more.

Less than two weeks into my practice of primarily silent prayer, the Spirit put these words in my mind (I say the Spirit because there is no way I would have chosen them): "It is time." Impulsively, I asked out loud, "Time for what?" The only inkling was that it referred to something I needed to surrender. I wondered what it was about but said nothing to God or to others. Over the next three months, through three unconnected individuals, in the most random of ways, it became clear to me what I needed to let go of. The third person, a dear friend now living in another state, used the exact same words: "It is time." This happened during a conversation after I had just taught a sermon on living in step with the Holy Spirit.

In my sermon I talked about all four stages of the butterfly life cycle in detail: egg, larva, pupa, and adult. Each stage has a different goal, and the last one is when the caterpillar has finished forming inside the pupa and the butterfly emerges from the chrysalis. As soon as the butterfly has come out, it will pump blood into its wings and set out to fly and reproduce. In my sermon on Romans 8, I opened my arms wide as I imitated a butterfly flying to encourage us to "fly" with the Holy Spirit wherever he wishes to take us, knowing he will make us fruitful.

My friend shared with me what the Holy Spirit had put in her heart: that my assignment at the chapel was complete, and it was time to "fly"; that is, to devote my time to taking care of my family and finally writing my first book. As I felt the Spirit's powerful prompting within me, my reaction was to burst out in a flood of tears. I then shared all of it with my husband, my sweet partner with whom I test anything I suspect is coming from the Lord.

After prayer, he agreed also that it was time. I cried again but proceeded with the process of communicating to my supervisors, the volunteer leaders, and eventually the congregation that the Lord was leading me in a different direction. Some people got it. Others were disappointed, sad, and confused. But they all trusted me and wished me well as they transitioned to the next pastor. Since then, in my new role as a teaching pastor, I still get to teach God's Word at

Mariners and other locations. I have remained in contact with many of my congregants, even officiating weddings and memorials. But it was essential to go from teaching almost every weekend (forty times a year) to a more manageable pace, considering what came next.

In the Bible, we see people leave things behind to make room for what God has for them in the future. Abram and Sarai, in their senior years and childless, left the safety of their land and relatives to travel to another land, where God promised they would become a great nation, blessed to be a blessing.[8] Ruth, a young and beautiful Moabite widow, made great sacrifices to follow her mother-in-law back to Israel. She left her country and people behind. She chose to make Naomi her family, and Naomi's God her God.[9] The disciples left their sources of income, their livelihoods, and provision to follow Jesus.[10] He became their source of provision.

All of these stories point to Jesus, "who, existing in the form of God, did not consider equality with God as something to be exploited. Instead he emptied himself by assuming the form of a servant, taking on the likeness of humanity. And when he had come as a man, he humbled himself by becoming obedient to the point of death—even to death on a cross."[11] He gave it all and reminded his followers that "a servant is not greater than his master."[12] These stories encourage us to operate out of an abundant and dependent heart, being stewards instead of owners of all that we possess. From the abundance of his forever presence, we can hold loosely everything, even some of those good things God gives us.

From the abundance of his forever presence, we can hold loosely everything, even some of those good things God gives us.

Even if all is going well on our journey of faith, that doesn't mean we won't have to leave some things behind. God often calls us to say "yes" to some difficult things and "no" to some good things. Knowing and discerning how to do this is challenging, especially when we fear missing out or being sidelined. When we strive and measure our fruitfulness only by comparison to others, we increase our fear, losing opportunities. All of this can lead us to hold on to good things and not experience the greater gifts God wants to give us and do through us, the gift of his presence and the joy of his promises. Additionally, the journey of faith includes spiritual warfare, bullets on the front line of life, injuries on the battlefields as we endure potholes and roadblocks. We need to discern if it is God or the enemy[13] who is vying for our obedience.

A lot was happening for our family that year I left the chapel, both good and bad. Our youngest daughter, Melissa, was married to a wonderful young man, Kasra, and my husband celebrated his sixtieth birthday with a huge party. He's the extrovert between us. Two of our granddaughters were born that year, making us the happiest grandparents to nine grandchildren. But also, two of our children's marriages were in crisis. Sadly, I also had some relationship issues to resolve with a few family members.

And most challenging was that my mother entered the late stages of Alzheimer's disease. I have no good words to say about this horrible way to die slowly. As much as my mom was struggling at the beginning of the year, it only got worse month by month. It was a long goodbye. My Mami went to be with the Lord on February 7, 2021, surrounded by her children, her "pollitos" (chicks) as she used to call us. I am extremely grateful for the incredibly painful and overwhelming season of helping her die with dignity and providing her with the best care I could. I am joyful I could focus on celebrating the various milestones of our family without distraction: weddings, births, and death. I am humbled that God helped me let go of something good, my pastoral role at church, for something he knew I needed to pay attention to, to be available for. It was the "better" for me in this season to be undistracted, even by the good gift of my previous work. Only he knew.

Then there was the call to start writing books, this one being my first. I was not sure I could even write that many words. There was no way for me to know if my writing would produce fruit, or if anyone would buy and be nourished by it. Aside from my family and friends who would get it as a gift, I wondered if anyone would want to read it. Who am I to write? What do I have to say? Why should anyone listen to me or spend precious time reading my words? These were the doubts that plagued my mind. I was concerned that leaving something so good and fruitful would be the wrong choice. But as I look back, I see that choosing a surrendered posture toward even the good things God had put before me was best. In an act of obedience, I took a deeper dive into the sea of faith, knowing the better way may not be for my benefit, but for others.

Again, the better that God gives us may not be *for* us.

Typical of God's ways, we will experience a blessing as well, but it is not predictable what the blessing will be like. We may give of our finances and receive a heart of contentment. We may sacrifice our time for others and receive the blessing of peace. We may give up the thing we count on for our security and experience joy. Jim's mom modeled for us a life of sacrifice. She was doing well in her interior decorating business when family members who lived in Virginia called for help. After much discussion and prayer, Carol decided to leave her home and business in California to move in with her family. For over ten years she gave of herself. She would say that those years were challenging but also a huge blessing in the realm of relationships.

When It Comes to Jesus, *Loving* Means *Obeying*

On our journey of faith, our commitment to Jesus should correlate with our willingness to walk in obedience to him. In other words, if we do not obey Jesus, it reveals that we are not committed to *him.* The more we obey, the stronger our commitment. The stronger our commitment, the more we obey. Jesus said, "Why do you call me

If we do not obey Jesus, it reveals that we are not committed to him.

'Lord, Lord,' and don't do the things I say?"[14] He is not our Lord if we do not obey him. Sometimes people ask me, "How have you built such a strong rela-

tionship with God?" My answer is simple but hard to live out, and I mean that for myself as well: "Obedience." When I have managed to obey Jesus, even if imperfectly and especially when there is nothing in it for me, I have grown in my faith. Our willingness to obey is directly related to our faith in God's promises. Do we believe that God is faithful, that he keeps his promises? In a way, we all struggle with promises because life has pounded on us enough times to make us skeptical.

When I was little girl, all my friends at school used to get a few cents a day as an allowance. That was a lot of money for a kid. My, how things have changed! This is going to give you a hint of my age and where I grew up. In Puerto Rico during the late sixties, with one penny you could buy a little square of Bazooka gum. It was the hardest gum to chew, more like sweet plastic, but it came with a comic strip in full color. With one cent, you could buy a Tootsie Roll lollipop or a Red Vine.

My mom promised us that she would give us an allowance someday, just like the other kids at school. I wanted an allowance so bad, but we didn't have any extra money. We were extremely poor. But she would promise us all the same, saying, "I'm going to get to the point where I can give you five cents a week." We would beg her, "Mom, when are you going to make that promise true? We want our allowance." But it never happened.

Today, I give my mom an enormous amount of grace for having such tight finances back then. A five-cent candy allowance probably wouldn't have been the best use of her resources. Other broken promises in my life have been less easy to accept. Like when my father stopped visiting me when I was nine years old. He promised to visit us, but he did not follow through. That really hurt!

How about you? Has someone ever made you a promise and failed to deliver on it? Even a small promise unfulfilled can leave a scar on our hearts and condition us to withhold our trust. How have your past experiences in life had an impact on your ability to trust?

When those closest to us betray our trust, the disappointment and disillusionment we feel can spill over into all our relationships, including our relationship with God. This is especially true when God calls us to do things that are hard for us while we are waiting on him to fulfill his promises in our lives. So if you struggle, listen: You're not alone. I pray you would be encouraged to see how God responds even to your struggle to obey. He is "slow to anger but great in power" and "abounding in faithful love and truth."[15] That is because he desires for us to become who he created us to be.

Keep in mind also that when we obey, there is no guarantee that the next event or season of our lives will be smooth and easy. In fact, things could get harder for us. Oh, this is hard to write, but it's true. Looking back to Abram and Sarai's story starting in Genesis 12, we're reminded that they trusted and obeyed God, but things got immediately challenging.

There was a "severe" famine in the land, so Abram and Sarai had to go to Egypt to survive. Remember, Abram was given a promise by God that he would be blessed, that his name would be made great, that he would have land, and that he would be a great nation. God couldn't do those things if Abram were dead, but Abram was fearful for his life nonetheless.

When they arrived in Egypt, Abram came up with a plan to lie about Sarai's status as his wife, telling the Egyptians that she was his sister. Sarai was taken to Pharaoh's household and Abram was treated well because of her. But then Pharaoh's household was hit with severe plagues because of Sarai. They were kicked out of Egypt, but at least with some provisions. God rescued Abram and Sarai and put them back on track. But this scenario happened again—and again. Yet even still, God came through for them.

Maybe you've said yes to God, but you've found yourself off track. Maybe you were walking in obedience for a while and then turned away. Perhaps you think it is now too late. You fear that the promise is now behind you or that God is tired of working with you because you're just impossible. Is that you? I hope you are encouraged by the story of Abram and Sarai, because God kept rescuing them from

God pursues us and continues to work in our lives so that his promises are fulfilled.

problems of their own making and putting them back on track toward the promise that he'd made them. I am so grateful that God pursues us and continues to work in our lives so that his promises are fulfilled.

Do we make it harder for him? Do we make it harder for ourselves? Most likely, yes. But do you know what's awesome? Even in those bumps along the journey, God is teaching us along the way. He uses everything to prepare us for the fulfillment of the promise.

Years went by, and even though Abram and Sarai became wealthy, they were unable to conceive a child. How was Abram supposed to start a nation without the ability to bear children? God repeated his promises to Abram, this time giving him a beautiful picture to remember it by: "'Look at the sky and count the stars, if you are able to count them.' Then he said to him, 'Your offspring will be that numerous.'"[16] Abram believed again, but the journey was far from over.

It would take twenty-five years before Abram (now renamed Abraham) and Sarai (now renamed Sarah) had their son Isaac. And again, things got difficult, for God tested Abraham by asking him to sacrifice Isaac. Abraham's willingness to obey such a huge ask was the result of years of practicing obedience along the way. The angel of the Lord stopped Abraham from harming his son and provided a substitute for the sacrifice. Abraham was commended for his faith and for not withholding his son from God.[17] Abraham and Sarah's story is a beautiful picture of obedience even in the face of constant struggle and imperfection. They didn't always do it well, but their "long obedience in the same direction"[18] birthed a nation blessed to be a blessing.

Christ, Who Is Our Life

The first time I sensed the calling to become a writer and teacher was in March 2005. It was such a strange thought to me, for I had yet to read the Bible in its entirety. (I had skipped some of the minor prophets.) That year, the church was doing an annual read that included a psalm and a section of Proverbs every day. We were encouraged to write a prayer each day based on what we read. One day in March, I wrote a prayer that has become my reminder of God's promise that I would eventually teach his word and write books. It has been sixteen years since that call. Jim and I were enjoying a fruitful season of ministry, travelling around the world delivering wheelchairs through the Free Wheelchair Mission,[19] but God had other plans.

The journey took me to seminary in my mid-forties. I remember sitting at a bench one day, memorizing Hebrew words and thinking that I had lost my mind. I told my friends that God called me to write a book, and for years I had nothing to show for it. It felt like I was believing and telling a lie for a long time. I left many good and bad things behind along this journey. I have not always been

III. Blessing through Obedience

obedient, but I see how God has been working in me and blessing others along the way. Our obedience to God, our willingness to let go of even the good gifts he gives us, first does a work in our hearts and then it blesses others.

This prayer remains my prayer, for the Lord is not yet done with me. I offer it to you. May it help you surrender a little more today.

> *Lead me, Lord, to a blameless life. Nurture me to a loving relationship so that I may do what is right by loving others and telling your truth. May the light of your glory shine through your work on me.*

God has a part for you and me in his grand story, even if our journey does not look like anyone else's. At times, we will leave the good we can create to join the better he is unfolding. It may not be for us, and it could be worse before it gets better. But in the long run, it is the best because it is from the Lord and for the Lord. This requires a shift from earthly thinking to a heavenly mindset, as Paul writes: "Set your minds on things above, not on earthly things. For you died, and your life is hidden with Christ in God. When Christ, who is your life, appears, then you also will appear with him in glory."[20]

God has a part for you and me in his grand story, even if our journey does not look like anyone else's.

And we don't run our race alone: We are part of a community that is on this faith journey together. We'll talk more about what it means to journey in community in the next chapter. Because if there is one thing Jesus calls all of us to leave behind, it's the idea that we can be self-sufficient on the faith journey.

Meanwhile, we must remember that all of what we have is ultimately his. This mindset shift will encourage us for the rest of our lives to remain committed and content in seasons of plenty or wanting. Practicing stewardship and pursuing generosity are ways to remind our souls that we have more than enough—and yet, God wants to give us more. He is the one we must follow—he is the only influencer that matters. And even though following Jesus means sacrifice, because we must walk the way he walked, our measure of grace can increase. Our measure of faith can increase. Our measure of faithfulness can increase. Take inventory of what you are clutching onto so tightly. Take heed that you hear from God above the noise of this scarcity-minded world. Then, let go to receive what you will share with others.

SPIRITUAL PRACTICES: STEWARDSHIP AND GENEROSITY

Once again, I have coupled two spiritual practices here. They are often combined into one practice, as Calhoun does, but I think they are two different but correlated actions. Stewardship is the responsible management of our resources. Generosity is the releasing of resources. As you can see, they are not the same. You can give generously without managing your resources well. And you can manage your resources well but give nothing. God has entrusted us with the role of stewarding the resources of this earth, as well as those of our own household. Resources include more than just money. Other examples include our relationships, personal possessions, opportunities, connections, freedoms, and our time and talents. Trusting in God to guide us, we can use these resources to benefit others in many ways. Good stewardship creates fertile ground for generosity.

Sometimes God prompts us to give more than we feel comfortable giving. But we must remember that all we have is his to begin with, and he promises to faithfully provide for all of our needs. When we give generously out of any of our resources, we remember that we are dependent upon a good, loving, and powerful God. Our struggle with generosity reveals what is in our hearts that may be grasping for control and certainty within our own power. Generosity has the power to cleanse our hearts from unhealthy attachments. Intentionally sharing our resources liberates us from greed, selfishness, and lack of love toward others. Generosity begets generosity and transforms our hearts to be more like God's. He is generous in every possible way, including giving us eternal life through Jesus Christ.

The Process

Stewardship and generosity are intentional practices. You can review your assets (remember they are more than money) and reflect on how you utilize them. Perhaps you can create a ledger that lists assets you are managing well and those where you have room for improvement. Then, challenge yourself to move items from the "needs improvement" side to the "well done" side. Make it fun and reward yourself in some way for accomplishing each milestone.

Think of ways to invest your resources so they may grow and increase your ability to be generous with them. Look for ways to share what you have with others. Even a smile is an act of generosity. It can change someone's moment or day. Give often and watch as your heart is transformed by the Holy Spirit to ever-increasing joy. Every person can be generous, even those who have few monetary or material resources. Generosity reflects the kindness and goodness of

God. Ask him to suggest ways to be generous and to give you the courage to trust him with everything he has entrusted to you. It is the best way to live!

Prompting Scriptures

I will sing to the Lord because he has treated me generously.

—Psalm 13:6

You may say to yourself, "My power and my own ability have gained this wealth for me," but remember that the Lord your God gives you the power to gain wealth, in order to confirm his covenant he swore to your ancestors, as it is today.

—Deuteronomy 8:17–18

The one who loves silver is never satisfied with silver, and whoever loves wealth is never satisfied with income. This too is futile.

—Ecclesiastes 5:10

A rich person is wise in his own eyes, but a poor one who has discernment sees through him.

—Proverbs 28:11

Instruct them to do what is good, to be rich in good works, to be generous and willing to share, storing up treasure for themselves as a good foundation for the coming age, so that they may take hold of what is truly life.

—1 Timothy 6:18–19

A generous person will be blessed, for he shares his food with the poor.

—Proverbs 22:9

This is my command: Love one another as I have loved you. No one has greater love than this: to lay down his life for his friends.

—JOHN 15:12–13

The physical presence of other Christians is a source of incomparable joy and strength to the believer.[1]

—DIETRICH BONHOEFFER

CHAPTER 10

TRAVELING IN COMMUNITY

IMPERFECT, A PRIVILEGE, NECESSARY

The Hollywood Walk of Fame in Los Angeles showcases 2,725 stars[2] made of terrazzo and brass, installed on both sides of Hollywood Boulevard and Vine Street. Each star is engraved with the name and signature of an entertainment industry celebrity. Walking this long stretch of the city is a highlight for millions worldwide. I was sixteen when I set foot on the star on the corner of Hollywood and Gower that memorialized actor and singer Allan Jones. The eight-block walk on my first day of school was a memorable joy. I was giddy at the freedom of walking down a busy street full of people with the awareness that not even one of them knew my name.

As I walked down Hollywood Boulevard, it was a relief to be independent and unknown, separated from a community of people who monitored my every step. None of those people could now gossip about my homemade clothes or tell my mom the outrageous lie that I was pregnant after they had seen me cross the street holding a boy's hand. Never mind that Edwin was a gentleman who did not want me to get run over by the crazy drivers in our Naranjito neighborhood.

When Mami moved us to California, we all left that little town where every person knew our names, would show up at the house unannounced expecting coffee and bread, and had the scoop on our latest family drama. It was exhilarating to walk down the street with no one watching, but only because I didn't yet realize how much my soul would soon starve for community. It didn't take long for me to miss that small town and the richness of being seen, known, challenged, and accepted as a person who belonged.

All of us know that we need to do life with other people. As the old idiom goes, "Can't live with them, can't live without them."[3] Community is important for flourishing in life, but it is even more so on the faith journey. Oddly, when it comes to faith, we seem to think community is optional. It is not. Yes, a personal relationship with Jesus is essential, as we will stand alone before God when called by him to give an account. Yet even though our faith may be personal and individual, it is never private or meant to be so.

It is essential that we travel in community, not only because it's important but also because it is a privilege and command from God.

Our Western obsession with independence, however, makes it difficult to develop and keep friendships, let alone connect with fellow believers. Our lifestyle, which includes the ability to move from city to city and state to state, stretches our relationships over thousands of miles. This increases the difficulty of maintaining deep intimacy. People come in and out of our lives. But even if they don't, the design of our communities and homes with easy-to-open-and-close garage doors and internal access to the house do not engender casual connection. Developing deep relationships must be planned, initiated, and included on our calendars. Social media gives us a false sense of connection, making it difficult to distinguish between meaningful and surface relationships.

It makes sense to choose wisely whom we invite into our intimate walk with God, but this challenge is not an excuse to isolate ourselves from our brothers and sisters in Christ. The danger of being deceived or hurt by others can lead us to assume that it is safer to walk our faith journey as a solitary traveler. That couldn't be further from the truth. We live in a lonely world, and we need deep community with other Christians now more than ever. It is essential that we travel in community, not only because it's important but also because it is a privilege and command from God.

Obstacles to Community

There are a lot of obstacles to building a deep faith community. The most obvious culprit is the devil. Christians have a real enemy who desires nothing more than to divide God's people from God and each other. The word "devil" comes from the Greek word *diabolos*. It can also be translated as "adversary, backbiting, slanderer and accusing falsely."[4] Clearly, the devil doesn't want people to be in harmony. He loves chaos. He wants to "steal and kill and destroy."[5]

Naturally, division (i.e., encouraging distrust and maybe even hatred against other people) is his number one tactic. Jesus warned us about the devil, saying, "He was a murderer from the beginning and does not stand in the truth, because there is no truth in him. When he tells a lie, he speaks from his own nature, because he is a liar and the father of lies."[6] Paul warned us not to allow anger against others to go unresolved because it gives "the devil an opportunity."[7] The devil loves it when we stay isolated so he can lure us into sin, and "sin demands to have a man by himself. It withdraws us from the community."[8] It's a vicious cycle that leads to disastrous effects.

But even if we manage to get past the obstacle of false independence and our enemy the devil, we then face a bigger one.

People.

When we travel on our spiritual journey, it's important to remember that the people in our lives are one of the greatest treasures we have. After all, they're the ones who will support and encourage us along the way. But at the same time, people can also hurt us, discourage us, and abandon us. The brokenness in the human heart contributes to difficult moments and deep wounds. We, too, are capable of hurting others. All of us have parts of our personality that could be difficult for some others to deal with. And guess what? People with difficult personalities come to church too!

My mother did not take us to church when we were children. She refused to set foot inside the little church in the pueblo of Naranjito. Anytime we questioned why, she would go on a long tirade about the people who sat in the front pews, banging their chests, crying "Mea culpa! Mea culpa! Mea culpa!"[9] and who then started gossiping about others the moment after they shook the priest's hand and before the holy water evaporated from their index fingers. Mami refused to join a Christian community because she felt all Christians were hypocrites, and she didn't want to be around them. She would say, "I don't need them. I have my own relationship with God." This is how my mother lived most of her faith until she was in her mid-seventies.

Years after we moved to California, after all her kids were married and we were on our own, my mother moved back to Puerto Rico to be a caregiver to her parents. After fifteen years of being a full-time sole caregiver, she was burned out and decided to move back to California. I had just recently married Jim, and we invited her to live with us until we could find a permanent place for her. She loved being independent. Jim and I were just starting our journey with Jesus (me for the first time, Jim rededicated his life) and reading the Bible.

We started a small group Bible study in our home, as the pastor of our church made it clear that we must all join a small group. He said that if we wanted to experience the greatest blessing of our faith journey and grow in it, we needed to be in community with others in a small circle. Our group was only a few months old when my mother moved in. At first, she was skeptical and just sat there listening. But then she purchased a new pink-covered Bible at the church store and joined our study every Wednesday with enthusiasm. The following year, Jim was privileged to baptize my mother, and thereafter she started her own Bible study group with the neighbors around her new home. Those women became her companions to the end.

Sometimes it is not the people who are currently in our communities who are our obstacles. For many of us, it is the people who *were* in our communities who are still standing in the way of us forming deep, healthy connections in the church. Our deep relational wounds from that past most certainly affect our ability to connect with others in the present. I struggle to open my life to others because I was deeply hurt from a young age by the one person I thought should never hurt me so.

My father left our home and family when I was less than a year old. The earliest memory I have of him was of a time he came to visit me. I was eight years old. My mother sent a few of us children to stay at our grandparents' house during summer break. I was staying at my father's mother's home when he came to pick me up. I don't remember seeing him before then, and I can't remember why I was the only one he was spending time with.

In truth, I was thrilled to have my father to myself. He took me to San Juan, the capital of Puerto Rico. We rarely visited San Juan because my mom had no car, and it was too expensive and time-consuming to go by bus. After walking around the city, my father took me on a boat ride in the San Juan harbor to enjoy the city lights from the water. Another new experience for me. Unfortunately, that is when I learned that I easily get motion sickness. To this day, I often get carsick, even when I'm driving.

As the boat ride progressed, so did my dizziness and stomach pain.

We drove home in silence, me hoping my stomach and headache would soon calm down. When we arrived at my grandmother's, my father lifted me up on his shoulders and started doing circles in the middle of the street. I held my arms stretched out as if I could fly. It was fun. Until I threw up on myself and all over him. He quickly put me down, mumbled a slew of complaining words, and dropped me off at the door, leaving before my grandmother opened it. There I was, drenched in tears and vomit. That was the first and last time my father and I had time alone. For years my broken relationship with my father made it hard for me to allow others access to my most intimate self.

I know a young lady who grew up in a Christian cult. Her father was spiritually abusive to her, often using Bible verses as tools for manipulation, and the people in their small inward-focused church were no better. She had many painful experiences at the hands of people who professed to follow Jesus. You can imagine how hard it is for her to get vulnerable with other Christians.

Jesus knew that people were going to let him down, yet he walked with others in vulnerability.

Some people struggle to walk into church without getting sick to their stomachs because they cannot deal with people's strange behavior or because they experienced mental, spiritual, or physical abuse or neglect by the clergy.

Without a doubt, if you are in an abusive and dangerous situation, seek help and immediately remove yourself from harmful people. But as soon as possible, it is wise to purposefully look for a safe Christian community to receive the help and support needed for healing. Despite these and many other obstacles, we must all resist the natural urge to withdraw into ourselves. If you have been out of a Christian community for a while, "you may have isolated yourself from the very things God wants to use to help you grow."[10]

Community Is Imperfect

How delightfully good when brothers live together in harmony!

—Psalm 133:1

Even when we are among healthy, holy people, we can find that others put obstacles in our path. The apostle Paul traveled with a team, and sometimes things got messy between them too. Paul and Barnabas, two godly men who loved Jesus and the church, did not always see eye to eye. Acts 15 documents a conflict over bringing John Mark on their second missionary journey. Paul was upset with John Mark for abandoning the team halfway through the first missionary trip, so he did not want to count on him again. The disagreement between Paul and Barnabas was so sharp that they "parted company"[11] and went different ways.

Barnabas took John Mark with him and sailed to Cyprus, and Paul chose Silas and went toward Syria and Cilicia. Eventually, Paul hints that the conflict may have been healed, as he commends John Mark in his second letter to Timothy.[12] Despite the many challenges he faced when working with others, Paul was committed to a band of brothers and sisters. Jesus also relied on his disciples, inviting them to pray with him before he was arrested and crucified. He modeled to us the importance of traveling in community. Jesus knew that people were going to let him down, yet he walked with others in vulnerability.

It is easy to embrace relationships within our Christian community when people are nice and cool to hang around with. I have a dear friend who is very encouraging and always says the nicest things. One time, as we enjoyed lunch together, I paid special attention to the way she used the most encouraging words. I would like to learn to be as kind as she is. I have another friend who has a way of engaging people in conversation. Anytime we're together, I find myself telling her about everything that's going on in my life. She has a way of asking questions without making me feel interrogated. She makes me feel welcomed and safe to share. I want to learn how to ask questions the way she does. Sometimes I find myself doing all the talking. She challenges me to grow more and more like Christ.

It's easy to be generous to grateful people. It's fun to be around joyful people. It is wonderful to be with loving people. It feels safe to be with reliable people. All of this is a privilege indeed!

However, walking the faith journey with others can be enormously difficult because it involves sinful people trying to get along. Like familial brothers and sisters, we are all prone to compete, fight, disagree, and even become rivals. For this reason, we may create tactics that help us avoid community, treating others as problems to be solved or elevating ministry goals over the importance of good fellowship.

But we must hold on to the fact that community is still good, even when it is not perfect. If even Jesus, the perfect Son of God, desired to spend time with his disciples, surely we, imperfect as we are, need the strengthening presence of our brothers and sisters.

Community Is a Privilege

Therefore encourage one another and build each other up as you are already doing.

—1 Thessalonians 5:11

Some of the most impactful books I have read on the importance and meaning of walking the faith journey together as a family of faith were written by Dietrich Bonhoeffer. Living in community was something he thought deeply about. At twenty-one, Bonhoeffer presented his doctoral thesis entitled "The Communion of the Saints." He later published *The Cost of Discipleship*, contending that being a disciple means giving up your life and living for Christ, something he did himself. But my favorite book, *Life Together,* was born from the years he led a fugitive or "illegal" community of twenty-five seminarians to live as a family of faith in Christ.

In the introduction of *Life Together,* we get to know Dietrich Bonhoeffer. He was born into a family of seven children in Germany and raised in Berlin. From a young age, he studied

> *If even Jesus, the perfect Son of God, desired to spend time with his disciples, surely we, imperfect as we are, need the strengthening presence of our brothers and sisters.*

theology. "For him, Christianity would never be merely intellectual theory, doctrine divorced from life, or mystical emotion, but always it must be responsible, obedient action, the discipleship of Christ in every situation of concrete everyday life, personal and public."[13] He was a vicar, a theology professor, and a pastor to students, and later led a congregation during the time of Hitler's regime.

Eventually, the German Gestapo forbade him to write or publish any more works and closed the seminary. Bonhoeffer also found himself at odds with some of his fellow Christian leaders, as he refused to participate in the "German-Christian" compromise. He had an opportunity to leave Germany permanently during an assignment to Union Theological Seminary in New York. Instead, he decided to return and participate in finding a solution to the problem of evil in his country, which included some involvement in a secret plan to overthrow Hitler.

Bonhoeffer "acted in accord with his fundamental view of ethics, that a Christian must accept his responsibility as a citizen of *this* world where God has placed him."[14] Even after he was arrested, he continued to write letters, and due to his good relationships with the guards, his papers, essays, and poems were preserved. On April 19, 1945, Bonhoeffer was executed by the Nazis in Flosenberg.

Bonhoeffer modeled for us what it looks like to be formed into the image of Christ by walking in community with other believers, no matter the cost. He discourages us from believing that the journey can be for us and God alone. He wrote, "You are not alone, even in death, and on the Last Day you will be only one member of the great congregation of Jesus Christ. If you scorn the fellowship of the brethren, you reject the call of Jesus Christ, and thus your solitude can only be hurtful to you."[15] You're never alone when you're in Christ. We may not have much in common with those God puts in our path, but what brings us together is Jesus—what he has done for us, and what he calls us to do with him.

We may not have much in common with those God puts in our path, but what brings us together is Jesus—what he has done for us, and what he calls us to do with him.

The gift of community is experienced in a variety of forms. Joining a small group of believers to do life together, visiting one-on-one, worshiping together during a service, and sending letters of encouragement and support are all ways to connect with other Christ followers, no matter where they live or how far the distance between us. We're connected to brothers and sisters, broken as we are, and God chose to do that because it is through that union, partnership, and community that he makes us like Christ and uses us to bring healing to one another. To me, this is truly remarkable.

I think of my own life and my own deficiencies. How can I be used to help another person grow or heal? I'm a hot mess over here. Then I think about some of you, and I wonder how it will all possibly work out. All kidding aside, it's hard to wrap my mind around the fact that even Jesus was willing to suffer and endure so much at the hands of people.

The other benefit of walking the journey of faith in community is how we can hold each other up. There will be times in your life when you will need your Christian community in a way that you cannot rely on anyone else. When my son, Chad, was going through a difficult season, I was desperate. I tried to help him, but I could not solve his situation. I had to give him to the Lord and rely on the prayers of my Christian brothers and sisters. Our small group prayed for my son every single Wednesday and whenever else I called upon them. I felt like a broken record asking for the same prayer request. They prayed with me Wednesday after Wednesday after Wednesday.

God did a miracle in my son's life and his situation improved. I believe it was an answer to our prayers. But my time with that community and their willingness to hear my request repeated every week surprisingly ministered to my heart and grew my faith. Their constancy pointed me to the faithfulness of God. That's what the Christian community does. It holds us strong when we feel weak.

Community Is a Necessity

We are forbidden to neglect the assembling of ourselves together.[16]

—C. S. Lewis

In Northern California, we have a wonderful national treasure called Muir Woods. This redwood forest is composed of giant and beautiful trees that have survived for hundreds of years. They grow 250 to 300 feet high, and some of them have been there for over 600 years. Walking among the giant trees takes your breath away. These trees have survived many seasons of life, insects, fungi, storms, and fires. How do they survive for so long? They are remarkably resilient.

The redwood tree is resistant to insects, including termites. Secondly, they seldom die from attacks by fungi due to their high percentage of tannin, the chemical responsible for the reddish color of the wood and bark. Fire struggles to kill these trees, as they contain neither pitch nor resin, and their bark grows to at least one or two feet of thickness. But, even if the redwood is killed by a fire, the tree continues to reforest by forming sprouts around the base of the parent tree. So resilient is this tree that after years of attempts to clear one from the land, sprouts continue to grow in its stead.

It is reasonable to assume that for such tall trees to endure so many hardships, their roots must go very deep into the ground. But redwoods do not have deep roots. They survive by interconnecting their shallow roots that go down only about six to ten feet into the soil, extending them out sideways about one hundred feet from the trunk, and fusing them with the roots of neighboring trees. The convoluted network of roots travels for miles, increasing the stability of the entire forest. The trees support one another. Christians do the same. Community is necessary *because it is how God designed us to grow.*

Community is necessary because it is how God designed us to grow.

Without Jesus, we could not have his peace within ourselves to offer to others, let alone get to know one another at the level of intimacy God intends for us. We learn to love each other the way he loved us. His love is active and perfect. As Paul describes it,

> *Love is patient, love is kind. Love does not envy, is not boastful, is not arrogant, is not rude, is not self-seeking, is not irritable, and does not keep a record of wrongs. Love finds no joy in unrighteousness but rejoices in the truth. It bears all things, believes all things, hopes all things, endures all things. Love never ends. But as for prophecies, they will come to an end; as for*

tongues, they will cease; as for knowledge, it will come to an end.

—1 Corinthians 13:4–8

We intentionally work at accepting one another, just as Jesus accepted us, in order to bring praise to God.[17] For, as Bonhoeffer wrote, "even when sin and misunderstanding burden the communal life, is not the sinning brother still a brother, with whom I, too, stand under the Word of Christ?"[18] Human love is about us. Genuine love is about Jesus Christ.

Unlike the "I did it my way" of my early journey, when I used to think I had control over every aspect of it, the lessons I learned and my experiencing God with a group of people led me to a deeper openness to the voices and encouragement of others. Isolation can hurt us. Jim and I have been involved in a life group since we started our faith journey together. Although the individuals and our groups have changed for various reasons, we cannot imagine walking out our faith without carrying each other's burdens.[19] We are regularly "teaching and learning, forgiving and being forgiven, representing Christ" to each other, and interceding for each other's needs.[20]

The idea of remaining faithful to God with a "just me and God" mindset is our invention. It is not God's intention. Many of my past mistakes and shameful actions came about because I was unwilling to let trusted sources in on my faith journey. I have learned to rely on a community of believers to encourage and hold me accountable. We need other Christians to speak words of truth to us, especially when we feel uncertain or discouraged. This is essential for us to walk our journey faithfully. But also, it is a privilege to care about the present and eternal well-being of another believer. We must come to the Christian community with a posture and heart of a servant, ready to offer our lives as a service to others.

As C. S. Lewis so beautifully states it:

The load, or weight, or burden of my neighbour's glory should be laid on my back, a load so heavy that only humility can carry it, and the backs of the proud will be broken. It is a serious thing to live in a society of possible gods and goddesses, to remember that the dullest and most uninteresting person you can talk to may one day be a creature, which, if you saw it now, you would be strongly tempted to worship, or else a horror and a corruption such as you now meet, if at all, only in a nightmare. All day long we are, in some degree, helping each other to one or other of those destinations . . . You have never talked to a mere mortal.[21]

The Christian community is the body of Christ, and God uses that community to form us.[22] We must enter the lives of others and invite them to join ours so we may strengthen one another as "iron sharpens iron."[23] It is the place where we can make true emotional connections with the right people so our relational wounds can heal, and we can replace loneliness with community. Whole books have been written on the process of finding a community of faith to walk with. A very practical method is offered by Jennie Allen in her excellent book, *Find Your People.*[24] Check it out.

The faith journey reaches maturity when we stop trying to protect ourselves from people and instead focus on protecting them, as we compassionately live with and for others. We need people in our lives, and people need us in theirs.

The faith journey reaches maturity when we stop trying to protect ourselves from people and instead focus on protecting them, as we compassionately live with and for others. We need people in our lives, and people need us in theirs. I hope you have captured a vision of the importance of seeking people with whom to walk this amazing faith journey. I wish to encourage you to choose to fight for the depth and longevity of your relationships.

Model vulnerability and transparency as much as possible. Don't expect the group to be your all, and don't dump your life on others. It should be a give-and-take experience, not necessarily at the same time. Give and receive generously. Seek your people in your time of need, giving them a reason and opportunity to care for you. Respect the confidential nature of your conversations and expect the same from others. Serve and play together. Let others hold you accountable and do that for them in kindness and humility. Deal with conflict instead of burying the issue(s) under the rug. And try and try again.

Community is imperfect, but it is good, and it is necessary. And it can be a bulwark when our faith journey gets foggy and our direction becomes unclear—we'll talk more about those times of obscurity and confusion in the next chapter.

Oh, my friend. Don't give up. Walk in community until your last breath. That is when our *unique* journey becomes a blessing outwardly. That is when we may "be mutually encouraged by each other's faith."[25]

SPIRITUAL PRACTICES: HOLY COMMUNION AND PRAYER PARTNERS

Holy communion has been central to the worshiping life of Christians from the beginning of the church. The Christian practice dates back to the last Passover meal Jesus ate before he was arrested, beaten, crucified, buried—and raised to life. Jesus instituted this sacrament for us to remember him and what he did for us. It helps us rejoice in the presence of God in the person of Jesus Christ, and in the redemption he secured through the shame of the cross.

Communion is, by its nature, a sacrament done with others, as Paul makes clear in his letter to the Corinthian church: "Because there is one bread, we who are many are one body, since all of us share the one bread."[26] We gather with other believers for this practice because it also reminds us that together we make up the body of Christ. The gathering does not have to be large. It can be as little as two people, which is why I have coupled it here with the practice of prayer partners. Communion in community and having prayer partners reminds us that the journey of faith is not a solo endeavor.

Prayer partners agree to support each other and pray

together in shared intercession. Such a practice allows us to be witnesses to God's work in each other's lives. Sometimes we need a prayer partner to remind us that we gave that request to the Lord already, and we can walk in freedom. Prayer partners don't mind hearing the same prayer requests again from us; they will pray with us no matter how long it takes for a prayer to be answered. They rejoice with us when things go well and lament with us when they don't. Knowing that others are praying with us and for us helps us gain confidence and peace no matter the circumstances.

The Process

The practice of communion requires some bread and some grape juice (or wine), and a Christian brother or sister or many of them. That is it! Spend some time in prayer, confession, worship, and Scripture reading before taking the elements. Pray that the Lord will remind you of his presence, love, and redemption as you do. Of course, you can practice this at your local church as often as they offer it. We have already covered the practice of prayer in a previous chapter, but here we are to pray with someone in person or via technology.

Prompting Scriptures

> For I received from the Lord what I also passed on to you: On the night when he was betrayed, the Lord Jesus took bread, and when he had given thanks, broke it, and said, "This is my body, which is for you. Do

this in remembrance of me." In the same way also he took the cup, after supper, and said, "This cup is the new covenant in my blood. Do this, as often as you drink it, in remembrance of me." For as often as you eat this bread and drink the cup, you proclaim the Lord's death until he comes.

—1 Corinthians 11:23–26

Every day they devoted themselves to meeting together in the temple, and broke bread from house to house. They ate their food with joyful and sincere hearts, praising God and enjoying the favor of all the people. Every day the Lord added to their number those who were being saved.

—Acts 2:46–47

Now I appeal to you, brothers and sisters, through our Lord Jesus Christ and through the love of the Spirit, to strive together with me in prayers to God on my behalf.

—Romans 15:30

We always thank God for all of you, making mention of you constantly in our prayers.

—1 Thessalonians 1:2

Therefore, confess your sins to one another and pray for one another, so that you may be healed. The prayer of a righteous person is very powerful in its effect.

—James 5:16

Pray constantly.

—1 Thessalonians 5:17

So we fasted and pleaded with our God about this, and he was receptive to our prayer.

—Ezra 8:23

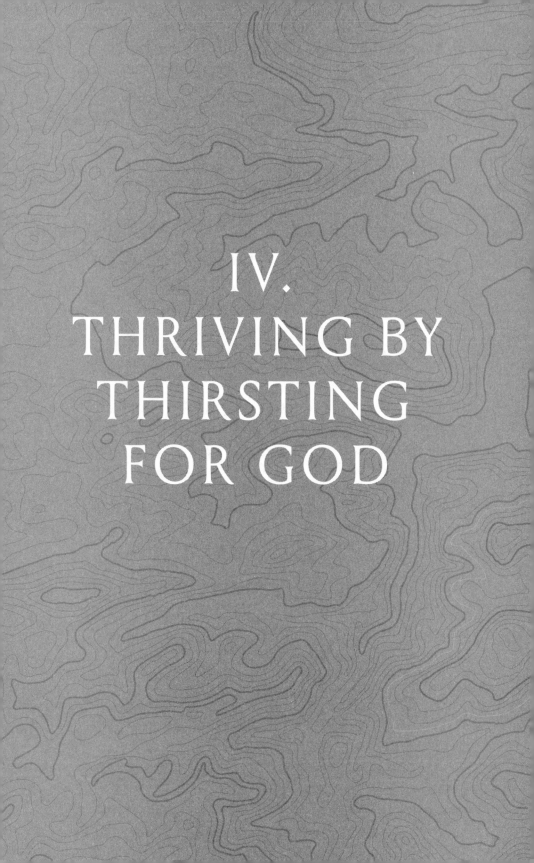

IV.
THRIVING BY
THIRSTING
FOR GOD

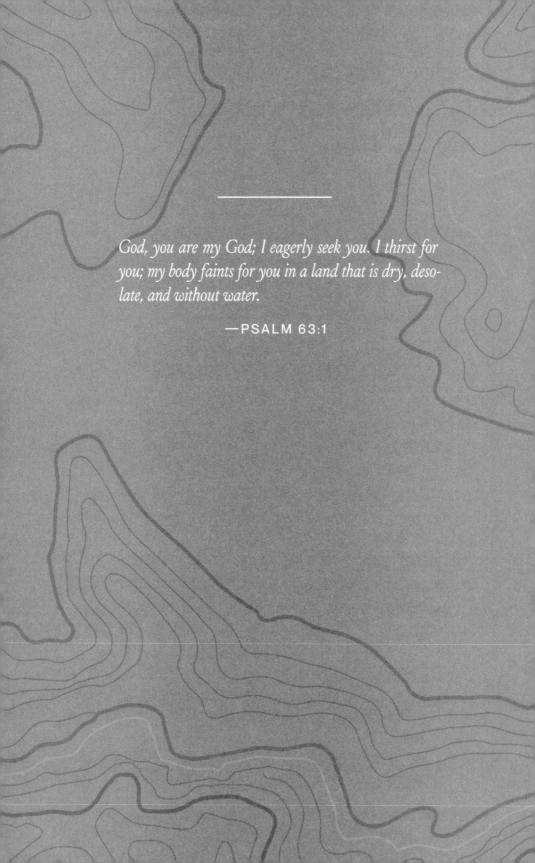

_____

God, you are my God; I eagerly seek you. I thirst for you; my body faints for you in a land that is dry, desolate, and without water.

—PSALM 63:1

CHAPTER 11

AMBIGUITY IS INEVITABLE

FINDING PEACE IN THE FOG

On a hot summer afternoon in 2014, Jim and I arrived at the Trivandrum International Airport in Kerala, India. Our ministry partner's son, Sam, was there to greet us. As he loaded our luggage into his brand-new Toyota SUV, young Sam told us he was taking us to visit a seminary up in the mountains. This special school in Idukki trained young men to become pastors and prepared them to serve the people living in Northern India who had never heard the good news of Jesus Christ. "We're going to drive up the mountain, arrive at our hotel tonight, get a good night's rest, and then tomorrow, we'll visit the students," he said. We were tired, but Sam convinced us it was worth the long drive.

Jim and I settled in our seats and chose to enjoy our time with Sam as well as the scenery. India is an incredible country! We were fascinated by the beautiful people and exotic buildings, the bright colors, and arresting smells. Sacred cows ran free on the streets, donkeys pulled carts, and all sorts of other animals mingled with the people walking by. Sam was explaining many things to us but also stopped every so often to talk to people. He spoke in Malayalam, the local language of Kerala, but we soon realized he was asking for directions. Jim and I glanced at each other, concerned that he did not know where he was going. After several stops, I couldn't contain my curiosity any longer and asked Sam if he was lost. He said he knew where we were going but that this route was new to him. Then he said, "In India, we trust each other for good directions."

We trusted Sam, Sam trusted the people he was asking, and off we went to a place we had never seen before.

As Dependent as a Baby in a Car Seat

As Sam was driving up the mountain, we entered a very narrow road that curved and twisted and made me feel carsick. I was uncomfortable in the back seat but was grateful that the road was smooth compared to some of the rough roads we had already traveled. Sam was very proud of the road and told us that his uncle was the one who made sure this part of the road had asphalt and was well maintained. It had lines painted on the sides and center lines. It felt safe even though there was a steep drop to an unseen valley on our right. Even when it started to rain, we were not concerned because we knew exactly which way to go.

Then the night grew dark, and a thick fog developed. We were feeling more nervous than before, but at least the lines were still visible. Jim and I were now paying special attention to the ground ahead of us. I was no longer sitting comfortably in the back seat, enjoying the scenery. I leaned forward as close as possible to Sam while still wearing my seatbelt. From behind his shoulder, I stared at the lines, assisting Sam with my eyes—as though he needed them. It was my desire to be one with Sam, but only so I could control his driving. I will tell you more about this adventure in a moment, but this part reminds me that sometimes, I do the same with God. Even in my surrender, I try to exercise my dominance.

When we move in active surrender to God, we will have

innumerable blessings, powerful moments, and increased joy along the faith journey. It's not hard to fully give God the reins when good things are happening. But we will also experience all kinds of troubles. If you have been on your faith journey for a while, you know this to be true. Jesus warned his followers that they would experience division, hatred, and persecution. He did not promise a journey free of suffering.

When those experiences come, it's hard not to get anxious and want to take control of the wheel, so to speak. But God gives us the peace that "surpasses all understanding,"[1] which undergirds our soul, especially in moments of struggle. To endure on our faith journey through the high and low moments requires us to discern between what God invites us to do and what our own controlling desires and mindset tell us we ought to do. We must grow to desire God's heart and his ways, at least a sliver more than we want our own.

Since God's desires for you are many, and they are all good, thirsting for God is the only way to thrive in and throughout every part of the faith journey.

This is why Jesus called his followers to think of themselves as branches on a vine.[2] God wants us to produce good and lasting fruit with our faith, but we can only do so by remaining dependent on his nourishment. Since God's desires for you are many, and they are all good, thirsting for God is the only way to thrive in and throughout every part of the faith journey.

The Only Thing That Helps: Water from the Well

Thirsting for God in a spiritual sense is a theme found throughout Scripture.[3] David thirsted for God "in a land that is dry, desolate, and without water."[4] Through the prophet Isaiah, God promises to pour out not only thirst-relieving water but also his Spirit as though it is water to the soul.[5] Think about "thirst" for a moment. What comes to mind? I think of dryness, emptiness, and a burning desire. Just thinking about it makes my mouth feel dry and causes my tongue to stick to the roof of my mouth. Water is essential for human survival. Among its many benefits, it helps us improve our overall well-being, makes up most of our body weight, helps our body function, protects our tissues and joints, and regulates our body temperature. None of us like to thirst, not even Jesus.

Jesus used our physical experience of thirst as a metaphor for spiritual desire. The conversation he had with the woman he met at Jacob's well started by him asking *her* for a drink. The woman was not there looking to meet the awaited Messiah. She just wanted to fetch water for herself with as little interaction with others as possible.[6] Because of her shame, it was likely her daily practice to retrieve this all-important resource during the hottest part of the day when few people would be around. It's no wonder that when she heard Jesus talk about a "spring of water" that would end human thirst, she was eager to receive it.[7] Wouldn't we all be?

But here is where the story gets interesting.

After the woman asks Jesus for the *magic water,* Jesus confronts her with the truth of her story. Knowing everything about her, Jesus offered her life-giving grace. What does this have to do with living water? It turns out, everything. Jesus self-discloses to the woman that he is the coming Messiah, the one who came to satisfy the human *thirst* for salvation.[8]

Our eternal salvation is secured through Jesus's life, death, burial, and resurrection. However, this does not mean that we will stop thirsting for more of God on our faith journey. The Christian faith journey leads you to the heart of God. It starts with believing in Jesus as Lord and Savior[9] and accepting his gift of life and the indwelling of the Holy Spirit. It is the Spirit who will teach us everything we need to know and remind us of everything Jesus did and said.[10] It culminates in the glorious eternity with God in his new heaven and new earth.[11] In between these two points is the challenge. In between these two points, we labor as unto the Lord[12] and live with a thirst for more of God. We continue to thirst to behold his glory and experience the fulness of eternal shalom. We will thirst to live as Paul exclaimed: "I consider that the sufferings of this present time are not worth comparing with the glory that is going to be revealed to us."[13] As we grow in wisdom and understanding of the truths of God's Word, the Holy Spirit moves us from milk to solid food.[14] But as we discussed, this growth is hardly ever linear. The in-between time we live in can be messy, turbulent, mucky, and dry.

Growth is hardly ever linear.

Times of Vulnerability

Back in India, we had driven for what seemed like hours when suddenly Sam slowed down to less than five miles per hour, and for good reason. The lines on the sides of the road disappeared completely. Now we could easily fall off the edge or crash against the mountainside. We were all getting nervous. "Sam, what happened to the lines?" I asked. A little annoyed, he replied, "My uncle was the one who helped make the roads better back there, but now we're in a different district, and they didn't keep this up."

Okay. At least the middle lines were still there. We were living from one dash to the next dash, hoping no car would come down the mountain in the opposite direction. At this point, we were just plain scared. And then the dashes disappeared. Gone. All we saw was a wall of white fog in front of us. The wall felt so close to the front windshield of the car, we did not know which way to go. We could not turn around in the middle of the mountain on the narrow road. Now we were terrified.

I kept asking Sam if he felt okay driving, offering my husband's help. Sam was in his early twenties. Was he experienced enough for these conditions? My mind was racing, and I became convinced that we would not make it to the top of the mountain. If a car were coming down, we wouldn't know it until it was too late and we collided head-on with it. But Sam kept saying, "It's okay. We're going to get there. We just must keep moving forward. We can't turn around." The danger was real, and I knew Sam could feel it, but he at least knew what to do; he knew how to go forward, and we had to trust him. It was a real testing of my faith to let Sam be the one in control along this journey. It was hard to go with "the flow."

Have you ever been in a situation like this where you felt extremely vulnerable?

The journey of faith includes periods or seasons of ambiguity when our experience can be interpreted in a variety of ways, or where it may be difficult to understand its meaning. Along the path, as I have said before, sometimes we may think we have misunderstood God's direction or missed a turn. This can happen especially when our circumstances are working out differently than we expected or when we are not hearing God's voice clearly. We can get so confused and may be tempted to give up on what we thought we were supposed to do. We thirst.

Sometimes we may think we have misunderstood God's direction or missed a turn.

But then, when we thirst for God to give us clarity and get nothing in response, our desperation increases. It can feel like driving without any guidance and facing a thick wall of fog ahead. We might wonder if God is punishing us for something we did wrong—or worse, that he's given up on us. Some refer to this as "the dark night of the soul," a time of searching and not finding, of sitting alone in dark ambiguity.[15] I have experienced this several times, especially while planning and writing this book. I had multiple seasons when

I begged God to give me clarity on what to write about, or even if I was to write at all.

As a pastor, I have walked with people who enter this agony for various reasons, such as the loss of a loved one, a devastating diagnosis, a disappointment in business, or the pain of someone's moral failure. This is the stressful stuff no one likes to talk about. Where do people who are confused or feel like they are lost on the journey go for help? This is when we need the support of the faith community the most. The way through is to embrace God's plan for our lives above all else—more than our idols but also more than our dreams, ideas, people, work, and parts of ourselves.

We can get through every white-knuckle experience by trusting God to guide us in his wisdom.

The apostle Paul said this of himself: "I have been crucified with Christ, and I no longer live, but Christ lives in me. The life I now live in the body, I live by faith in the Son of God, who loved me and gave himself for me."[16] This means that nothing we go through, not even a season of ambiguity, is futile, but instead will have an eternal and lasting effect. We can get through every white-knuckle experience by trusting God to guide us in his wisdom.

When the Fog Lifts

Sam was trustworthy. He knew which way we had to go. He had been on this road before. He had already traveled these mountains in these conditions. Yet, unlike Sam (who's an imperfect person who could've easily made a mistake), we have a Lord who is perfect and all-knowing. He doesn't leave us. He doesn't forsake us. He's certainly not going to lead us the wrong way. But I get it. Sometimes, it feels like God is toying with us. But he is not. That's not in his nature.

Jim and I kept asking Sam, "Are we there yet?" like little kids on a family vacation. Sam's responses were short and to the point:

"Twenty more minutes." Another forty-five minutes passed, I asked again, "Are we there yet?" He repeated his response, "Twenty more minutes." We complained, "Sam, you said twenty minutes forty-five minutes ago!" He said, "I know. Twenty more minutes."

After a long while, we got to the town where we were supposed to stay. Once again, we noticed that Sam seemed a bit lost. He stopped at one hotel, checked in with them, and returned to the car. He stopped at another hotel, checked in with them, and returned to the car. I asked, "Sam, do you not know which hotel we're staying at?" He responded, "Well, actually, I haven't made any reservations at any hotel. I'm just trying to see what hotel has space for us." I couldn't help myself. I barked back, "What, we just *drove* here? It took us twelve hours to get up the mountain, barely alive, and you're telling us you don't even know where we're going to stay?" Sam remained unusually calm for such a young fellow facing a tired and freaked-out Puerto Rican woman. He said, "Don't worry. We'll find a place. It's not a problem."

When we arrived at the third hotel, it had a very ugly fence and gate. We were so anxious, thinking to ourselves that the hotel probably had fleas and who knew what else. Sam could see our faces twisting in desperation, and he told us, "Trust me. This place is good. They're going to have room. I know this place. Just trust me. I want you to have a good night's sleep. I know that you're tired. I'll take care of you." He kept saying, "Trust me." All I could think was, "Easier said than done, buddy! Prove yourself."

Has any part of your journey with God felt like this—like he's feeding you morsel by morsel, asking you to trust him with what comes next? Chances are it has, because that is how we see God at work in the lives of many people in the Bible. He didn't tell Abraham, Noah, or Mary every detail ahead of time. It took years of walking with God, step-by-step, for these people and many others. In these anxious moments, we might feel tempted to turn around, jump out of the car, or quit altogether. But if we did, I'm convinced we would miss out on the joy he has set before us and the blessing of walking with him.

We looked out our window as soon as the gates were open to see that the hotel was gorgeous. The view, the rooms, the service, the grounds . . . everything was a wonderful surprise. The next day we went to the seminary to enjoy time with the students. We heard their stories and encouraged them. These young men were trained and, for graduation, received a bicycle and a Bible. They would soon be sent off with a small amount of money to start churches in the region of India that was most hostile toward Christians, places where you can be decapitated even today for admitting to be a follower of Jesus. These young boys were so courageous, and we were encouraged to be with them.

And driving down the mountain after the fog had lifted was a treat. It was a beautiful day, and the scenery was unbelievable. We were driving through the tea-growing region of India, in the southern part of the country. The beautiful countryside was peppered with farms with neat rows of plants and millions of tea leaves. We would not have seen all of this had we not trusted Sam to take us up the mountain. Granted, the journey was not what we expected, and the experience was a bit terrifying for a while. We doubted Sam many times, but he got us to our destination.

That ride has become, for me, a metaphor for a life that thirsts for God above all else.

Choosing Daily (You Are Always at the Fork in the Road)

I'm not going to lie or sugarcoat this. The journey of faith can be rough. My story in India is a cakewalk compared to what some people have experienced—maybe to what you have experienced. In my library, I have a book called *Jesus Freaks*,[17] which tells the stories of people with unashamed faith who paid the ultimate price for following Jesus. It sits prominently by my computer screen. I never want to forget the men and women in the past and present who are willing to follow Jesus no matter the cost. These people were not called to a comfortable faith walk or a high-profile honor, but to the privilege of shining a light on the faithfulness of God and the love of Jesus. It reminds me that we will be challenged and scared at times. Sometimes we may be tempted to say, "I'm going to stay at the bottom of the hill." But we may not know that God is taking us to a good place until we're on the other side of this earthly life.

When Jesus invited the twelve disciples to follow him, they left everything to walk with Jesus. They went where he went and everywhere he sent them. Even when Jesus tried to go off alone, they looked for him. But not everybody followed Jesus. Some people listened to Jesus's teachings, followed him for a while, and then left. One of the reasons I am writing this book is to encourage you (and myself) not to be one of those people. My prayer is that we commit to staying on the path.

Jesus asked his disciples, "You don't want to go away too, do you?" Peter rightfully said, "Lord, to whom will we go? You have the words of eternal life. We have come to believe and know that you are the Holy One of God."[18] That's it. We're going with Jesus! After three years, Jesus knew there was so much more he wanted to teach them, and he told them that he would be sending the Holy Spirit, the "living water," to continue to guide each of his followers. Once we put our trust in Jesus and his saving grace, the Holy Spirit guides our journey. He is the one who leads and directs us in the ways that are pleasing to God, even if, for now, things don't make any sense.

The Holy Spirit will encourage us to stay all in. He is closer than the pillar of cloud and fire the people of Israel followed in the wilderness, because he is resident in our hearts and speaks to us Spirit to spirit.[19] He will tell us what we need to hear and do, but often one step at a time, through the thick fog.

Are we going to follow our God, or are we going to follow the culture, the world, and the things people say? Will we choose to live by the Spirit or live by our own desires? Remember the words from Galatians 5:17, when Paul tells his people, "For the flesh desires what is against the Spirit." The flesh and Spirit conflict with one another. We can't choose to go both ways. We're either led by the Spirit, or we're going to be led by our earthly mindset. They're going to take us in different directions.

Let us remember that God is in the proverbial driver's seat of our eternal life. He is trustworthy to take us where it is best, where we will experience the peace we desperately need. That doesn't mean we will hear every single answer from God the minute we want to. There are times when we will be asking for God—asking, asking, asking—and all we will hear is silence. Or maybe we will hear something akin to Sam's response of, "Twenty minutes," meaning, "Not yet." Our part is to keep taking steps toward him, thirsting for more of him daily.

His Presence Is Our Peace

There is a beautiful quote from C. S. Lewis that encourages me when I am in a season of ambiguity: "God cannot give us a happiness and peace apart from Himself, because it is not there. There is no such thing."[20] Remember, there's no peace apart from God. Even if he's silent, he's silent for a reason, but it doesn't change the fact that you've never left his sight.

In Scripture we see a God who is always present with his people. As frustrating as they get to be, as badly as they misbehave, as disobedient and rebellious as they are, God is always with them. The whole story of Scripture is about a God who loves us so much that, even though we disobey, even though we are sinful people, he pursues us, saves us, and guides us. You and I are image bearers of a good, loving, and powerful God. He is going to lead his creation to his fullness. That's his intention.

Confidence on our journey comes with letting go of our demand for clarity and letting God unfold his plan for us, accepting that God has a purpose for our lives even if we don't understand it or see growth.

Confidence on our journey comes with letting go of our demand for clarity and letting God unfold his plan for us, accepting that God has a purpose for our lives even if we don't understand it or see growth.

Our planning and plotting must not become our god. We must leave room for things not to happen the way we planned and allow that we may not always understand the providence of God. We may be like most of the people mentioned in Hebrews 11, who did not fully know, and most of whom never saw, the fruit of their labor and faith. What if we, like them, remain committed?

These people were living by faith until the end. Faith ruled their lives through the ambiguity and the fog of the journey. They may not have received the things promised to them in their lifetimes, but they endured in their journey because they embraced the trustworthy promises of God. They accepted their lots as "foreigners and strangers" on earth.[21] They looked ahead for a heavenly city prepared for them by God.

What was the outcome of such sterling faith? Despite their many failings (all of them failed in various ways), God was not ashamed to be called their God. He was delighted to be known as their God. One of the two women mentioned by name in Hebrews 11 is Rahab.[22] Her story is told in Joshua 2. It, too, reminds us to act on the faith we already have. We do not need big faith to move mountains and take down walls.[23]

Trusting until Faith Becomes Sight

The people of Israel had been in the wilderness for forty years, but now it was time to enter the Promised Land. God called Joshua to be "strong and courageous"[24] because he and his people were about to do battle for this gift. The first battle was with Jericho, a highly fortified city. The king of Jericho had built two great walls, one inside the city surrounding his palace and homes and another around the entire city. Joshua secretly sent two spies to scope out the city and the extent of the enemy's power.

Upon entering the city, the spies stopped at the house of a prostitute named Rahab. What were they going to learn there about Jericho? Who knows! But Rahab turned out to be a non-Jewish or pagan woman who was interested in the God of the Israelites. She lived on the outer wall, far from the city's center. She was probably separated from her family and anyone in high society due to her profession. Yet she became the woman who gave the two spies the gift of life and encouraged the Israelites to pursue the land God had already given them.

Word got out that the men were hiding in her home, so the two men hid on her roof from the city guards. Rahab then made a declaration about the God the Israelites worshiped. She had heard about him and the things he had done. That was enough for Rahab to risk everything and trust that their God was able to give her life. She made a deal with the men to keep secret their spying in exchange for her life and the lives of her family. Her sign of faith in the God of Israel's ability to conquer a very powerful city was a scarlet rope hung from her window.

If you read the story in Joshua 1–6, it takes the Israelites a long time to arrive ready for battle. Joshua first assembled the people, crossed the parted waters of the Jordan, created a monument to the miracle, worshiped, circumcised the warriors, and waited for them to heal. Then they set off toward Jericho, but following God's instruction, they circled the city once a day in silence for seven days. I can only imagine what Rahab must have felt. Her declaration of faith was on full display, her family inside her home probably wondering why they trusted her to begin with.

Then on the seventh day, after going around the city seven times, the Israelite troops shouted and blew their ram horns, and the walls collapsed. Rahab lived on the wall. Think of the stress she must have felt as the city wall collapsed around her and the troops advanced into the city, destroying everything.[25] She may have been pacing the house, sweating, and biting her nails. What if her house also collapsed? What if the warriors did not get Joshua's memo to leave Rahab and her people untouched? Would the two young spies keep their word? Was the God of the Israelites trustworthy? These are questions I would have asked myself if I were in her situation, along with many others. So many things could have gone wrong. Rahab's life was on the line, literally!

But she hoped in the Lord above all else. So her hope was steadfast. Her thirst for God was so great that she risked it all. But she risked it all for the one thing she was certain to receive, because the One she trusted was trustworthy.

The story of Rahab and her scarlet rope—which she hung from her window to remind the Israelites of the promise made—gives us hope to trust God's infinite wisdom and power and his long-term goals. She had no idea when God would come to her rescue, though she hoped he would. She hung the scarlet rope in trust, risking everything, thirsting for the God of the Israelites, not knowing what the future would hold.

Even when the walls around us fall (the things we put our trust in, the certainties that gave us clarity), God holds us by his grace and eternal plans. Thirsting for God is the wisest way to walk the journey of faith and finish well, even when part of the journey feels like driving through deep fog.

What is the greatest uncertainty in your life right now? Do you wish you could grab the driver's wheel of your life and make your own way through the fog?

A scary trip on the roads of India revealed to me that I wanted God not just to remove the fog that was blocking the view in front of our car, but to remove all ambiguity from my journey of faith. I heard no audible voice, but the answer was clear. Ambiguity—driving through the fog— was the way this trip was going to go.

Thirsting for God is the wisest way to walk the journey of faith and finish well, even when part of the journey feels like driving through deep fog.

Slowly, turn by turn, we kept driving until we reached our destination. I submitted to the reality of the ambiguity before me and realized that the same posture was necessary on my faith journey in order to increase my trust in God and remain faithful to him. Increasing our thirst for God helps us practice detachment from the things of this world. We must practice saying no to self and yes to God, fasting from our need for clarity.

And one of the times we thirst most for clarity is when we find ourselves face-to-face with suffering. We will talk about how to handle that next.

SPIRITUAL PRACTICES: SUBMISSION AND DETACHMENT/REST

I hope it is obvious why I combined these two spiritual practices for this chapter. Ambiguity is so uncomfortable; it leads us to clasp things that give us clarity much harder than usual. Submission leads to peace because it is an intentional posture to seek alignment of our will with God's will. We submit to God because we know he is above it all, and his love always wants good for us. God's holiness means that he is perfect in every way—in his love, goodness, and power. His intentions are always for our ultimate good.

The reason we struggle to submit is that so much of our world and so many people have let us down repeatedly. But God never does! He is faithful. When Jesus is our King, that is freedom. Obeying other people can lead to disaster, but when we obey God, we obey someone who is completely trustworthy. We can lay aside our anxiety and rest in his wisdom. The practice of submission to God increases our ability to learn from him and experience his ways.

Detachment is a different posture than submission, but I think of them as cousins. The very act of detaching from the things of this world leaves us in the right posture to submit to the Creator, who is above it all. Detachment helps us let go of the little gods we have bowed down to. This helps us live in the freedom of being a child of God.

The Process

When we practice submission and detachment, we identify the things that have taken priority over our relationship with the Lord. We confess that we have put our trust in things like money, status, stuff, beauty, health, success, and even our religiosity. We confess that we have desired to have ultimate control. We remember that our identity is rooted in Christ and nothing or no one else. This can be done alone or with a prayer partner, or through journaling.

Ask the Holy Spirit to help you identify what area(s) of your life you need to submit to God and what one thing you need to detach from to experience more of him. To practice submission, take the one area of your life the Holy Spirit has identified, and consciously follow a specific scriptural command that applies to that area.

To practice detachment, share something you own (house, car, your time, etc.) that has value to you with someone else. This practice can help you hold it less tightly when you invite God into the experience. Notice the feelings that come up when you do this exercise and pray to the Lord to help you release your attachment to the item you shared.

Prompting Scriptures

Therefore, brothers and sisters, in view of the mercies of God, I urge you to present your bodies as a living sacrifice, holy and pleasing to God; this is your true worship.

—Romans 12:1

Adopt the same attitude as that of Christ Jesus, who, existing in the form of God, did not consider equality with God as something to be exploited. Instead he emptied himself by assuming the form of a servant, taking on the likeness of humanity. And when he had come as a man, he humbled himself by becoming obedient to the point of death—even to death on a cross.

—Philippians 2:5–8

For whoever wants to save his life will lose it, but whoever loses his life because of me will find it. For what will it benefit someone if he gains the whole world yet loses his life? Or what will anyone give in exchange for his life?

—Matthew 16:25–26

For those who live according to the flesh have their minds set on the things of the flesh, but those who live according to the Spirit have their minds set on the things of the Spirit. Now the mindset of the flesh is death, but the mindset of the Spirit is life and peace. The mindset of the flesh is hostile to God because it does not submit to God's law. Indeed, it is unable to do so. Those who are in the flesh cannot please God.

—Romans 8:5–8

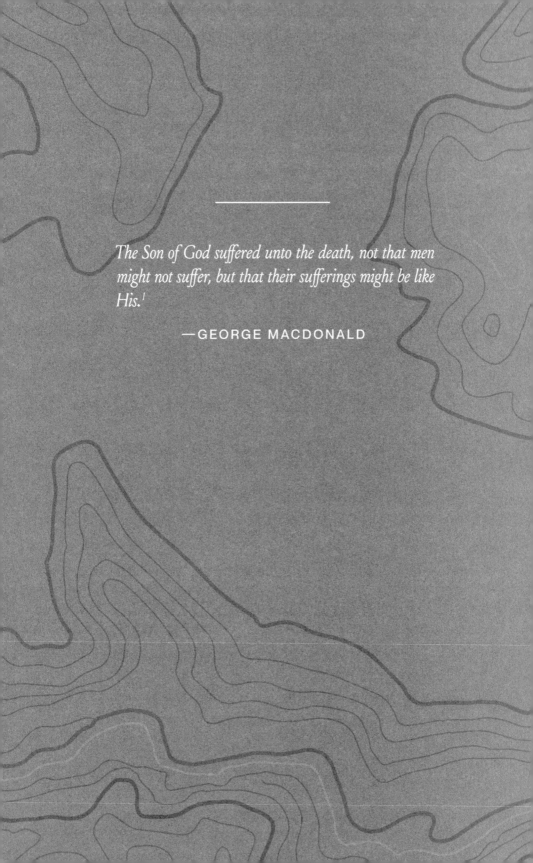

The Son of God suffered unto the death, not that men might not suffer, but that their sufferings might be like His.[1]

—GEORGE MACDONALD

CHAPTER 12

THE
JOURNEY IS
MYSTERIOUS

WHAT TO DO WITH SUFFERING

We don't have to search for suffering.

Dangerous things hurt. Suffering is real. Pain is pain. Sometimes the suffering is so deep that we are likely to question if we will make it through. And when we do make it to the other side of the struggle, we are not the least bit interested in going through it again.

The pain of suffering affects every area of our lives, sometimes resulting in post-traumatic stress, depression, and physical illnesses. It can even affect our faith journey, for it confronts us with the paradox of the existence of a good God amidst an unjust world. Yet it is through the cruel suffering of our good and loving God (Jesus Christ) that our own suffering will eventually be overcome and undone.[2]

Our common mistake is to think that God will keep us from suffering and that our lives will be pain-free. This mindset is, at a minimum, bad theology, and at worst, a lie from the pit of hell. God is after something better than our temporary happiness and comfort. At the heart of the Christian faith is the belief that no suffering is meaningless, and that none needs to be wasted. Even deep suffering has the potential to produce in us "strength, fulfillment, and personal development."[3] Christians who endure suffering with the help of God, the community of faith, and sometimes therapists, grow in resilience and the capacity to comfort others in their suffering.

I do not seek, celebrate, or enjoy suffering, but I desire to have a faith that endures through the toughest moments in life. I want a faith that gets me through struggles in such a way that it increases my courage and my confidence. I want a faith that can withstand the ultimate test of all: seemingly sense-less suffering. I call this a *thriving faith*. I believe it is the kind of faith we all want. It's the kind of faith the apostle Paul modeled and that helped him fin-ish the race well. We want to join him by one day saying, "I have fought the good fight, I have finished the race, I have kept the faith."[4]

At the heart of the Christian faith is the belief that no suffering is meaningless, and that none needs to be wasted.

Paul suffered greatly. He recites a long list of his woes to the Cor-inthians[5] and ends with the key to his endurance. What is it Paul did with the suffering in his mysterious faith journey? Here he is in his own words: "I will most gladly boast all the more about my weak-nesses, so that Christ's power may reside in me."[6] According to Paul, the way to make it through all manner of suffering with an intact faith is to accept our vulnerability and increase our dependence on the God and Father of the Lord Jesus.

The apostle James teaches us the same, and it is his instruction we will unpack in this chapter.

James's letter is about thriving on our faith journey. He makes the point that it is through suffering that the genuineness, strength, and health of our faith are revealed. James was the half brother of Jesus. His sermon-like letter addresses "the twelve tribes dispersed abroad."[7]

Because of their faith, Jesus-following Israelites were pushed out of their towns and forced to leave their homes. They moved among people of other nations to unfamiliar places and, even there, experienced more persecution and increased challenges.

In the first section of his letter, James teaches these believers four essentials of a thriving faith that initially seem counterintuitive. His words challenge us, but for good reason. James wrote to encourage, give hope, and strengthen the faith of people like us who were struggling to endure and stay the course.

Essential for a Thriving Faith #1: A Joyful Attitude

Consider it a great joy, my brothers and sisters, whenever you experience various trials, because you know that the testing of your faith produces endurance.

—James 1:2–3

The Greek words for "whenever you experience various trials" (*hotan peripipto poikilos peirasmos*) paint a picture we don't get from the English language. In Greek, the word *peripipto* (experience) means "to fall around someone, to embrace someone ... and in the [New Testament], to fall into the midst of something so as to be totally surrounded by it, to fall into or among."[8] Surrounded by many trials! This makes me think of the way an army encircles its enemy, or the way water encloses and applies pressure to anything thrown into it.

James calls believers to "consider," to rethink or think differently about the many struggles they are experiencing. Under tremendous pressure, James calls them to rejoice in their suffering; not because suffering is good, but because they had already suffered greatly and made it to the other side stronger and more resilient. They had reason to rejoice because their current suffering also would produce increased endurance. James paints the picture of a faith that will prove itself to be genuine and strong under pressure and adversity.

It's only when we get through those difficult seasons that we can see the condition of our faith. We can talk about having faith in Jesus any day, any time. I can give you a long list of why I believe what I believe, and I'll appear theologically sound, but you will not know the validity of my words unless you see my faith tested. Our faith cannot be fully revealed until we go through some challenges and it gets put to the test. That's when we will see if it is real or strong. That is why rejoicing is in order. When our faith is proven to be resilient, we have reason to celebrate.

Peter puts it this way:

> *Dear friends, don't be surprised when the fiery ordeal comes among you to test you, as if something unusual were happening to you. Instead, rejoice as you share in the sufferings of Christ, so that you may also rejoice with great joy when his glory is revealed.*

> —1 Peter 4:12–13

Again, Peter is not claiming that suffering is good; rather, he is saying that on the other side of suffering for our faith, we will experience great joy. We need to learn "to rest in the mystery of ambiguity and intuitive guidance from God,"[9] especially in our suffering.

As I write this chapter, our dear friend Bob Shank is celebrating his one hundredth day after a bone marrow transplant to fight acute myelogenous leukemia. Today, we celebrate that his body produces bone marrow and blood that is 100 percent from his granddaughter's donated marrow. None of his "former but corrupted material is present." For six months, Bob's life was completely reoriented, and his faith was put to the test with this unexpected challenge. Talk about being "surrounded" by trials!

The transplant and the months of doctor appointments, blood tests, and numerous evaluations before and after were arduous but necessary to increase his chance of survival. Bob and Cheri self-isolated away from their huge circle of friends, and he resigned his role as CEO of his ministry. This was necessary to focus on the treatments and protect him from infections and diseases, including COVID.

Bob and Cheri's page on CaringBridge.org was their megaphone where they shared their journey vulnerably with friends from all over the world who were praying for the entire family, but especially for Bob's healing. Nothing was for certain. It still isn't. Acute leukemia is a menacing health crisis. But Bob's faith, Cheri's faith, and their family's faith are shining like the brightest stars. This was not the first huge battle they have endured. Years ago, Bob was in a terrible car accident that almost took his life. Bob contends that "rescue is not the promise of God; His presence in any Class of Life challenge is what He's committed to provide."[10]

Cry if you have to. But do not miss the good thing God is doing in and through you.

Writing this is emotional for me. Bob and Cheri have been spiritual parents to Jim and me ever since we dedicated our lives to Jesus almost twenty years ago. Over the years, they have nurtured our faith and challenged us to live for Jesus purposefully and boldly toward eternal significance. We are both graduates of The Master's Program for Christian leaders, which Bob and Cheri founded. They have modeled resilience for us, and they have done so with a joyful attitude.

If Bob wrote this chapter, I think he'd say to you and me, "Get on that roller coaster. Don't close your eyes. Keep your hands up in the air. Scream if you must. Cry if you have to. But *do not* miss the good thing God is doing in and through you." In fact, he just now texted me this: "There is messaging from Him in every situation; we're often too distracted to discern His wisdom!" Bob gives me a hint about the posture Job must have had when he tore his robe in suffering, shaved his head, fell to the ground, acknowledged his pain, and worshiped by saying, "Blessed be the name of the Lord."[11]

Can you think of a time when you were able to find joy in the midst of suffering? What helped you do that?

I am also praising God for his provision and encouragement. My heart is full of gratitude for Bob and Cheri's endurance and faithfulness. I see in them a thriving faith that, like Paul's, leads to finishing the race by trusting in God's abundant grace through Jesus. They remind me that we're already living in the eternal realm, though our time on this side of eternity is limited and fragile. Have you seen this kind of mature and joyful faith in others? I sometimes struggle to match the spiritually mature joy of my suffering friends, but I know that their example is something to cling to. Whose example of joy in suffering encourages you?

Remember that nothing can snatch us from the hand of God. Nothing. Ever. Hallelujah! We cannot find—we cannot even see—the quality of our faith unless we lean into the unexpected trials in our lives.

Essential for a Thriving Faith #2: A Surrendered Will

And let endurance have its full effect, so that you may be mature and complete, lacking nothing.

—James 1:4

We must be open to experiencing the best God can bring from

our greatest challenges. God is always at work to bring about good. Perhaps we can proclaim like Paul:

> *We also boast in our afflictions, because we know that affliction produces endurance, endurance produces proven character, and proven character produces hope. This hope will not disappoint us, because God's love has been poured out in our hearts through the Holy Spirit who was given to us.*
>
> —Romans 5:3–5

I take great comfort in the fact that God does not waste *anything.* We know this is true, but I wonder if you're like me, wondering if there is another way. There is not. My friend, strap yourself to God.

A beautiful example of a life lived this way is that of Joni Eareckson Tada. After fifty-five years of living in a wheelchair after a terrible accident left her a quadriplegic, "two bouts of cancer, severe breathing issues, COVID-19, and chronic pain," Joni speaks of still not having all the strength she needs and of "needing God desperately."[12] Like Paul, Joni boasts about her weakness and rejoices in the God who has brought her further than she could imagine. She strapped herself to the words of Paul in Acts 20:24 (NIV):

> *I consider my life worth nothing to me; my only aim is to finish the race and complete the task the Lord Jesus has given me—the task of testifying to the good news of God's grace.*

She has dedicated her life to the work of providing support to people living with disabilities in the US and abroad. Her suffering is hard to grasp for any of us who have not experienced anything like her journey. But her words are fit for all of us:

I try not to grasp at my fragile life, nor coddle it or minimize my activities . . . just because I'm getting older, getting weaker, and dealing with more pain. Rather, I find great comfort and joy in dying to self and living every day to serve the Lord Jesus and others around the world whose disabilities are far more profound than mine. What else could be more important than practicing Christianity, with sleeves rolled up, among the needy?[13]

In a video update after her battle with COVID-19, Joni shared[14] about this surrendered state. Struggling to breathe, she cried out to God, fearing that this virus would end her life, but trusting God to see her through this new battle even if it meant death. She felt the Lord take a "gentle, firm possession" of her affliction and "begin to do a work" in her.

God called Joni to deeper surrender, further than she had ever gone before, to a place free of doubt: "Do you believe me . . . ?" Imagine that! Joni's response seared deep into my mind and heart: "I believe you."

Oh, that all of us who put our trust in Jesus would have her mindset when our suffering becomes unbearable. Joni "felt a wonderfully odd calmness and almost indifference to how much it might hurt or how it would end and felt perfectly still under the hand of God, resting in the shadow of the Almighty . . . blessed."

Very few of us are quadriplegics, but all of us have experienced pain and doubt. Can you think of a time when you were suffering and were able to surrender the outcome to God? If not, what do you think might have helped you come to that place of surrender? Think of that time in your mind and reimagine it. Picture how it might have gone differently. Act out in your imagination what surrendering to God in that moment of pain might have looked like. As I look back at my own responses to past sufferings, I am reminded that this is an area with maturing opportunities for all of us.

Whatever our suffering may be, no matter its source or length, we can surrender it to the Lord to work his best will on us. G. D. Watson wrote it this way:

> When the suffering soul reaches a calm, sweet carelessness, when it can inwardly smile at its own suffering and not even ask to be delivered, then it works its blessed ministry. Then the cross you carry begins to weave itself into a crown.[15]

When we yield ourselves completely to God and trust him with every part of our faith journey, through every circumstance and in every step, he can do the greatest miracle: he can transform our life into a remarkable act of worship, just as he has with Joni's—but even more so, as he did with Jesus when he surrendered his will to the will of the Father.[16]

Essential for a Thriving Faith #3:
Dependance upon God's Wisdom

> Now if any of you lacks wisdom, he should ask God—who gives to all generously and ungrudgingly—and it will be given to him.
>
> —James 1:5

I would have expected James to say something like, "If you're struggling, if you're going through a trial, if you are suffering, ask God for comfort, peace, strength, endurance, patience, and joy." Isn't that what we pray for when we're suffering? We pray for those things for our friends. But that's not what James tells us to pray for. It's quite fascinating that he instructs us to pray for *wisdom* instead.

There's no doubt that when we suffer, a lot of questions come up for us—questions of meaning, such as, "God, why is this happening to me? Why now?" Suffering also transforms our sense of self from pride to humility. It leads us to examine ourselves and re-evaluate our vulnerabilities and weaknesses. Do we respond to suffering with anger and a greater need for control, or are we prone to getting stuck in self-pity? Our

Depending on God's wisdom amid suffering can help us find sources of joy even in the darkest shadows.

deep struggles also cause us to explore our attachments, for we may have been relying too much on them. For all of this, we need God's wisdom. Depending on God's wisdom amid suffering can help us find sources of joy even in the darkest shadows.

Think of a time of recent suffering—or of suffering you're experiencing right now. Pray for wisdom—now, for this exact thing. This is a time when you don't just have to practice! You can actually stop and ask God for wisdom in this very moment. As God to help you see your situation from his divine perspective. What does the Lord bring to mind? If nothing seems obvious to you, decide when you're going to pray about it again, and remain open to hearing—we must ask, and keep asking!

Considering stories like those of Joni and my friend Bob, we might be tempted to think that God has a special heart for those suffering huge battles and gives them a special kind of wisdom. The surprise, however, is that while our individual experiences may be teaching us different things, the wisdom of God is the same for Joni, Bob, you, and me. The Lord is generous!

James tells us that wisdom is the first thing we should ask for. We need wisdom so we don't waste the opportunity to mature in our faith. The teacher in Proverbs reminds us:

If you call out to insight and lift your voice to understanding, if you seek it like silver and search for it like hidden treasure, then you will understand the fear of the Lord and discover the knowledge of God. For the Lord gives wisdom; from his mouth come knowledge and understanding.

—Proverbs 2:3–6

When we humbly ask God for this kind of wisdom, he gives it.

We must depend on him daily, hourly, and sometimes, minute by minute. Like the Israelites received manna from heaven, rationed for the day but always enough, we can receive the wisdom we need bit by bit. Jesus said, "I am the bread of life"![17] We can count on him to feed our souls and get us to the other side of our afflictions.

And here is another source of hope. When we get off the "roller coaster" of our current suffering, we will have wisdom that can be a benefit to others. At a minimum, we become more compassionate toward the suffering of others when we, too, go through our own trials. For example, we will better empathize with a person's struggle as she undergoes cancer treatments when we find ourselves in that clinic waiting room wearing our own chemo beanie. Suffering can create wisdom in us if we let it and resist closing our hearts in bitterness.

So I gaze on you in the sanctuary to see your strength and your glory.

—Psalm 63:2

When I went through seminary, I fulfilled my internship requirement by working as a chaplain in our local children's hospital, Children's Health of Orange County, California. There, I watched families deal with incredibly difficult seasons of life. There was a noticeable difference between the families who depended upon God for support and wisdom and those who did not. I was very insecure about my ability to be of help to these families walking through experiences I had never walked through. My supervisor trained me and prepared me for a variety of situations by having me read books about this type of work.

After spending one day with him visiting families, watching him gently guide them through their most painful moments, deep doubts, and stressful decisions, I was convinced I was the worst person possible for this role. The next day, I showed up hoping to get further training, but it was a very busy day at the hospital. The moment I walked in, my supervisor gave me my first assignment. It was an emergency, and he could not go with me because he was needed in another room.

My walk to the NICU felt like it took forever, even though I was practically running and the building I was in was not that big. I was praying all the way there, asking God for wisdom on what to do and say. Never in my life had I seen a child so small die in front of me. I hoped I never would. As soon as I arrived at the tiny bed, all the nurses and doctors stepped back to reveal his little body and the crying mom by his side. I motioned the staff not to stop their work. Prayer and medical care can go hand in hand.

But the mother told everyone to move away and let the woman she had never met and knew nothing about pray for a miracle over her dying son. Trembling, I approached the mom and put my hand over her shoulder with her permission. We looked at each other only briefly before closing our eyes to the troubles of this world to seek the eyes of God amidst that dark moment.

Just as I was about to start, she herself began praying boldly and joyfully. She told God how much she looked forward to seeing her son play sports, attend school, and get married. She rejoiced that God gave her such a perfect and beautiful son. She thanked God for the doctors, nurses, and for me. Her prayers showered God with accolades for his faithfulness and goodness. There was so much rejoicing in her prayers that did not match the circumstances at that moment. Yet, this I knew: Her dependence on God

Her intimacy with God's Word prepared her for this moment of adversity.

through her suffering was already becoming a surprising gift to all of us. Her intimacy with God's Word prepared her for this moment of adversity.

Her son lived through that crisis, and through many other times when his frail body threatened to shut down. She and I prayed so many times together, I lost count. Each time, I prayed for wisdom, and I think she did the same. We both grew in our faith, dependence, and trust in God simultaneously as her son grew in weight and health.

If in our times of suffering (or that of others) we pay attention and ask God to teach us along the way, we will learn things we would not learn any other way. And some times of suffering will be worse than others; some parents will pray for their children and not see them live. I prayed with parents and stood by them as they watched their baby take one last breath in their loving arms.

For two friends of mine, their suffering began during pregnancy when their doctor diagnosed their unborn child with a condition that guaranteed either a stillbirth or only a few hours or days of life after birth. I watched as they leaned on God heavily for wisdom, each in their own way. Here, too—here *especially*—we must throw ourselves on the mercies of God. There is no one else big enough to possibly be able to comprehend such sorrow. In my own life, the most powerful lessons have come in seasons of struggle, suffering, and testing. It is there that God gives me the wisdom I depend on to mentor and help other people who are in similar situations today.

Essential for a Thriving Faith #4:
A Trusting Heart

But let him ask in faith without doubting. For the doubter is like the surging sea, driven and tossed by the wind. That person should not expect to receive anything from the Lord, being double-minded and unstable in all his ways.

—James 1:6–8

James instructs us to pray with confidence, with unwavering faith. He uses an image of ocean water manipulated by the wind. It's not fun to be in an environment where we are tossed about. Suffering is the worst time of all to be in that state. It is there that we need the most confidence and strength. But our posture can be as honest as the man who asked Jesus to heal his son who was possessed by spirits. The boy's father cried out, "I do believe; help my unbelief!"[18]

God does not expect us to ignore our pain, minimize our suffering, or cover our afflictions with positive thinking. He sees us and our pain.

In his book *Walking with God through Pain and Suffering*, Pastor Tim Keller observes that a common metaphor used in the Bible for facing affliction is "*walking*—walking through something difficult, perilous and potentially fatal."[19] He points to the many passages in Scripture that compare suffering to walking "in darkness" or "through deep waters" or "slippery and dangerous mountain paths," many of which are found in the Psalms, Isaiah, Job, and Lamentations. This means God does not expect us to ignore our pain, minimize our suffering, or cover our afflictions with positive thinking. He sees us and our pain. As the psalm of David exclaims, we can say, "I follow close to you; your right hand holds on to me."[20]

This reminds me of the story of Hagar, an Egyptian slave who suffered much.[21] Abram and Sarai were not yet pregnant as God had promised, so they decided to take matters into their own hands. Sarai convinced Abram to take Hagar and conceive a child with her. After Hagar got pregnant, Sarai turned on her, treating her with contempt. Things got so awful that Hagar ran away from her mistress. Yet God met Hagar in her suffering, sent her back to Sarai, and promised to "greatly multiply" Hagar's offspring. She named the Lord "El-roi," meaning "the God who sees me."

Hagar is the first person in the Genesis narrative to name God. Walking with God in suffering is perhaps the most powerful way to know him and his heart.

The writer of Hebrews implores us to trust in God even in our suffering by keeping our eyes fixed on Jesus: "Consider him who endured such hostility from sinners against himself, so that you won't grow weary and give up."[22] Isaiah 53 gives us a list of some of his sufferings, and they were awful.

The key term is "endured." In other words, our focus is not on controlling our emotional response, the details of our circumstances, or the environment we find ourselves in; rather, our focus is on the One who *walked* through deep suffering and made it to the other side. He enters the fiery furnace with us, as he did for the three young men who refused to bow down to King Nebuchadnezzar.[23] Like my mentor, Pastor Kenton Beshore, says, they walked with "double-fisted faith": They trusted in God's wisdom and believed that he had the power to rescue, and even if he did not, he was the only one deserving worship. Honoring God was their extraordinary joy. We can do the same.

The Goodness That Can Come after Sorrow

Blessed is the one who endures trials, because when he has stood

*the test he will receive the crown of life that God has promised
to those who love him.*

—James 1:12

James teaches us that we can have a thriving faith by maintaining a joyful attitude, a surrendered will, a dependance on God's wisdom, and a trusting heart. There is a great reward: life for us and life for others. When we walk through our challenges with Jesus, he equips us to walk with others and bring life-giving hope to them. Some of us have experienced the great mysteries of God along our journey of faith, particularly when we were in deep suffering, and we should share them with others in humility and wisdom because they point to the wonders of the mind of God.

A joyful attitude, a surrendered will, a dependance on God's wisdom, a trusting heart. Which of the four is the hardest for you to lean on? May I encourage you to circle one? Maybe the one that's the hardest for you could be the very thing God wants to use in your faith journey to minister to others in their suffering.

Be still.

Rest.

Remember God's faithfulness. Make a list of his work in your life. Identify what scares you and give it to God in prayer. Find encouragement by reading stories of people who trusted God through suffering.[24] Keep your focus on God's promises and fix your eyes on Jesus.

Walk.

SPIRITUAL PRACTICES: MEDITATION AND SERVICE

Okay, I admit it. Meditation and service might be the strangest combination of spiritual practices, especially when you consider I am connecting them to the topic of suffering. But I have a point to make here.

Meditation is the practice of intently gazing on God through Scripture and God's creation. It involves slowing down and looking deeply with the eyes of our spirit for the divine imprint in all things and people. Every person is made in the image of God. His attributes, such as wisdom, love, creativity, joy, gentleness, etc., are reflected through people. His relational nature is demonstrated in the fact that people are relational. His missional purpose is reflected in our desire to create things and to manage and order our world. When we meditate, we seek to set our mind on heavenly thoughts and wisdom. We set out to look beneath the surface, to see as God sees all things. Focusing on God directly, or as we are inspired to by his creation, has a calming effect and helps us feel connected to him.

When we serve, we choose to give of ourselves, our time, treasure, talent, and energy to care for and support another person or group of people. It is "loving our neighbor" as Jesus called us to do. The act of service has the power to transform our hearts and develop our character. Service increases our joy, and compassion grows our sense of love. Most of what we do all day is for our own benefit.

We can get so preoccupied with our own lives and problems and suffering that we do not see the suffering of others. But when we put down our own needs and agenda and make another person the recipient of our resources and time, we release ourselves from the tight grip of self-focus. Our problems get bigger the more we stare at them, and they get smaller when we compare them to the great God who loves us. By the power of the Holy Spirit, it can be deeply refreshing to shift our gaze toward the problems of others and help them.

The Process

Now here is why I have put these two practices together. This was not my invention. Jesus put them together when he reminded his disciples of the greatest two commandments (see the Prompting Scriptures). If meditation is fixing our eyes on Jesus and Jesus calls us to love our neighbor through acts of service, especially for the most vulnerable in society, then there is a way to find relief from our pain and suffering.

As I mentioned in this chapter, a most beautiful example of this is Joni Eareckson Tada. She suffers greatly from physical pain and trouble breathing every day, but she seeks Jesus in the eyes of every person to whom she provides the gift of a wheelchair. Her determination to put her suffering in the hands of God is inspiring. When we serve others, our problems tend to take a back seat, at least for the moment. This is especially true if we intently look for the image of God in those whom we serve, and we don't bring our problems to them. We serve with joy!

Look for someone to serve today. Perhaps someone who is suffering in the same way you are. If you're a single mom, help another single mom. If you are struggling with finances, help someone with theirs. If you are sick, call a friend who is bedridden. If you're lonely, spend time with someone you know is often alone. You get the picture. Stand with those who suffer and look for Jesus there. Remember, "The Lord is near the brokenhearted; he saves those crushed in spirit."[25]

Prompting Scriptures

> He said to him, "Love the Lord your God with all your heart, with all your soul, and with all your mind. This is the greatest and most important command. The second is like it: Love your neighbor as yourself."
>
> —Matthew 22:37–39

"For I was hungry and you gave me something to eat; I was thirsty and you gave me something to drink; I was a stranger and you took me in; I was naked and you clothed me; I was sick and you took care of me; I was in prison and you visited me." Then the righteous will answer him, "Lord, when did we see you hungry and feed you, or thirsty and give you something to drink? When did we see you a stranger and take you in, or without clothes and clothe you? When did we see you sick, or in prison, and visit you?" And the King will answer them, "Truly I tell you, whatever you did for one of the least of these brothers and sisters of mine, you did for me."

—Matthew 25:35–40

Therefore, since we also have such a large cloud of witnesses surrounding us, let us lay aside every hindrance and the sin that so easily ensnares us. Let us run with endurance the race that lies before us, keeping our eyes on Jesus, the pioneer and perfecter of our faith. For the joy that lay before him, he endured the cross, despising the shame, and sat down at the right hand of the throne of God. For consider him who endured such hostility from sinners against himself, so that you won't grow weary and give up.

—Hebrews 12:1–3

We are, not metaphorically but in very truth, a Divine work of art, something that God is making, and therefore something with which He will not be satisfied until it has a certain character.[1]

—C. S. LEWIS

My lips will glorify you because your faithful love is better than life.

—PSALM 63:3

CHAPTER 13

CERTAINTY HINDERS GROWTH

WANTING GOD MORE

There are people I know who are peaceful and content in their faith journey most of the time. They don't seem to have control issues with God. They have the same posture as the song "Que Sera, Sera (Whatever Will Be, Will Be)."[2] Let tomorrow be tomorrow. As you have probably noticed throughout this book, I'm not one of these people. While I do not consider myself a futurist, I prefer to know what's coming ahead of time. No surprises. Please don't get me wrong. I am confident about my ultimate salvation in Christ, through God's grace, and certain that nothing can separate me "from the love of God that is in Christ Jesus our Lord."[3]

But in my day-to-day life, I'm more like the psalmist. His words might as well be mine: "My eyes grow weary looking for what you have promised; I ask, 'When will you comfort me?'"[4] Using the words of Paul in Romans 8:22, I groan with the whole creation with "labor pains" for God's justice to come in this world, for the end of violence, for a breakthrough to happen in my life and in the lives of others, and for my sanctification to finally happen in its fullness.

I struggle with bearing uncertainty about how my life and faith journey will pan out. My struggle also shows up in the little things. I want the certainty that, by this time tomorrow, God will eliminate my awful tendency to spew out four-letter words when I get super angry or stub my toe. Old habits from my time in the South Bronx die hard. Believe me, I have prayed for this!

Sure, some level of certainty is needed for us to feel safe and enable us to operate in our daily lives. But Jesus made it clear that his followers must be willing to bear with uncertainty.[5] I've heard people say, "I am afraid that if I surrender my life to God, he will send me to be a missionary in Africa." First of all, this statement makes Africa sound like a terrible place to live. It is not. I've been to a few of the countries in Africa, know people who live there, and it's wonderful! But I get the sentiment behind this statement.

We all have "that place" we hope God will never send us, the cross we do not want to bear. We are anxious, thinking that if we surrender our faith journey to God, he will stretch us, take us through seasons of suffering, take away our favorite comforts of life, and expect us to do hard things—like loving our neighbor and praying for our enemies.

If I demand certainty from God over every detail of my life and journey, I am simultaneously buying into the lie that I cannot be fully dependent on our good, faithful, and loving Father.

Maybe if I knew where my provision was going to come from, or whether or not I am going to experience some terrible loss or disease, or if my Christian efforts are guaranteed to be fruitful, I could do something to alter the parts of the future I do not like. I could then pray to God to see if there is another way (like Jesus did in Gethsemane), or at least prepare my heart for what is to come. It's so hard for me to let the future be the future. It's so hard to let go of my craving for certainty.

Yet, I know my insistence on certainty hinders my spiritual growth on the faith journey. It disrupts my faith walk with Jesus, limits my relationship with the Father, and closes my ears to the prompting of the Holy Spirit. If I demand certainty from God over every detail of my life and journey, I am simultaneously buying into the lie that I cannot be fully dependent on our good, faithful, and loving Father. Doing so is akin to joining Adam and Eve as they stood in the Garden of Eden believing the serpent's lies: "Did God really say . . . ?"[6]

That is perhaps the biggest reason I have written this book: to remind myself, and you, that depending on God is the *only* source of certainty we can truly count on.

Wanting God More: Going from Control to Commitment

As they were traveling on the road someone said to him, "I will follow you wherever you go."

—Luke 9:57

The person who said this to Jesus was probably eager to follow the great teacher and miracle maker. But they likely didn't realize that Jesus was not only homeless, but his path was also headed toward a shameful death on an excruciatingly painful cross. If there was any certainty for Jesus in his life, it was that he came to die to himself so that others might live in him. Rather than being filled with fear and anxiety, Jesus was filled with fiery passion for his journey: "I have a baptism to undergo, and how it consumes me until it is finished!"[7] That is the passion I pray God will grow in our hearts.

There is such a thing as believing without commitment. Faith takes our beliefs to another level, and Jesus knows that about us. In John 2:23–25, we're told,

While [Jesus] was in Jerusalem during the Passover Festival, many believed in his name when they saw the signs he was doing. Jesus, however, would not entrust himself to them, since he knew them all and because he did not need anyone to testify about man; for he himself knew what was in man.

What is in "man" or humanity? A tendency to believe yet fail to commit. Jesus knows we tend to believe, but when things get hard, we are tempted to bolt. Jesus understands our human condition. He knows our hearts; he knows we struggle. To trust or have faith in something requires sacrifice from us. We're told in this passage that people began to trust Jesus, but Jesus did not trust them.

The word for *trust* in Greek is *pisteuō* (pronounced *pist-yoo-o*). Doesn't that sound like "peace to you"? This word essentially refers to a conviction that something you believe is true, reliable, and trustworthy enough for you to act despite any present uncertainty. Not just believing, but putting our whole weight behind trusting something, acting with commitment, and not holding back. This word was important to all of the gospel writers, but John used it more than the others. Luke used it eight times, Matthew ten, Mark fourteen, but John, in this gospel alone, used it ninety-six times! John is a short gospel calling us to a deeper way of believing, so the heavy usage is even more noteworthy.

For example, in John 4, we read the story of Jesus healing an official's son who was about to die. The story presents a progression of faith, a picture of how it begins and how it grows. A man came to Jesus believing Jesus could do for him something of great importance. He was a "royal official," someone accustomed to making things happen by his authority. If you look at the Greek word behind this title, *basilikós*, anyone familiar with the language would have understood that the man had power; he was a man "belonging to a king." The term was used for someone who worked for the king, and considering the area Jesus was in, this man very likely worked for the feared Herod Antipas. John the Baptist confronted King Herod for marrying his half brother's wife. Herod's response, influenced by his wife, was to have John the Baptist beheaded in prison and his head brought on a platter to Herod's wife.[8]

The high-ranking official came to Jesus in his hour of most desperate need. Imagine someone of such stature leaving his sick son behind and traveling a long distance to humble himself and ask for a miracle from Jesus of Nazareth, the man everyone was talking about. That must have taken great courage. This man came to Jesus fully committed, knowing he had no other place to go. Everyone would see him humble himself, and he didn't care. His commitment overtook his fears.

As I have already mentioned, my own commitment to faith came shortly after I turned forty years old. I believed in God and that Jesus's life, death, and resurrection were real, but I did not put my faith in him. I tried doing life my way, only to make a huge mess and hurt many people, including my children and myself. It was at my hour of deepest need when I recognized I had to humble myself if I wanted my life to change. I needed to take a step of faith.

The royal official's step of faith was believing that Jesus could do the impossible: save his dying son's life. As a mother and grandmother, a chaplain, and a pastor, I know this type of desperation. I have prayed like this for my son during his season of drug addiction. For seven years, I did not know if my son would live. His life hung on the line, and only a miracle of God could have restored him as he is today.

I have joined families in petitioning for the healing of a dying child. We all deal with many stressful situations, but nothing comes close to the stress of the impending death of a child, our own or not.

Jesus's response to the royal official's humble petition was rather unwelcoming and seems to be addressed to both the man and the bystanders: "Unless you people see signs and wonders, you will not believe."[9] Jesus is making a statement about humanity, about us. Some of us, especially some of us who think of ourselves as science-minded, want to see concrete proof. We will not grow in our faith unless we see proof of what God can do. Again, we seek certainty. Although Jesus's statement was spoken in a matter-of-fact way, and maybe with a little bit of a rebuke, the royal officer didn't let that stop him.

The man's commitment to faith was evident as he implored Jesus to act by declaring publicly his full dependence on Jesus's power to heal. He was certain his son would die if Jesus did not come with him.

He was certain.

He was wrong.

Jesus once again responded differently than expected. He answered the royal official's pleading with a command and a promise: "Go ... your son will live."[10] Jesus did not go with him, but he did the miracle at the very moment he spoke the promise. This reminds me of the language of Genesis 1, when God said, "Let there be . . . . And it was so."[11] Conversely, I am reminded of doubting Thomas, who refused to put his faith in Jesus unless he saw proof of his resurrection. Jesus's response to Thomas was to state how "blessed are those who have not seen and yet believe."[12] Indeed, blessed or happy is the person who has faith even when all evidence points to the contrary. The chasm between our faith and God's faithfulness is huge. But, here again, God is faithful to help us. Jesus loved Thomas enough to show himself and allow Thomas to touch his resurrected body and

If you struggle with trusting God with your future, you're not alone, and you are not a failure as a Christian.

examine the wounds he endured before death. "My Lord and my God!" Thomas exclaimed.[13]

Oh, the mercy of Jesus. Even as I type this, it warms my heart. This is what he does for you and me. If you are stuck in any stage of faith, perhaps craving certainty or demanding Jesus to prove himself to you in his mercy, he still does what is in accordance with his will. His desires for us, for his creation, and his dedication to his mission of salvation, are greater than our thirst for him. He responds to us, just as he responded to the royal official and the apostle Thomas, with an imperative to act on the faith we already have, and a promise to help us endure. What do you think it took for that man to leave Jesus, the miracle worker, the one who could save his son's life, and start walking back home fifteen, eighteen, or twenty miles, believing his son was healed? How much faith did he need? Just enough faith to take the first step and keep walking.

Some First Steps

Years ago, I was having issues with my blood sugar levels. I experienced nausea, fatigue, dizziness, shakiness, and a slew of other symptoms as a result of low blood sugar levels. I craved sugary foods and drinks and would run to them, believing they were the solution to my problems. My doctor explained that I was experiencing the symptoms of hypoglycemia. She educated me on the roller coaster I was putting myself on every day, starting with my orange juice and sugary cereal for breakfast and continuing with my affinity for regular cola as a companion to every meal. For an antidote, my doctor recommended I start the day by eating more protein and fibrous foods and switching my cola to unsweetened iced green tea. Sure enough, my sugar cravings were subdued and, with time, so was my blood sugar roller coaster. I had to correct how I fed myself to change my body's cravings.

If you struggle with trusting God with your future, you're not alone, and you are not a failure as a Christian. The spiritual practices I have highlighted in this book (though there are many more for us to choose from) are my way of silencing the craving of my broken heart for certainty. They are the spiritual "protein and fiber" that has a lasting effect on the health of my faith journey. God uses even our most uncertain seasons as powerful opportunities for us to experience his presence and grow our trust in him.

Jon Bloom put it this way in his book *Not by Sight*:

> *The uncertainty we are faced with is only apparent uncertainty. Our future and our provision and our ultimate triumph are certain to God. He has all the foreknowledge, power, and resources necessary to insure these . . .*[14]

Unfortunately, I have learned that knowing this as truth is not enough. We need to practice letting go of our craving for certainty and security, because the more we feed the craving, the greater our fears, doubts, bitterness, and anxiety will become. We get rigid, less graceful, controlling, and at times abusive. It injures us on our journey of faith, and it threatens our commitment. The bottom line is that dependence on certainty hinders our growth in Christ.

We might think it takes extraordinary faith to move from control to commitment, but all we need is enough faith to take one step in the direction God is calling us. Then, take the next one. You already have what is needed to take each step.

Remember the things that we have learned together so far and be encouraged:

1. Your journey matters to God. He has desires for you, and you can know them.

2. God knows how your story will go, but you don't (and can't). Therefore, you must give up the craving for *control* of your life and embrace *commitment* to God.

3. Instead of following your own formulas, you can build a *relationship* with Jesus. Instead of being passive, you can *actively* surrender, and this means walking with him in trust.

    We might think it takes extraordinary faith to move from control to commitment, but all we need is enough faith to take one step in the direction God is calling us.

4. There will be many obstacles on your journey of faith, but God will be with you as you face them.

5. There will be disorientation on your journey of faith, but God has given you tools to keep you steady and will help you to continue moving forward. Also, he can handle your questions, so you shouldn't be afraid to ask.

6. You may mess up on your journey of faith, but God has given you a way to recover. Remember that Jesus paid the price for your sin. Repent and confess your sins to him, and turn to trusted fellow believers for help in walking in holiness.

7. Godless shame lies. You were made in the image of God, saved from the penalty of sin by grace through Jesus, and he wants you to walk in freedom.

8. You will be tempted to compare yourself to others, and to rely on your own expectations of how your life should go. Both of these temptations are a trap. Instead, seek to actively trust God and *his* plans for your life.

9. Loving Jesus means obeying him. You must be willing to let go of even the *good* things in your life if he tells you to do so. He always wants the *best* for you.

10. You cannot walk the journey of faith alone. Seek to live your life in community with fellow believers.

11. Ambiguity is inevitable. But God does not change, and he will be with you in your times of vulnerability. Increasing your thirst for God will help you find peace in this troubled and confusing world.

12. Suffering is part of the journey. But you can face it with a joyful attitude, a surrendered will, a trusting posture, and a dependent heart. The God of comfort will comfort you and help you endure.

And here are the spiritual practices you've learned that will help you apply the concepts we've discussed:

1. Practicing the presence of Jesus.
2. Simplicity and slowing.
3. Worship.
4. Prayer.
5. Spiritual direction and discernment.
6. Truth-telling and confession/self-examination.
7. Gratitude.
8. Examen and journaling.
9. Stewardship and generosity.
10. Holy communion and prayer partners.
11. Submission and detachment/rest.
12. Meditation and service.

And at the end of this chapter, we'll learn about:

13. Teachability and humility.

These principles and practices are tools that you can return to again and again on your faith journey.

Tightrope Walking

Once we're walking in faith, thriving in our faith requires a deeper thirst for God, a deeper commitment to obedience and to believing in his promises. Sometimes our circumstances feel manageable, and it feels easy to have faith because we can sense how things will likely work out and can easily recognize God's actions. It might be a situation like when a tightrope walker faces a tightrope that is not too far off the ground. In those moments, it doesn't seem hard to commit to Jesus and trust him more, for if things don't happen as we expect, we can always just hop off the tightrope. Sometimes that's as far as we go with our faith.

Other times our challenges are bigger. We might find ourselves in a situation when "solid ground" is way down below, but we're tethered by something. We are trusting in our finances, past successes, current wisdom, or our network of friends. Although our challenges create anxiety for us, we have a backup plan, something to hold on to other than Jesus.

One Sunday morning before I preached my sermon, a woman approached me and asked me to pray for her ailing mother. The woman was a doctor, and she had been trying to save her mother, using all of her energy, education, influence, and finances. But nothing was working. She was in tears and clearly desperate. There was no "tethered line" for her anymore, so her faith reached a higher level. Maybe that's where you are today. You struggle to commit to God more fully, but you also have nothing else to hold on to.

That royal officer had nowhere else to go but where Jesus sent him. Perhaps he walked home feeling like a failure. He walked all the way to Cana to humiliate himself before Jesus, and then he walked home with a command and a promise. His son could have still died. Perhaps he felt like a fool for believing and trusting in Jesus. I imagine the torment he felt on that walk home—the torment we might feel if we were on a very high tightrope without any tether.

With eleven Guinness World Records to his name, Nik Wallenda has done world-record tightrope walking with no protection, earning him the title of "King of the High Wire."[15] He was the first to walk across Niagara Falls without a net and without a tether. He walked across a portion of the Grand Canyon. He crossed from one high-rise building to another in Chicago, a unique tightrope walk because it had a 19-degree incline (from 588 to 671 feet), and the wind was roaring that day. If you watch the videos online, you will notice that the walk got harder as he went.

If you're a little afraid of heights, I'll give you a fair warning: this is a tough video to watch. Fifty thousand people were below, watching and wondering if he would make it. Nik said, "You guys watching think I'm crazy, but this is what I was made for." His father spoke to him as he walked, encouraging him, and giving him direction. At one point, his father told him that the wind was about to get stronger, and Nik responded, "It's all good … God is in control." When he reached the solid ground of the rooftop, he exclaimed, "Praise God! To God be the glory!"

Nik has publicly professed his faith in Jesus Christ. While he has trained for his sport and has worked hard to be fit, he knows he cannot control everything that is happening when he is on the tightrope. No one can give him 100 percent certainty that he will make it safely to the other side. Not even the fact that he is a Christian guarantees a specific result.

He is committed to trusting God beyond himself, no matter the outcome. Hebrews 11:1 says, "Now faith is the reality of what is hoped for, the proof of what is not seen." Sometimes we want people to tell us exactly what to do and how to live the journey of faith. We desire to avoid doubts and struggles. We believe that we are growing if we become more certain and fixed in our practices. That could not be further from the truth. For Nik, walking with "man-made" certainty is not enough, as he would likely make foolish mistakes. He walks both in skill and in trust. Having a thirsty faith includes waiting on God to help us while acting on what little he gives us until we know more. "If God is to be God in our lives, we cannot remain in control."[16]

Having a thirsty faith includes waiting on God to help us while acting on what little he gives us until we know more.

God called Abraham to go to a distant land and gave him little information as to what would happen and how things would develop. Abraham went.[17] He accepted God's command and tried to live by doing what God desired, which included making huge sacrifices and living with constant uncertainty.

Likewise, we must tear down our attachment to the idol of certainty in this life. There is something better: God's faithful love. In Psalm 63:3, the psalmist praises God's gracious *hesed*,[18] translated as "faithful love," far above the gift of life. Spiritual maturity is living fully committed to trusting our loving God with all our moments, the highs and the lows, and every step. This broken world needs us to continue growing in our faith and living like Jesus, revealing both his character and his actions.

Right now, you might be giving all you've got to Jesus on the faith journey, and you are surprised to still feel the tension of uncertainty. You feel the pressure of the unknown. You feel the extra pain because you have nowhere else to go. I hope that you have been encouraged.

Remember that the royal official walked back to his son, probably feeling tension, anxiety, and fear the whole way. But Jesus did not wait for him to make it all the way home before giving him the good news. While he was still on his way, the servants came to tell him that his son was alive and well. That must have been an amazing moment of encouragement for him. His obedience, the promise, and the reality coalesced to form breathtaking joy. I'm assuming he ran to see his son—especially as his home came within sight—to see the miracle for himself.

The royal official took many steps of faith, not knowing what would happen, but already the miracle had been put in place by Jesus. The royal official went. He obeyed. He trusted. He thirsted for God's miracle to happen as he walked, demonstrating the beautiful tension between listening to the promise and acting upon it.

When the father realized that his son was healed the very moment Jesus told him it was to happen, he didn't say, "What a coincidence! I happened to visit Jesus, and my son got healed." He could have done that; sometimes we explain away God's miracles in a similar fashion. But he did not. His faith doubled down. Remember, first he believed "what Jesus said,"[19] and then he believed in Jesus.[20] His faith deepened, as did the faith of his whole household. It went to a whole new level.

The Fruit of Faith

Often in our faith journey it's not uncommon to wonder if we are where we're supposed to be or if we're making progress at all. This brings up anxiety for those of us who want to finish well but feel like we're running out of time. The Bible has numerous stories of people who did not finish well, like King Saul, King Jehu, and King Joash.[21] I don't want to be like them! I doubt you do either. But if we commit to walking with Jesus by faith, day by day, step-by-step, with our eyes wide-open to the work he is doing in our lives, he is faithful to produce in and through us good fruit by the power of the Holy Spirit.

God promises that your faith journey will be full of life; it will be fruitful. Fruit is a metaphor used in Scripture for a productive, significant, and successful life. The "fruit" we produce is consistent with God's character. God invites us to imitate him, to act as he does. We "belong to him who was raised from the dead in order that we may bear fruit for God."[22] In John 15, as part of his parting message, Jesus reminds his disciples to remain in him the same way a branch that is attached to a vine is dependent on that vine to bear fruit. God's desire for us is that we bear lasting fruit, and we cannot do it apart from him. Jesus said, "You did not choose me, but I chose you. I appointed you to go and produce fruit and that your fruit should remain."[23] But when we depend on our human-made certainty, we detach ourselves from the vine.

On one of our trips to Peru with the Free Wheelchair Mission,[24] we visited the humble and tiny home of a man who was living alone and could not walk. We did not know what his medical diagnosis was, but it was evident that he suffered from paralysis of his lower body. This meant that he spent most of his time alone in his bed. He was dependent on his family and neighbors to bring him food and provision.

Our group had already delivered wheelchairs that week and had grown more accustomed to the painful stories of people who suffered so much without the gift of mobility. All of us were feeling blessed by the privilege of bringing such wonderful hope to people in need. Despite our experience, when we entered Alberto's hot and humid room, we were instantly shocked.

Sitting in his tiny bed, Alberto raised high his hands and proceeded to loudly praise God for the visitors. I translated his words as quickly as they came out of his mouth, speaking with as much intensity as Alberto. He wasn't thanking God for the wheelchair. He was passionately grateful for God's faithful love and the presence of fellow believers. The team was overwhelmed by his joy. The fruit of faith in this man's life was incredible. He had been waiting for years for this promised gift, not knowing when it would come. Day by day, Alberto had to deal with the challenges of paralysis, including regularly soiling himself and having to wait for days for someone to clean up his body and bed. We came to bless him. But Alberto blessed us.

He taught us that thirsting for God is better than wanting for anything in this life. Like David, Alberto's lips glorified God because his faithful love is better than life.[25] Alberto wanted God more than he wanted his wheelchair. Imagine that! God desires our trust more than anything else, even more than our "correct" beliefs. The antidote to our craving for certainty is a nurtured, increased thirst for God—we must want to have a thirst like David's, like Alberto's. In tears, many of our team walked out of the room to collect themselves.

The antidote to our craving for certainty is a nurtured, increased thirst for God

Alberto's faith was so strong and evident, it was as though we walked into the most beautiful garden of flowers with joyful song.

Whatever time we have on this earth must be used to know the height, depth, width, and length of the love of God. If we walk in his love and release our journey of faith to Jesus, we learn to turn away from entrusting ourselves to powerless things or lesser things. This results in wisdom, gratitude, and joy. We increase our concern for the well-being of others because that is what is in his heart.

Identify the "certainty" idol you tend to rely upon. Prayerfully release control of it. Tell a trusted friend to pray with you and hold you accountable. Write about it in your journal or write a letter to God. Be specific about what you will trust to God's loving hands instead of your own.

Faithfulness to the faithful one is better than any other "certainty" that this world can offer. May God bless you as you move from control to commitment!

SPIRITUAL PRACTICES: TEACHABILITY AND HUMILITY

You cannot learn if you don't humble yourself. Teachability and humility are twin practices that work well together. The spiritual practice of teachability involves opening ourselves to learn from God and receive fresh guidance from the Holy Spirit. It does not just entail collecting more information; rather, it allows the information to transform us and move us from our wrong ideas, opinions, and perspectives. Jesus calls us to be his disciples, his learners. We must be in a constant posture of learning and receiving from the one who is wisdom himself. There is no end to what we can learn from Jesus through his sanctification process. To practice teachability is to be willing to change anything Jesus calls us to change and try anything Jesus calls us to consider, to be not a lifelong learner, but an eternal learner. Humility is at the core of teachability.

To practice humility is to practice becoming like Jesus, as Paul calls us to do in Philippians 2. Jesus gave in every area of his life, and he led us into life through his vulnerability. Andrew Murray wrote that "true humility comes when before God we see ourselves as nothing, have put aside self, and let God be all."[26] To be humble is to make our motivation God's glory and nothing else. It is to think of ourselves less and make the needs of others a higher priority. The fruit of humility is the company we keep. We get to walk with Jesus, who was perfectly humble in every way. Teachability and humility are the postures that help us want more of God. It doesn't get better than that!

The Process

To practice teachability, choose a passage that you find difficult to understand, and study it with the help of a few commentaries or online study tools. Listen to sermons on the passage or ask your pastor to help you with it. Reflect on what you have learned from Jesus but have not yet applied to your life. Is there one thing you can implement to learn the lesson deeper? Take inventory of your propensity to think you know enough to have complete certainty in any area of your faith journey. Ask God to help you release that false certainty to him and accept the vulnerable position of a student, that he may help you grow.

To practice humility, read and reflect on Philippians 2 and consider all that Jesus did that was humble. Try applying one of his actions to your own life. For example, what if you did not "exploit" the position you hold at work or home or in your community, and put down your titles and privileges instead for the benefit of others? Make space for someone who does not have access to your privilege. Serve someone today in a small or big manner. Consider the sources of your pride. Ask God to help you find humility in this area of your life by showing you more of his deep love for you.

Prompting Scriptures

Let no one deceive himself. If anyone among you thinks he is wise in this age, let him become a fool so that he can become wise.

—1 Corinthians 3:18

He leads the humble in what is right and teaches them his way.

—Psalm 25:9

For there is nothing hidden that will not be revealed, and nothing concealed that will not be brought to light. If anyone has ears to hear, let him listen.

—Mark 4:22–23

It is from him that you are in Christ Jesus, who became wisdom from God for us—our righteousness, sanctification, and redemption—in order that, as it is written: Let the one who boasts, boast in the Lord.

—1 Corinthians 1:30–31

Therefore, as God's chosen ones, holy and dearly loved, put on compassion, kindness, humility, gentleness, and patience, bearing with one another and forgiving one another if anyone has a grievance against another. Just as the Lord has forgiven you, so you are also to forgive. Above all, put on love, which is the perfect bond of unity.

—Colossians 3:12–14

He said to them, "It is not for you to know times or periods that the Father has set by his own authority. But you will receive power when the Holy Spirit has come on you, and you will be my witnesses in Jerusalem, in all Judea and Samaria, and to the ends of the earth."

—Acts 1:7–8

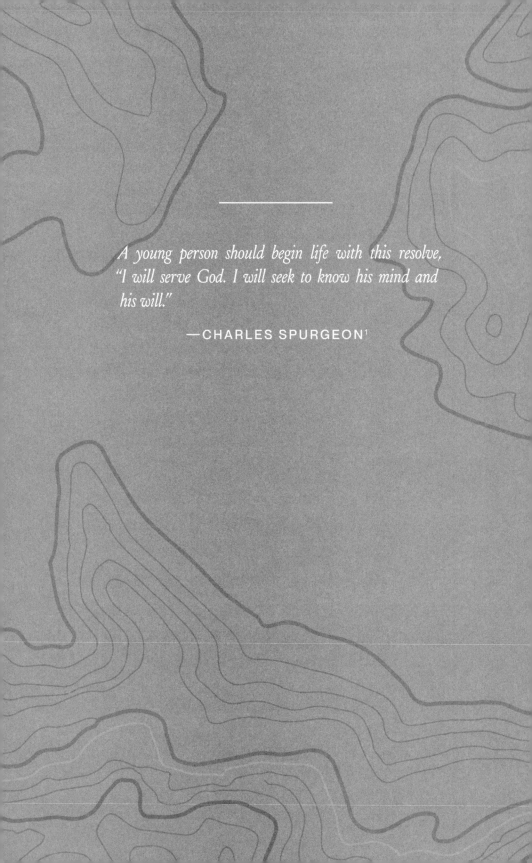

A young person should begin life with this resolve, "I will serve God. I will seek to know his mind and his will."

—CHARLES SPURGEON[1]

CHAPTER 14

THE OUTWARD JOURNEY

A COMMISSION

Three people I knew died in the span of a few weeks, all unexpected. At eighty-two years of age, Irene had the most engaging smile, the kind that lights up a room. The last time I saw her, she sat across from me during lunch at the memory care facility where my mom lived. We were laughing and enjoying ourselves as much as possible, despite the communication difficulties that come with advanced Alzheimer's disease. Then suddenly, Irene threw up her lunch, and we all motioned for her nurse to come. The head nurse quickly whisked Irene away, leaving behind a pile of cloth napkins on the floor over the smelly mess. That was the last time I saw Irene. Just a few days later, she took her last breath.

Kristin was only thirty-eight years old. I did not know her well, but my stepdaughter Jennifer went to school with her, and they remained friends into adulthood. She died in her sleep. In shock, her husband tried to bring her back to life but did not succeed. While trying to minister to Jen's sadness, praying for God to give her and her friend's family comfort, all I could think of was how unpredictable life can be.

Janice Freeman Neuble had a gifted and powerful voice. She was regularly invited to sing at our church, and when she was on stage, you couldn't help but get drawn into her heart. She pulled people from their deepest selves with the tears of her soul. Despite fighting cancer and lupus for years, she seemed able to manufacture energy out of sheer willpower. But one day, amid a bout of extreme pneumonia, a blood clot traveled to her heart and stopped the music. Her husband was left behind to care for their daughter. Janice was thirty-three.

I was not close to any of these women, yet their deaths in rapid succession were a collective wake-up call, a loud alarm clock to my distracted soul. They increased the volume of God's voice. He was calling me to increase my commitment to him.

Chances are that you also experienced a sense of urgency by simply reading their stories. Stories like these remind us that we are not guaranteed tomorrow. Life can end instantly via a car accident, illness, airplane crash, fall, or choking on a piece of food ... I don't mean to be depressing here, but our days are numbered. When our time is up, it's up.[2] We don't know the hour or the cause, but we all know that moment of transition is coming. We cannot live as though tomorrow is guaranteed. It's not.

The time to actively surrender and commit our life to the Lord is now—always now.

> *So I will bless you as long as I live; at your name, I will lift up my hands.*
>
> —Psalm 63:4

As I mentioned earlier in the book, every year I seek the Holy

Spirit's help in selecting a word and a Bible passage to reflect on over the next 365 days. The practice started shortly after I surrendered my life to Jesus and accepted his gift of salvation. I do not remember who recommended the idea, but it has become a beautiful rhythm of faith practice for me. My word for 2019, the year these three women died, was "listen," and my passage was Proverbs 4:20–21: "Pay attention to my words; listen closely to my sayings. Don't lose sight of them; keep them within your heart." In the book of Proverbs, a father instructs his son about wisdom and her[3] ways.

Throughout the book of Proverbs, an option is put before the reader to choose the straight path of wisdom or the crooked path of foolishness. The book ends by praising wisdom in action, this time personified as a "wife of noble character."[4] The writer calls us to pursue wisdom and listen to her voice.

By February 2019, as I daily reflected on the word and passage during my prayer and Bible study time, I sensed that God was whispering to me, "Time is short."

A call from God sounds like a straightforward thing, right? But what I want to emphasize now is that calls from God can take a long time to fulfill, but when the time comes, we must act.

The Lord got my attention. The sudden death of these women increased my motivation to reorganize my life, time, and priorities to finally write this, my first book. As I said before, eighteen years ago I sensed the Lord calling me to write and teach. It has never been a dream of mine to write books, and English is my second language. Yet, the whisper did not leave me; rather, it was confirmed multiple times over the next year by various sources and people. A call from God sounds like a straightforward thing, right? But what I want to emphasize now is that calls from God can take a long time to fulfill, but when the time comes, we must act.

At first, I downplayed the call, thinking it was a strange thought.

But this strange thought came with six book titles or subjects to teach about. I kept it to myself and continued praying about it for a year. During that time, many circumstances pointed me back to this nagging feeling that God was calling me to become an author. Finally, I told my husband, Jim, and asked him to pray with me about it. To my surprise, he encouraged me to pursue the next steps. My biggest challenge was that I had not yet read the entirety of the Bible. In my first year of reading it, I skipped a few of the minor prophets.

To speed up my learning, I joined a women's Bible study group. It was wonderful, except that they only studied one book a year, and it would take years before I knew enough to teach. The Bible has sixty-six books! That is when my friend Matt Olthoff recommended that I attend seminary. As I have shared with you, it took me two years to be accepted as a "Special Student" at Fuller Seminary. I went there to get educated to write books, and God equipped me to do so by transforming me into a pastor.

If I had known it would take so many years and a whole lot of life to get here, I may not have taken a single step. I often felt like a failure and was worried that I had let God down or frustrated him to the point that he would send someone else to complete the task he had set out for me. Several times I quit the project, either because I felt discouraged, overwhelmed, and exhausted, or because I was worried that the work was fueled by selfish ambition or my childhood desire to be seen. I was terrified to leave the good, successful, and familiar to embark on a foggy road.

What you have in your hands is a product of my own journey of letting go of the craving for certainty. The ideas for this book had been ruminating in my mind and keyboard for years. Thousands of words were poured out as wonderful, only to be discarded as useless a few weeks later, or sometimes soon after a good night's sleep. Numerous developmental editors and frame writers worked with me to give form to the fire that was burning in my heart, only for me to tear it apart with the knife of fear. Eighteen years of research, part-time writing, and telling my family and friends that God called me to write a book ended with a decision. God made it clear it was time. Inspired by God's "time is short" reminder, I committed.

Satan seeks to kill things even before they are born; to make our short time shorter. Pharaoh tried to kill Moses well before he had the opportunity to grow up and be used by God to set the Israelites free. Joseph was sold into slavery years before he provided food and safety for all his father's family in the land of Egypt. The devil tempted Jesus in the wilderness well before the Holy Spirit sent his disciples to all the corners of the earth to share the good news of salvation through Christ. Whatever we set our mind to do together with the Lord will be fiercely opposed by God's enemy. We must commit, sometimes with the help of others.

Three other women encouraged me to stay committed. The first two women simply reached out to me, saying the Lord put it in their hearts to pray for me. They did not know why or what to pray for, so for two months, we prayed for God's wisdom over my life. The third woman was my dear friend Sandy Almquist. Twice a month, Sandy and I connected by phone to debrief a few of my sermons. She used to do this in person, but we continued with the practice even after her family moved to Tennessee. Before we started our sermon review, Sandy said, "Inés, I must tell you something the Holy Spirit has put in my heart. I don't know if this will make any sense to you, but here it goes. It is time!"

"It Is Time."

As I look back now, I believe God was reminding me that the time is always now to actively surrender more of myself to him and embrace the uncharted journey ahead. No matter what happened yesterday, or what is coming tomorrow, this very moment is precious. We can open our eyes to see God's presence, our souls to thirst for more of him, and our hearts to love as he does.

As you can see, I've been on a long journey, slowly writing a book I am convinced God called me to write for you. I've been walking in obedience and struggling. After years of experiencing the faithfulness of God, I have no reason to doubt his call. It wasn't doubt that made this hard for me; it was fear. Fear of failure. Fear of rejection. Fear of public opinion. But fear has no air to breathe when time is up. Boldness kicks in, and a sense of urgency pushes through the interruptions. I needed the laser focus, and now that I have written the book, I know why.

Choose

One of the greatest gifts God has given us is agency, the ability to act autonomously and freely. God gave us the choice to obey or not, to trust him or not. In the Garden, humanity lived in perfect harmony with the Creator until they used this remarkable gift to choose against God and disobey.[5] I don't need to enumerate the slew of problems human choice produces when it is driven by pride, greed, and a thirst for power and control. I believe you know them well. But when our human choice is driven by a thirst to glorify the one true God of the Bible, the result is life-giving to ourselves and to others.

When our human choice is driven by a thirst to glorify the one true God of the Bible, the result is life-giving to ourselves and to others.

We are blessed to be a blessing.

The moment you surrendered your life to Jesus and accepted him as your Savior, he gifted you to serve him in his kingdom, for his glory, and the benefit of others. You received the gift of the Holy Spirit, through whom God equips you appropriately and specifically for the good works he has prepared ahead of time for you to do. God's gift transforms you into a gift to others. Jesus's death and resurrection is proof that God is much more powerful than anything you fear or are anxious about.

As Paul said in his letter to the Ephesian church believers, we must "pay careful attention, then, to how [we] walk—not as unwise people but as wise—making the most of [exploiting] the time, because the days are evil."[6] Paul reminds us that we must "exploit" the moment to the full. The Greek word behind exploit (*exagorazō*) refers to buying or redeeming something.

Redeem the time!

What a beautiful picture for us. We can spend our limited time worrying about stuff, trying to control circumstances, anxious about not having certainty and being frustrated by unreasonable expectations. We can pay the high cost of control, which tightens our grip on circumstances, isolates us from others, steals our hope, and worsens our problems. We can blame, throw a huge tantrum, or hide in our addictions. Or we can calm our anxiety moment by moment by opening our eyes wide to the wonder of Jesus and redeeming every moment in Christ. We do not have full "authority, power or influence over events, behaviors, situations or people."[7] Still, we do have the ability to commit our attention to the power and grace that comes from the Holy Spirit.

We who trust and follow Jesus can gobble up every opportunity to expose the darkness and participate in God's redemptive mission.

Increasing our sense of urgency is important, especially when we consider all the distractions, addictions, attachments, and false idols that vie for our attention and time. At a minimum, we all carry our computer, calendar, camera, Bible, games, banking, and a whole host of other things in a technological unit that fits into the palm of our hand; and too many of us are always staring at it! But the world around us is intensifying in darkness. The favor toward Christians in the West is waning, at least partly due to the increasing clash between secular and Christian values, politicization of faith, a constant stream of failures by spiritual leaders, perverted biblical teaching, and hypocritical behavior. We must choose obedience to God above all else.

It's not like Christian commitment is something we only do once and then never veer off the right path from that point forward. Every morning, we get to resolve again as we fix our eyes on Jesus. We can commit at lunchtime, and again at that pesky middle-of-the-night anxious hour, and let God feed our soul with his truth. With the help of the Holy Spirit and God's Word, we choose to trust God rather than test him when we're tempted to sin. We pray to Jesus to help us with our doubt when the gospel of Jesus Christ shocks us again. We resolve when we suffer, for pain squeezes to the surface fake commitment. We commit in confession and tears because we know how human we are, and how prone we are to wander. We preach to our soul when it finds itself dejected and in turmoil to keep our hope in God and praise him as our Savior and our Lord.

> *Let your eyes look forward; fix your gaze straight ahead. Carefully consider the path for your feet, and all your ways will be established. Don't turn to the right or to the left; keep your feet away from evil.*

—Proverbs 4:25–27

The faith journey begins the moment we say yes to Jesus as our Lord and Savior, and it continues forever in eternity. Jesus laid down his life for us, and in response, we lay down ours for him. We die to self and allow him to rebuild us fully into the image bearers we were intended to be from the beginning.[8] As we fix our eyes on Jesus, set our minds on heavenly things, and pattern our lives on Jesus himself,

Jesus continues the work of transformation, from glory to glory.[9]

There is a Japanese tradition of repairing pots with a resin infused with gold called kintsugi, which means "golden joinery." It refers to the art of fixing a broken ceramic pot in such a way that the cracks are highlighted by the golden resin instead of being hidden. The ceramic piece ends up looking more beautiful than before it was broken. This is a beautiful picture of what Jesus does in us throughout the journey of faith if we commit to him and let him into every aspect of our lives.

The favor toward Christians in the West is waning, at least partly due to the increasing clash between secular and Christian values, politicization of faith, a constant stream of failures by spiritual leaders, perverted biblical teaching, and hypocritical behavior. We must choose obedience to God above all else.

It amazes me how the Lord works together all things "for the good of those who love [him], who are called according to his purpose,"[10] even if we cannot sense it happening. He loves us more than we could imagine. He helps us "finish the race."

Aside from our experience of time and the advancement of technology, nothing else seems linear, not even the telling of our stories. Our journey might resemble that of Philip: following God's prompting, lacking foresight of the effect of our obedience.[11] Philip was called to leave the big revival in Samaria and go down a dusty road. His obedience transformed one man's life and, thereafter, an entire continent.

I wrote this book not knowing how your life would be affected but trusting that God can use even my obedience to bless and encourage you. I hope you will find inspiration in this book to celebrate the unique journey of faith Jesus has called you to live, and to remain committed to it. Additionally, I wrote this book to praise the Lord, to lift up my hands and bless his name, to sing of his goodness and faithfulness in my life so that you'd get to know the Lord whom you walk with, whom you are committed to, evermore. And so that you'd thirst for him without ceasing.

What a difference from the little girl that once stood on the roof of her concrete house in the Puerto Rican jungle, hoping to go to heaven and escape this earth. Then, all I was thinking about was myself. Oh, how the Lord has changed me, for now I wish to remain and, like Paul, "continue with all of you for your progress and joy in the faith."[12]

As I write this, I am praying for you. Maybe you know about Jesus, or believe and follow him, but have not actively surrendered your life to him. He is eager to receive you. The Creator is doing a "Divine work of art" in you. Every day is an opportunity to actively surrender more to his faithfulness.

You have done everything as far as you can—the wind is blowing, and your legs are probably wobbly. You may be experiencing uncertainty in your finances, a broken relationship, a scary health diagnosis, a painful loss, or an intense spiritual battle. All of these stressors will prompt you to seek certainty by trusting in things other than God.

Embrace the reality that the faith journey is uncharted (at least to us), and that our sovereign God has good desires for his children, including you and me.

But throughout this book I have encouraged you to embrace the reality that the faith journey is uncharted (at least to us), and that our sovereign God has good desires for his children, including you and me. I have recommended spiritual practices designed to help you increase your awareness of God's presence, purpose, and guidance, and decrease your craving for certainty and control. I have encouraged you to walk with Jesus on your uncharted journey, with wide-open eyes to see him at work by the power of the Holy Spirit. Together, we have reflected on God's sovereignty, mercy, justice, and faithfulness, through my personal story as well as those of biblical characters. All of this is to remind you that the Lord wants your commitment, and time is of the essence. Time is short!

You and I are part of God's redemption plan. He gives us new mercies every morning,[13] so if you fall, remember that you can get back up and stay on the path. No more waiting. No more shrinking. Someone's life may depend on it.

What if you believed this? Whose life might you enrich by your willingness? Whose life is waiting on you to model faithfulness?

If you feel God is calling you to do something, to be something, do it. Be it. Believe me, I know how hard it is to discern if it is God's calling or something we have made up. I know the doubts. I know the fears. I know the attacks that come every time you get serious about doing it. But do not let any of it stop you. The greater the calling, the greater the struggle.

Give birth to what God has put in your heart

For many of us, too much of our Christian journey is spent oppressing ourselves with worry and anxiety about the things we cannot control. The more we recognize our freedom in Christ, the more eager we are to serve one another with love. We are free to work for the good of all.

Do not let the enemy win the battle. Connect with faithful brothers and sisters to help you discern, then find a way to impress in your mind how essential it is that you push through all the obstacles. Lean on the love of Jesus and the power of the Holy Spirit to guide you. Let the unimportant things drop, maybe even a few important things too. Do what it takes. Start the journey and give birth to what God has put in your heart. Bring it to life by his power. Offer it to God and give it to the world.

My encouragement to you today is to take one more step toward Jesus. As the writer of Hebrews reminds us:

Since we also have such a large cloud of witnesses surrounding us, let us lay aside every hindrance and the sin that so easily ensnares us. Let us run with endurance the race that lies before us, keeping our eyes on Jesus, the pioneer and perfecter of our faith. For the joy that lay before him, he endured the cross, despising the shame, and sat down at the right hand of the throne of God. For consider him who endured such hostility from sinners against himself, so that you won't grow weary and give up.

—Hebrews 12:1–3

Oh, how wonderful it will be to finish our race well, to hear the words of our loving Father: "Well done, my good and faithful servant." That day will come, provided we daily celebrate our unique, imperfect journey of faith and trust Jesus to be our constant Savior. An honest faith journey is as brilliant as the sun, generously supporting life. Living out of God's calling and releasing our journey of faith to others will reveal that our relationship with Jesus is everything!

Go, my friend! Trust in Jesus a little more today than you did yesterday. Our time on earth is indeed short; our faith journey is for eternity. May we spend it rejoicing together with the great cloud of witnesses—including Abuelita!

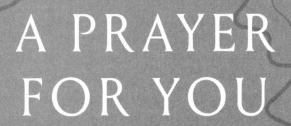

A PRAYER
FOR YOU

Here, at the end of the book, I wanted to close with a prayer. I'm honored to offer this poem by my talented friend Frank Carpenter as a closing meditation. Please feel free to read these words aloud, praying them as your own petition to God.

WHAT WOULD YOU HAVE ME SAY?

A POEM BY FRANK CARPENTER

Lord,
If I am to be your voice,
what would you have me say?
What is the message you would speak
through my words and deeds today?
What wisdom would you offer,
and whom is it directed to?
How would you lead your servant?
I submit my heart to you.
I submit my mind and spirit,
and my whole life willingly.
All I am and have is yours.
Do what you will with me.
Lord,
If I am to be your voice,
what would you have me say?
What is the message you would speak
through my words and deeds today?

ACKNOWLEDGMENTS

It takes a village to write a book. It took me years to research, write, and publish this one, and as I now offer my gratitude, I am sure I will miss someone who contributed to its completion. May the Lord bless each person involved for asking good questions, pushing back, and encouraging me to stay the course. A special thank-you to Dr. John Townsend for dutifully mentoring me for fifteen years on becoming an author. I am also grateful to Dr. Steve Halliday for telling me that I could write. Every writer needs to hear that, and it's especially uplifting coming from someone with your experience. Your red pen is always welcome to my work because I know it comes with your wisdom and kindness. Many thanks to Jessica Snell for helping me edit the earliest manuscript, and to my editor, Kyle Duncan, for sharpening the message. I hold eternal gratitude to my friend Chris Drobish for praying for me through all the hurdles and obstacles, and for celebrating the little victories. Major thanks to my focus reading group for your courage to read a messy pile of words and help me make it an encouraging and edifying read for others. Your incisive reflections and comments made this book better.

To my agent, Esther Fedorkevich, thank you for seeing something in me and my work that I could not, and for taking a leap of faith to publish it with excellence. Your entire team is fabulous!

Muchas gracias to my sweet friend and fiery Puerto Rican sister-in-Christ, mango-hot salsa, Pastor Bianca Olthoff. You spurred me into action and opened doors for me to make this book a resource for the next generation. Blessings!

Much of the content of this book stems from my life and my role at Mariners Church, where I have the privilege of writing, teaching the Bible, and pastoring. Thank you to our pastor emeritus Kenton Beshore for tapping me on the shoulder into my God-given calling to teach God's Word and to Sandy Almquist who encouraged me every step of the way by the power of the Holy Spirit. I am indebted to our senior pastor Eric Geiger, the directional elders and their wives, the staff, and my many friends there who guide my theological reflection and pray for my soul.

Thank you to my team at Trochia Ministries for encouraging me, making things happen while I was on writing sabbatical, and serving our community so well with your gifts, talents, and valuable time.

Also, a special thank-you to my children, Chad, Kayleigh, and Melissa; to my stepdaughters, Jennifer and Christina; to their spouses; and to our grandchildren (our "Smoothie Family"), for teaching me so much and cheering me on in this endeavor. I love you more than words can express. I'm grateful for our lab, Noelle, for being my constant companion as I wrote into the late night.

But to my sweet, fun, and wonderful husband, Jim, I must say a very special thank-you! I could not have done this without you, your support, wisdom, and encouragement. That one time you finished reading a chapter and clapped for me melted my heart. For years you have stood by me as I labored and struggled to get this book published. My office full of books is a testament to your generosity, patience, and kindness. This is our book. It contains more than our story, for it holds our passion for telling the world about the extravagant love of Jesus. Our love is forever.

ENDNOTES

Introduction

1 See, for example, Matthew 19:29, 25:46; Luke 18:29–30; John 3:14–16; Acts 13:48; 1 Timothy 6:12; Romans 6:22–23.
2 John 17:1–3.
3 Romans 11:25; 1 Corinthians 4:1; 14:2; 15:51; Colossians 2:2; 1 Timothy 3:16; see 1 Corinthians 2:7.
4 Spiros Zodhiates, The Complete Word Study Dictionary: New Testament (Chattanooga, TN: AMG Publishers, 2000).
5 Jeremiah 29:10.
6 Jeremiah 29:7.
7 James 1:2.
8 1 Peter 4:12.
9 John 13:16.
10 Joshua 21:45.
11 Hebrews 11:1, emphasis added.
12 See Mark 10:29–30, 2 Timothy 3:10–13, 1 Peter 4:12–13.
13 Proverbs 14:26.
14 See John 15:1–11.
15 John 15:11.

Chapter 1: Seeing the Invisible

1 St. Anslem of Canterbury, "A Prayer by St. Anslem of Canterbury," in Meeting Christ in Prayer, by John E. Sassani and Mary Ann Mclaughlin (Chicago: Loyola Press, 2008).
2 Genesis 2:7.
3 Genesis 1:26–29.
4 Genesis 3:7.
5 Romans 3:23.
6 Paul K. Presson and Victor A. Benassi, "Illusion of Control: A Meta-Analytic Review," Journal of Science Behavior and Personality 11, no. 3 (September 1996): 493–510.
7 Bilal Javed, Abdullah Sarwer, Erik B. Soto, and Zia-ur-Rehman Mashwani, "The Coronavirus (COVID-19) Pandemic's Impact on Mental Health," The International Journal of Health Planning and Management 35, no. 5 (September 2020): 993–96. https://doi.org/10.1002/hpm.3008.
8 Colossians 1:17.

9 Acts 17:28.
10 C.S. Lewis, Mere Christianity, rev. ed., (San Francisco: HarperOne, 1952), 153.
11 Howard W. Stone and James O. Duke, How to Think Theologically, 3rd ed., (Minneapolis: Fortress Press, 2013), 2.
12 Lewis, Mere Christianity, 6.
13 John 3:16.
14 Matthew 25:23.
15 John 1:12–13, 3:16–17.
16 It wasn't until she passed away at ninety-nine years and eleven months that we found out she had changed her own name from Isidora to Angela ("female angel"), because she desired to live an eternal life of purity before the Lord. She gave me the name of the Roman Catholic saint Inés, which, rooted in the Greek word hagnē, means "purity, sacredness, and holiness." For a middle name, she chose Socorro, which is part of the Roman Catholic title for the Blessed Virgin Mary ("Madre del Perpetuo Socorro"). It is a Spanish word meaning "help" (as in "Our Lady of Perpetual Help").
17 See Joshua 6.
18 Matthew 6:34.
19 Romans 8.
20 Psalm 144:9.
21 See Exodus 16:1–3.
22 Exodus 13:21–22.
23 Matthew 9:9; Mark 1:17; Luke 5:27; John 1:38, 43; 8:12; 21:22.
24 Acts 1:8, 1 Corinthians 6:19, 2 Timothy 1:14.
25 Numbers 9:19–21 NIV.
26 John 6:68–69.
27 Ephesians 1:14–19.
28 Ephesians 4:3-4, Romans 8:26, 1 Corinthians 12:4.
29 Galatians 5:25.
30 1 Samuel 3:10.
31 Dallas Willard, The Spirit of the Disciplines: Understanding How God Changes Lives, (New York: HarperCollins Publishers, 1988), 68.
32 Willard, The Spirit of the Disciplines, 121.
33 Angus Stevenson and Christine A. Lindberg, eds., New Oxford American Dictionary, 3rd ed. (New York: Oxford University Press, 2010).
34 Adele Ahlberg Calhoun, Spiritual Disciplines Handbook: Practices That Transform Us, rev. ed., (Downers Grove, IL: IVP Books, 2015), 21.
35 Willard, The Spirit of the Disciplines, 67.
36 Calhoun, Spiritual Disciplines Handbook, 71.
37 I researched for a source for this popular phrase used by the beloved Fred Rogers in the American television series Mister Rogers' Neighborhood, but I could not find one.

Chapter 2: Incomplete Maps

1 Revelation 22:20.
2 God speaks to his people. Here are twelve great examples of when God spoke: Genesis 2:16–17; Exodus 20:1–2; 2 Samuel 22:14; 1 Kings 19:12; Psalm 68:33; Psalm 29:3–9; Ezekiel 12:25, 43:2; Luke 3:21–22; John 10:27, 12:27–20; Acts 9:3–4.
3 2 Timothy 3:16–17.
4 Romans 8:22.
5 I want to be clear that this is what I heard to the best of my recollection. I do not hold these words as equivalent to the Bible, or even exactly God's words. I hold my understanding of these words humbly before the Lord. I'm grateful to him for his communication to me and trust him to forgive what is lacking in my understanding or memory. They have, however, guided me to Scripture to seek a better understanding of his heart for me at such a young age and throughout my life.
6 Genesis 39:2, 21, 23.
7 Genesis 50:20.
8 Romans 8:28–29.
9 Proverbs 3:5.
10 Matthew 16:24.
11 John 1:3.
12 Philippians 2:6–7.
13 John 7:6.
14 Philippians 4:12.

Chapter 3: Faith Is Not a Formula

1 See Galatians 5:17.
2 1 John 1:8.
3 See Matthew 24:9.
4 See Romans 5:3.
5 See 1 Peter 4:12–13.
6 See Matthew 26:39.
7 Ecclesiastes 1:14.
8 Jeremiah 29:11.
9 See Ephesians 1:3–14.
10 On August 5, 2010, thirty-three men were buried under the collapsed San Jose Mine in Chile, 2,300 feet underground for sixty-nine days. An international team and a record-breaking rescue mission resulted in the survival of all the miners.
11 See Isaiah 53:11.
12 John 4:28–30.
13 John 4:39-41.
14 See John 7:45-52.

15 My paraphrase of John 3:2.
16 John 4:14.
17 John 3:9.
18 John 4:15.
19 John 4:26.
20 www.freewheelchairmission.org.
21 Romans 12:1–2.
22 Colossians 3:2.
23 See Ephesians 2:8.

Chapter 4: Obstacles Are a Given

1 c. AD 540–604.
2 Timothy Keller, Walking with God through Pain and Suffering, (New York: Penguin Books, 2013), 47.
3 Marilyn McCord Adams, Horrendous Evils and the Goodness of God, (Ithica, NY: Cornell University Press, 1999), 28.
4 See Genesis 37, 39-50.
5 John 10:10.
6 1 Peter 5:8.
7 Ephesians 6:12.
8 Ephesians 6:13.
9 Ephesians 6:18.
10 2 Corinthians 11:16–33.
11 Acts 20:23.
12 2 Timothy 4:7–8.
13 2 Timothy 4:5.
14 Genesis 3:1.
15 Matthew 4:2.
16 Matthew 4:4.
17 Matthew 4:5.
18 Matthew 4:6.
19 Deuteronomy 6:16.
20 Matthew 4:8.
21 Matthew 4:9.
22 Matthew 4:10.
23 Galatians 2:20.
24 Romans 16:20, Revelation 12:12, 20:10.
25 Luke 22:42.
26 Romans 8:37.
27 Dr. Jordan Metzl and Claire Kowalchi, Running Strong, (New York: Rodale Books, 2015).
28 2 Timothy 4:6–7.
29 Nehemiah 4:11.

30 Nehemiah 4:12.
31 Nehemiah 4:4.
32 Nehemiah 4:9.
33 Nehemiah 6:9.
34 Nehemiah 4:14.
35 See 1 Samuel 4.
36 See 1 Samuel 6.
37 1 Samuel 7:12.
38 Nehemiah 4:21.
39 Nehemiah 6:15, 16.
40 1 Corinthians 9:24)
41 Mark Batterson, The Circle Maker: Praying Circles Around Your
    Biggest Dreams and Greatest Fears, expanded ed., (Grand Rapids, MI:
    Zondervan, 2016), 15.

Chapter 5: Questions Are Essential

1 A. J. Swoboda, After Doubt: How to Question Your Faith without Losing
   It, (Ada, MI: Brazos Press, 2021),
2 Walter Brueggemann, The Message of the Psalms: A Theological
   Commentary, (Minneapolis: Augsburg, 1984), 51.
3 See the full interview I did with Pastor Mike Erre on YouTube: https://
   www.youtube.com/watch?v=6wFaWWSqyx8.
4 https://www.faasafety.gov/files/notices/2014/Dec/SA17_Spatial_
   Disorientation.pdf.
5 Genesis 3:9.
6 Judges 6:10.
7 Judges 6:12.
8 Judges 6:1–2.
9 Judges 6:13.
10 Judges 6:14.
11 Judges 6:15.
12 Judges 6:16.
13 Judges 6:17.
14 Matthew 28:20.
15 Genesis 3:9.
16 Genesis 3:13.
17 Exodus 4:2
18 1 Kings 19:9.
19 Mark 10:18.
20 Mark 8:29.
21 Matthew 16:26.
22 Matthew 16:26.
23 Luke 12:51.

24 James 4:14 ESV.
25 Job 38:4.
26 Isaiah 6:8.
27 Romans 8:1.
28 Matthew 11:28.
29 John 10:27.
30 John 10:10.
31 Psalm 121:8.
32 See Luke 6:46–49.
33 Acts 1:8.
34 2 Corinthians 5:20.
35 1 Corinthians 6:19.
36 John 16:13.
37 Romans 8:16.
38 1 Corinthians 6:11.
39 Galatians 5:16.
40 John 14:26.
41 Acts 1:8.
42 Acts 16:6.
43 Romans 8:26.
44 John 16:8.
45 Galatians 5:16–26.
46 Brueggemann, The Message of the Psalms, 51.
47 Psalm 119:11.
48 Matthew 14:30.
49 See Romans 8:26–27.
50 1 Thessalonians 5:17.
51 See 1 John 5:14–15.
52 Galatians 6:2.
53 Ephesians 6:19, Matthew 26:40–41.
54 Proverbs 3:5–6.
1 Quoted by Andrew Murray in Humility: The Journey Toward Holiness, (Minneapolis: Bethany House, 2001), 67.

Chapter 6: Recovering from Wrong Turns

2 1 John 3:4.
3 Romans 3:23.
4 1 John 3:5.
5 Hebrews 4:15.
6 Romans 7:15.
7 2 Corinthians 5:17.
8 Galatians 5:16–25.
9 2 Samuel 11:4–5.

10 2 Samuel 11:2.
11 Dietrich Bonhoeffer, Life Together: The Classic Exploration of Christian Community, (New York: HarperOne, 1954), 112.
12 Psalm 51:4.
13 Psalm 32:1.
14 Murray, Humility, 55.
15 Romans 8:29.
16 Psalm 32:10.
17 Romans 3:24.
18 Romans 6:23
19 2 Corinthians 5:15.
20 Romans 8:37.
21 Exodus 20:2–17, Deuteronomy 5:6–21.
22 Matthew 5–7.
23 James 3:6.

Chapter 7: Shame Will Enslave You

1 Lewis B. Semdes, Shame & Grace: Healing the Shame We Don't Deserve, (New York: HarperCollins Publishers, 1993), 31.
2 "Brené Brown: Listening to Shame," YouTube video, 20:22, posted by TED2012, https://www.ted.com/talks/brene_brown_listening_to_shame.
3 Semdes, Shame & Grace, 40.
4 Semdes, Shame & Grace, 37.
5 "Brené Brown: Listening to Shame," (14:13).
6 Revelation 12:10.
7 Geoffrey W. Bromiley, ed., The International Standard Bible Encyclopedia, rev. ed., (Grand Rapids, MI: William. B. Eerdmans Publishing , 1979–1988).
8 Genesis 1:26.
9 Genesis 3:7.
10 Genesis 3:5.
11 Genesis 3:7.
12 Genesis 3:8.
13 Romans 1:21–22.
14 Romans 3:23.
15 John 5:18.
16 Luke 7:18–23, 48, Matthew 9:1–2.
17 John 3:16, 14:6.
18 John 6:48, 8:58.
19 John 5:17.
20 Matthew 26:67; 27:28–29, 44.
21 Hebrews 12:2.

22 2 Corinthians 5:17.
23 Dietrich Bonhoeffer, The Cost of Discipleship, (New York: Simon & Schuster, 1959), 45.
24 Deuteronomy 31:6.
25 Romans 8:1.
26 Luke 15:3–7.
27 John 13:36–38.
28 John 18:17, 25–27.
29 John 18:17.
30 John 18:25.
31 John 18:26.
32 Genesis 3:9.
33 John 10:10.

Chapter 8: What Not to Pack

1 A.W. Tozer, The Knowledge of the Holy, (New York: HarperOne, 1961), 2.
2 Matthew 3:11.
3 David Gibson, Living Life Backward: How Ecclesiastes Teaches Us to Life in Light of the End. (Wheaton, IL: Crossway, 2017), 54.
4 Ecclesiastes 3:1.
5 1 Kings 18–19.
6 1 Kings 19:9.
7 Quoted from Ann Voskamp's ministry email "When You Pray but God Doesn't Answer with the Miracle," dated September 22, 2022.
8 John 17:21.
9 Jeremiah 29:11.
10 Proverbs 3:5–6.
11 1 Corinthians 10:13.
12 2 Thessalonians 3:3.
13 Isaiah 43:2–3, Philippians 4:13.
14 Hebrews 6:10, Luke 16:9.
15 John 10:28.
16 Philippians 3:12.
17 See Hebrews 13:5; Deuteronomy 31:6, 8; Joshua 1:5.
18 Jonah 1:1–3.
19 Jonah 1:9.
20 Jonah 3:2.
21 Jonah 3:4.
22 Jonah 4:1.
23 Genesis 1:26, Isaiah 41:10, 1 Corinthians 13:4–7.
24 Adele Ahlberg Calhoun, Spiritual Disciplines Handbook: Practices That Transform Us, rev. ed., (Downers Grove, IL: IVP Books, 2015), 21.

Chapter 9: A Heavenly Mindset

1 Look for the image by searching the internet for "Jesus holding a bear."
2 Michael Maccoby, "Why People Follow the Leader: The Power of Transference," Harvard Business Review, September 2004, https://hbr.org/2004/09/why-people-follow-the-leader-the-power-of-transference.
3 Luke 9:23–24.
4 Dietrich Bonhoeffer, The Cost of Discipleship, (Minneapolis: Fortress Press, 2003), 87.
5 See Mark 1:18.
6 Bonhoeffer, The Cost of Discipleship, 32.
7 These are the words I have prayed through each year: 2003, Believe; 2004, Do; 2005, Release; 2006, Trust; 2007, Perfection; 2008, Submit; 2009, Grow; 2010, Act; 2011, Courage; 2012, Faithfulness; 2013, Grace; 2014, Present (as in "God's presence"); 2015, Warrior; 2016, Arise; 2017, Joy; 2018, Unexpected; 2019, Listen; 2020, Prophesy; 2021, Fire; 2022, Consuela (my first in Spanish).
8 Genesis 12:1–3.
9 Ruth 1:15–18.
10 Matthew 19:27, Luke 5:1–11.
11 Philippians 2:6–8.
12 John 13:16.
13 John 10:10.
14 Luke 6:46.
15 Nahum 1:3, Psalm 86:15.
16 Genesis 15:5.
17 Genesis 22:15–18.
18 This is a term used by Eugene Peterson in his book Long Obedience in the Same Direction.
19 https://www.freewheelchairmission.org/.
20 Colossians 3:2–4.

Chapter 10: Traveling in Community

1 Dietrich Bonhoeffer, Life Together; The Classic Exploration of Christian Community, (New York: HarperOne, 1954), 19.
2 "Holly Robinson Peete," Hollywood Walk of Fame, June 21, 2022, accessed July 1, 2022, https://walkoffame.com/holly-robinson-peete/.
3 The idiom is an adapted version of Desiderius Erasmus's observation, "Women, can't live with them, can't live without them."
4 Spiros Zodhiates, The Complete Word Study Dictionary: New Testament, (Chattanooga, TN: AMG Publishers, 2000).
5 John 10:10.
6 John 8:44.

7 Ephesians 4:27.

8 Bonhoeffer, Life Together, 112.

9 "Mea culpa" is a Latin phrase that means "through my fault." It is said as a prayer of confession in the Roman Catholic Church during the mass (service) as an expression of remorse for sins committed.

10 Jennie Allen, Find Your People: Building Deep Community in a Lonely World, (Colorado Springs, CO: WaterBrook, 2022), 217.

11 Acts 15:39.

12 2 Timothy 4:11.

13 Bonhoeffer, Life Together, 8.

14 Bonhoeffer, Life Together, 12.

15 Bonhoeffer, Life Together, 77.

16 C. S. Lewis, The Weight of Glory, (New York: HarperOne, 1980), 158.

17 Romans 15:7.

18 Bonhoeffer, Life Together, 23.

19 Galatians 6:2.

20 Lewis, The Weight of Glory, 167.

21 Lewis, The Weight of Glory, 45–46

22 1 Corinthians 12:20.

23 Proverbs 27:17.

24 If you do not know where to start to build community, I recommend a wonderful book written by Jennie Allen: Find Your People: Building Deep Community in a Lonely World.

25 Romans 1:12.

26 1 Corinthians 10:17.

Chapter 11: Ambiguity Is Inevitable

1 Philippians 4:7.

2 John 15:1–8.

3 cf. Psalm 42:2, 63:1, 143:6; Isaiah 55:1; Matthew 5:6.

4 Psalm 63:1.

5 Isaiah 44:1–4.

6 John 4:7.

7 "Jesus said, 'Everyone who drinks from this water will get thirsty again. But whoever drinks from the water that I will give him will never get thirsty again. In fact, the water I will give him will become a well of water springing up in him for eternal life'" (John 4:13–14).

8 John 4:14, 6:35, 7:37; Rev 7:16, 21:6, 22:17.

9 Romans 4:25, Colossians 2:14, Acts 4:12.

10 John 14:26.

11 Revelation 21:1.

12 "Whatever you do, do it from the heart, as something done for the Lord and not for people" (Colossians 3:23).

13 Romans 8:18.
14 Hebrews 5:13–14.
15 Janet O. Hagberg and Robert A. Guelich, The Critical Journey: Stages in the Life of Faith, (Salem, WI: Sheffield Publishing Company: 1973), 120.
16 Galatians 2:20.
17 D. C. Talk and Voice of the Martyrs, Jesus Freaks: Stories of Those Who Stood for Jesus, (Tusa, OK: Albury Publishing, 1999).
18 John 6:67–69.
19 Romans 8:11.
20 C. S. Lewis, Mere Christianity, (New York: HarperOne, 1980), 50.
21 Ephesians 2:19.
22 Hebrews 11:31.
23 Matthew 17:20, Hebrews 11:13.
24 Joshua 1:6, 9.
25 Joshua 6:21.

Chapter 12: The Journey Is Mysterious

1 George MacDonald, Unspoken Sermons, First Series, (Eureka, CA: Sunrise Books Publishers, 1989), as cited in The Problem of Pain by C. S. Lewis, (New York: Macmillan, 1947), vi.
2 Timothy Keller, Walking with God through Pain and Suffering, (New York: Penguin Books, 2013), 163.
3 Keller, Walking with God through Pain and Suffering, 164.
4 2 Timothy 4:7.
5 2 Corinthians 11:16–12:10.
6 2 Corinthians 12:9.
7 James 1:1.
8 Spiros Zodhiates, The Complete Word Study Dictionary: New Testament, (Chattanooga, TN: AMG Publishers, 2000).
9 Janet O. Hagberg and Robert A. Guelich, The Critical Journey: Stages in the Life of Faith, (Salem, WI: Shelfield Publishing Company), 118.
10 From Bob's Point of View email, dated January 24, 2002.
11 Job 1:20–22.
12 Joni Eareckson Tada, "New Resolve After 55 Years in My Wheelchair," The Gospel Coalition, July 30, 2022, accessed July 30, 2022, https://www.thegospelcoalition.org/article/new-resolve-55-years-wheelchair/.
13 Joni Eareckson Tada, "New Resolve After 55 Years in My Wheelchair."
14 "COVID-19 Health Update from Joni Eareckson Tada," YouTube video, 3:25, posted by "Joni and Friends," https://youtu.be/squAX6IV2Aw.
15 G. D. Watson, Soul Food, (Jawbone Digital, 2015), 39.
16 Luke 22:42.
17 John 6:35.
18 Mark 9:24.

19 Keller, Walking with God through Pain and Suffering, 226.
20 Psalm 63:8.
21 Genesis 16:1–15.
22 Hebrews 12:3.
23 Daniel 3:24–25.
24 Here is one I keep handy to help me remember what others have endured: Jesus Freaks: Stories of Those Who Stood for Jesus, the Ultimate Jesus Freaks, revised and updated edition by D. C. Talk and the Voice of the Martyrs.
25 Psalm 34:18.
1 C. S. Lewis, The Problem of Pain, (New York: HarperOne, 1940), 34.

Chapter 13: Certainty Hinders Growth

2 Link to the song and lyrics: https://www.songfacts.com/facts/doris-day/que-sera-sera-whatever-will-be-will-be .
3 Romans 8:38–39.
4 Psalm 119:82.
5 See, for example, Matthew 6:34, 10:16–19, 24:36.
6 Genesis 3:1.
7 Luke 12:50.
8 Read the story of the death of John the Baptist in Matthew 14:1–12.
9 John 4:48.
10 John 4:49–50.
11 See, for example, Genesis 1:6–7, 9, 14–15, 24.
12 John 20:29.
13 John 20:28.
14 Jon Bloom, Not by Sight: A Fresh Look at Old Stories of Walking by Faith, (Wheaton, IL: Crossway, 2013), 57.
15 https://nikwallenda.com/.
16 Janet O. Hagberg and Robert A. Guelich, The Critical Journey: Stages in the Life of Faith, (Salem, WI: Sheffield Publishing Company, 1973), 116.
17 See Genesis 12.
18 The information that the Hebrew word hesed refers to mercy, loyalty, faithfulness, goodness, graciousness, and loving kindness is taken from a definition by James Strong, Enhanced Strong's Lexicon (Woodside Bible Fellowship, 1995).
19 John 4:50.
20 "The father realized this was the very hour at which Jesus had told him, 'Your son will live.' So he himself believed, along with his whole household" (John 4:53).
21 King Saul, 1 Samuel 15:11; King Jehu, 2 Kings 10:29–32; King Joash, 2 Chronicles 24:22, 25.

22 Romans 7:4.

23 John 15:16.

24 For more information about this wonderful ministry that provides the "transforming gift of mobility to people with a disability living in developing nations, as motivated by Jesus Christ," visit www. freewheelchairmission.org.

25 Psalm 63:3.

26 Andrew Murray, Humility: The Journey Toward Holiness (Minneapolis, MN: Bethany House, 2001), 55.

Chapter 14: The Outward Journey

1 Charles Spurgeon, "The Affliction of Ahaz Sermon on 2 Chronicles 28:22," from The Lost Sermons of C.H. Spurgeon: His Earliest Outlines and Sermons Between 1851 and 1854, vol. 1, (Nashville, TN: B&H Academic, 2017).

2 Job 12:10, 14:5; Psalm 90:10–12, 139:16; Matthew 6:27; James 4:14.

3 Wisdom is not literally a woman, but the Hebrew word for wisdom (חָכְמָה, hokmāh) is a feminine noun. Wisdom is also personified by the writer of Proverbs, who describes it as if it were a real person. See, for example, Proverbs 4:8–9.

4 Proverbs 31:10–31.

5 See Genesis 3.

6 Ephesians 5:15–16.

7 APA Dictionary of Psychology, s.v. "control," accessed August 21, 2022, https://dictionary.apa.org/control.

8 Colossians 3:10.

9 See Hebrews 12:1–2; Colossians 3:1–4, 12–17; 2 Corinthians 3:18.

10 Romans 8:28.

11 Acts 8:26–40.

12 Philippians 1:25.

13 See Lamentations 3:22–23.